Surviving the Induction Years of Language Teaching

Surviving the Induction Years of Language Teaching
The Importance of Reflective Practice

Thomas S. C. Farrell

Published by Equinox Publishing Ltd.

UK: Office 415, The Workstation, 15 Paternoster Row, Sheffield, South Yorkshire S1 2BX
USA: ISD, 70 Enterprise Drive, Bristol, CT 06010

www.equinoxpub.com

First published 2024

British Library Cataloguing-in-Publication Data
A catalogue record for this book is available from the British Library.

ISBN-13   978 1 78179 551 4   (hardback)
          978 1 78179 552 1   (paperback)
          978 1 78179 553 8   (ePDF)
          978 1 80050 459 2   (ePub)

Library of Congress Cataloging-in-Publication Data

Names: Farrell, Thomas S. C. (Thomas Sylvester Charles), author.
Title: Surviving the induction years of language teaching : the importance of reflective practice / Thomas S.C. Farrell.
Description: Sheffield, South Yorkshire ; Bristol, CT : Equinox Publishing Ltd, 2024. | Series: Reflective practice in language education | Includes bibliographical references. | Summary: "Surviving The Induction Years of Language Teaching is unique to the language teaching profession because it outlines the detailed experiences of one ESL teacher during his first year and then during his third year to see what challenges he encountered during these important novice years. It is important for teacher educators, teachers and administrators to understand what novice teachers experience so that they can better be supported to become teachers for many more years to come"-- Provided by publisher.
Identifiers: LCCN 2023028138 (print) | LCCN 2023028139 (ebook) | ISBN 9781781795514 (hardback) | ISBN 9781781795521 (paperback) | ISBN 9781781795538 (pdf) | ISBN 9781800504592 (epub)
Subjects: LCSH: English language--Study and teaching--Foreign speakers. | Reflective teaching. | Language teachers--Training of--Evaluation.
Classification: LCC PE1128.A2 F2886 2024 (print) | LCC PE1128.A2 (ebook) | DDC 428.0071--dc23/eng/20231016
LC record available at https://lccn.loc.gov/2023028138
LC ebook record available at https://lccn.loc.gov/2023028139

Typeset by Sparks Publishing Services Ltd – www.sparkspublishing.com

Contents

Series Editor's Preface

Surviving The Induction Years of Language Teaching: The Importance of Reflective Practice by Thomas S. C. Farrell begins by setting the scene for novice language teachers in their early careers and the 'reality shock many are immediately exposed to on entry because the ideals that they may have formed during their education programs are often replaced by the harsh 'realities' of the classroom, and social and political contexts of the school in which they find themselves teaching in these early career years. This is an unfortunate reality for many because more often than not they are left to cope on their own in a 'sink-or-swim' type existence, with some ultimately deciding to leave the profession either in their first year or in the immediate years that follow. So, in *Surviving The Induction Years of Language Teaching: The Importance of Reflective Practice,* Farrell enters the lived experiences of one English as a second language (ESL) teacher, Roger (a pseudonym), in Canada during his first year of teaching and then his third year of teaching to explore the various experiences and challenges he faced as a backdrop for other teachers to reflect on their early careers as language teachers.

The 15 chapters reconstruct events that for the most part remain hidden with the aim of providing a real-life account of what it means to be a novice ESL teacher. Indeed, as Farrell points out, rarely is the research conducted *with* novice teachers to get *their* story in *their* teaching environment. *Surviving The Induction Years of Language Teaching: The Importance of Reflective Practice* thus gives voice to a novice ESL teacher that may otherwise go unheard, and it also outlines and discusses how his personal tacitly held beliefs were made explicit through discussions and journal writing and how he began to theorize from this new knowledge of what he does (his practice) in his classroom and how he critically reflected beyond practice.

Chapter 1, setting the scene, is an introductory chapter and sets the scene for the book that details not only the lived experiences of one novice ESL teacher during his first year of teaching, but also returns to investigate the lived experiences of this same novice ESL teacher in his third year (on his request) during his third year of teaching. Chapter 2, the induction years, outlines and discusses the transition from the teacher education program to the first year of teaching, the first year of teaching and the early career years after that to the third year of teaching. Chapter 3, reflecting on philosophy, outlines and discusses the topics related to philosophy that the Roger reflected on during his first year. Chapter 4, reflecting on principles, outlines and discusses the topics related to principles that the novice ESL teacher reflected on during his first year. Chapter 5, reflecting on theory, outlines and discusses the topics related to theory that he reflected on during his first year. Chapter 6, reflecting on practice, outlines and discusses the topics related to classroom practice during his first year. Chapter 7, reflecting beyond practice, outlines and discusses how Roger critically reflected on his work both inside and outside the classroom during his first year. Chapter 8, analyzing the first year, includes an exploration of what he has realized about himself as a teacher such as his insights and includes self-reflexive questions about his practice. Chapter 9, reflecting on philosophy, outlines and discusses the topics related to philosophy that Roger reflected on during his third year. Chapter 10, reflecting on principles, outlines and discusses the topics related to principles that Roger reflected on during his third year. Chapter 11, reflecting on theory, outlines and discusses the topics related to theory that Roger reflected on during his third year. Chapter 12, reflecting on practice, outlines and discusses the topics related to classroom practice during his third year. Chapter 13, reflecting beyond practice, outlines and discusses how Roger critically reflected on his work both inside and outside the classroom during his third year. Chapter 14, analyzing the third year. Chapter 15, professional development through reflective practice reviews the key patterns that emerged from the analysis of the first- and third-year experiences of the novice teacher.

Throughout *Surviving The Induction Years of Language Teaching: The Importance of Reflective Practice* the reader gets a real sense of the lived experiences of one ESL teacher during his first and third year teaching and his real challenges during his 'slump' in his third year and the importance of reflecting on practices throughout a teacher's career. As Roger, the teacher remarked, I now realize that the process of reflection helped me 100%. If I hadn't sat down and reflected on the past and things now, I don't think it would have been the same."

Pre-service and in-service language teachers, language teacher educators, and teachers and teacher educators beyond language education and program administrators and school principles will find the details about the life of a real early career language teacher outlined and discussed in this book a very useful, engaging and enlightening window into the real experiences and challenges that many teachers face in these early important years. Farrell agrees with Fanselow (1988: 115) when he noted: "Here I am with my lens to look at you and your actions. But as I look at you with my lens, I consider you a mirror; I hope to see myself in you and through your teaching...Seeing you allows me to see myself differently and to explore variables we both use." Farrell ends by encouraging all TESOL teachers regardless of their experiences but especially early career teachers such as Roger, to (re)construct and (re)adjust their personal beliefs and practices to better provide optimal learning conditions for students within their classrooms. *Surviving The Induction Years of Language Teaching: The Importance of Reflective Practice* will certainly benefit all teachers and other education stakeholders to become (more) reflective throughout their lives.

Thomas S. C. Farrell
Series Editor, *Reflective Practice in Language Education*

Chapter 1

Setting the Scene

INTRODUCTION

Like novices in many professions, novice teachers face considerable challenges as they transition from teacher education programs into the teaching profession. For many novice language teachers as well the transition from their teacher education program, be it a Certificate or MA graduate program, to their first year(s) of teaching can be a challenging experience as they face many obstacles with the transition. It has even been characterized as a "reality shock" for many because the ideals that novice teachers may have formed during the education program are often replaced by the harsh "realities" of the classroom, and social and political contexts of the school in which they are teaching (Farrell, 2016). One reason for the initial shock of going from training course to first year teaching may be a result of teacher education programs that do not provide suitable preparation for what novice teachers will face in real classrooms (Farrell, 2008). In addition, even though some schools have novice teacher induction programs with a mentor in place, many of these do not work because they do not really serve the everyday needs of the novice teacher (Farrell, 2022). It is unfortunate because many novice teachers are often left to cope on their own in a sink-or-swim type situation, with some ultimately deciding to leave the profession either in their first year or in the immediate years that follow. Yes, we all know that *all* teachers must experience life as novice teachers when they begin their teaching careers in real classrooms, and so I hope the contents of this is the book will better illuminate this under-researched area within language education. This book enters the lived experiences of Roger (a pseudonym), a teacher of English as a second language (ESL), in Canada during his first year of teaching; and then his third year of teaching. The various experiences, encounters and challenges he faces are explored, to see how he adapts during these early years.

Readers may wonder why I focus on the first year and the third years. The first year is a real reality shock for many novice language teachers (Farrell, 2022). Indeed, if they survive this important inaugural year, it does not mean the danger is over or that they will continue to develop as teachers because research indicates that that more novice teachers drop out after their third year of teaching. In fact, the percentages are staggering with 24% dropping out of teaching within the first year, and even more leaving after three years of teaching, 33% in total (Ingersoll, 2015).

Surviving the Induction Years of Language Teaching: The Importance of Reflective Practice is unique to the language teaching profession because it outlines and discusses the detailed experiences of one ESL teacher during his first year, and then during his third year, as a novice ESL teacher. We see life through his eyes and experiences so that we can better understand many of the realities novice language teachers encounter along their way to becoming career language teachers. It is important for language teacher educators, teachers and administrators to understand what novice teachers experience so that they can better be supported to become teachers for many more years to come.

RESEARCH APPROACH

Research in the field of general education related to novice teachers (and all teachers really) has been conducted mostly by outside experts *on* teachers rather than *with* teachers. In other words, it is something *done* by others *to* teachers – but rarely *for* teachers – in that the results almost never get back to the actual teachers after the study and academics leave the site. A common approach to most of this research is where academics develop a detailed questionnaire about the experiences of novice teachers during their first years of teaching, mostly based on questions developed from searches of literature related to "one size fits all" approach to learning to teach. While these questionnaires can be helpful to trigger initial thoughts and reflections of novice teachers about their experiences, the answers they provide may be true, imagined or indeed thoughts about "correct" answers and/or what they perceive the researchers want.

A teacher's knowledge is structured best through their narrative accounts of their lived experiences or through telling *their* story. As Elbaz (1991: 3) notes, "story is the very stuff of teaching, the landscape within which we live as teachers and researchers, and within which the work of teachers can be seen as making sense. This is not merely a claim about the aesthetic or emotional sense of fit of the notion of story with our intuitive understanding of teaching, but an epistemological claim that teachers' knowledge in its own terms is ordered by story and can best be understood in this way." Because I entered the life of one ESL teacher during his first year and third year of teaching to get *his* story, I gained far more knowledge than reading answers from a pre-prepared survey or questionnaire. Indeed, such a focus means that I must pay, as Stake (1995: 43) says, "continuous attention" to *his* story, "an attention seldom sustained when the dominant instruments of data gathering are objectively interpretable checklists or survey items."

I aim to provide a space for Roger to tell the story of his experiences and how he interprets various events he encountered both inside and outside the classroom during his first and third years of teaching. Through the reconstruction of these events that for the most part remain hidden I aim to provide a real-life account of what it means to be a novice ESL teacher. Indeed, rarely is the research conducted *with* novice teachers to get *their* story in *their* teaching environment. In English language teaching, Freeman (1996) has pointed out the importance of listening to teachers' voices about what they do because he says that it is necessary to put teachers at the center of telling their stories. Freeman (1996: 89) maintains that putting teachers front and center in terms of listening to what they do actually follows the jazz maxim. "You have to know the story in order to tell the story." I hope to present Roger's voice in the pages that follow.

Thus, one of the main purposes of this book is to give this voice to novice ESL teachers or, more specifically, to one novice ESL teacher's lived experiences in his first year and then in his third year of ESL teaching. *Surviving The Induction Years of Language Teaching: The Importance of Reflective Practice* is unique in that the research reported is not what researchers perceive as the experiences of novice teachers but the actual lived experiences of a novice ESL teacher at two crucial points in his early career: the first year and the third year of teaching ESL in Canada as relayed through interviews, discussions, journal writing and classroom observations. I (as author and facilitator) have been given permission to tell his story. By documenting Roger's journey and experiences, I hope readers will be able to get a sense of *his* professional world from *his* perspective as he reflects on the use of a holistic framework on different aspects of this practice (see Chapter 2 for more details on the framework used for reflection).

Surviving The Induction Years of Language Teaching: The Importance of Reflective Practice thus gives voice to a novice ESL teacher that may otherwise go unheard, and it also outlines and discusses how his personal, tacitly held beliefs were made explicit through discussions and journal writing and how he began to theorize from this new knowledge of what he does (his practice) in his classroom and how he critically reflected beyond practice. I believe all novice teachers have a personal framework of how languages should be taught and learned, and these can come from their initial teacher training and education and/or from their initial experiences teaching in real classrooms during their first years. In other words, my role as facilitator throughout the reflective project, as reported on in this book, was to help Roger make his tacitly held prior beliefs explicit. I shall address my role in more detail later in this chapter.

SOME BOUNDARIES

This book portrays the lived experiences of one novice ESL teacher in his first year and then in his third year while teaching ESL in Canada. It highlights the teacher's journey during these important years and celebrates his "local" understanding of his practices. Of course, I realize that this "local" understanding may have limitations in terms of generalizability because the reflections are specific to one teacher in one context. As a qualitative researcher I would like to point out that I usually do not focus on the generalizability of research findings because I am trying only to convey "local" understandings and interpretations with "thick" descriptions of what is. Indeed, Creswell (1994: 159) has pointed out that the purpose of qualitative research is "not to generalize findings, but to form a unique interpretation of events." Lincoln and Guba (1985: 316) have also argued that a qualitative researcher "cannot specify the external validity of an enquiry; he or she can provide only thick description necessary to enable someone interested in making a transfer to reach a conclusion about whether transfer can be contemplated as a possibility." I have attempted to provide such a thick description with the details presented in each chapter of this book.

Throughout *Surviving The Induction Years of Language Teaching: The Importance of Reflective Practice* I have also attempted to live up to my responsibility to provide a large enough data base with specific examples of the teachers' direct quotes and writings "that makes transferability judgments possible on the part of potential appliers" (Lincoln & Guba, 1985: 316). Thus, researchers, teacher educators, and teachers can make their own judgments regarding the data and any interpretations made by this author. Indeed, I hope many more language teacher educators replicate this work so that they can compare their findings to those reported on in this book and add to the corpus of the actual lived experiences of novice ESL teachers.

How reliable are the results reported on in this book? The reliability of any qualitative research really depends on whether the findings would be repeated if the study were replicated in similar conditions (with similar subjects and context). As with the problem of external validity, the specificity of a qualitative study makes it difficult to replicate. Following Creswell (1994: 159), I have stated "the researcher's position, the central assumptions, the selection of informants, and the biases and values of the researcher" in order to increase the chances of replicating the study in another setting. Hence, future studies can address this issue by using a comparative approach to demonstrate the similarities and differences across a number of settings.

That said, I believe that much of what is described and discussed in this book may have relevance for an individual language teacher's practice and context as well as teacher educators and administrators. Thus, by writing this book I have attempted, as Meister and Ahrens (2011: 1) have noted, "to enter the conceptual world of the participant to understand it as he does and to portray that understanding so that it will be insightful and illuminating for others." Researchers, teacher educators, and teachers can also enter Roger's world by reflecting on the details presented in each chapter.

This book is also for administrators. Many books for teachers tend to forget those that work closest with teachers: their administrators. Some administrators are excellent while others are not so helpful for teachers and this may be because they are under pressure from ministries or school owners to look at the financial bottom line rather than the individuals who work from them. This book can help administrators see what novice ESL teachers actually experience and what issues are important for them because these issues can also be very important for the institution/school. Indeed, if institutions want to encourage their novice ESL teachers to perform better, they should find ways to support and boost their morale by recognizing and affirming (verbally or otherwise) their important role within that institution. This support can come from the administration by providing regular time for novice teachers to meet together and with other teachers so that they collaborate and build supportive bonds with other more experienced teachers and the administration as they develop in their novice years.

ROGER: WHO AND WHY?

Surviving The Induction Years of Language Teaching: The Importance of Reflective Practice reports on some of the intense critical reflections of one novice ESL teacher, Roger, in his first and third years, using regular discussions, regular writing in a teacher journal, and classroom observations and interviews before, during and after the first year and third year of his practice. Who is Roger and why Roger are also valid questions to ask?

Who is Roger?

Although the setting of Roger's ESL teaching is Canada, he was not born there but moved to live there with his family when he was three years old. Roger said that his family was very conservative Christian and strongly adhered to the Christian faith. He continued: "I was raised to be respectful and to follow rules, in a sense; now I'm not as conservative as my family is, but still hold on to the basic principles of the

Christian faith; I've learned to be tolerant of others and to be respectful of people from different backgrounds; honesty, integrity, a strong work ethic, and patience are qualities that I've developed as a result of my faith." He had to learn English while in school from four years old and he said that he and his family "worked very hard to adapt to Canadian culture." As time went by, he said that he slowly stopped using his native language at home (I purposely do not specify his native language, and the country of his birth, for privacy reasons) although he did take many trips back and kept in touch with his L1.

Roger said that he may have been influenced to become a teacher based on his experience of his excellent grade schoolteachers both in elementary and high school whom he said, "had a real passion for teaching and I could see their joy when teaching us." Roger said that he noted that they "cared more about their students, cared more about how they taught (they were more interactive and valued input from students), and they cared to know more about their students' personal lives and interests." As a result, Roger notes these qualities influence him as a teacher. He said: "I always make a point to find out more about my students interests and personal lives and try to incorporate that into my lessons." I provide more detailed information about Roger in Chapter 3 when I talk about his philosophy influences during his first year.

I first met Roger in university where he was an undergraduate and graduate student in some of my classes. Roger graduated with a BA in Applied Linguistics and a further qualification teaching certificate at a more advanced level (Certificate in Teaching English as a second language), he then completed an MA degree in Applied Linguistics with a major in teaching English to speakers of other languages (TESL). It was during this time that Roger would drop into my office from time to time to discuss reflective practice. So why do I report on Roger's experiences?

Why Roger?

The genesis of the research reported in this book may be unique in some ways because I was approached by Roger just as he was beginning his first year of teaching. He asked if I would be willing to facilitate his reflections because he had taken some of my prior graduate classes. As Roger said, "the main thing is that I want to be able to step back and take a look at what I'm doing. Like, I mean, we often do so many things where we just do it and you don't think about it when you're doing it or after you're doing it and you just move on and that's it." Thus, Roger wanted to reflect on his practice in order to have "a different point of view of why I'm doing things the way I do and what kind of things I do and where do I learn to do those types of things." His interest in learning about what he was doing coincided with my own interest in reflective practice: I was curious about what he was doing in his first year, and where these things came from. As Roger himself asks: "is it things that I just made up or things that I learned from my classes or things I just learned from life experiences or from watching other people?"

Later, Roger again approached me at the beginning of his third year of teaching because he said he was eager to engage in further reflective practice during this year (I explain more about these circumstances in Part II of the book). Roger looked and sounded a bit "down" when we met. He told me he had just finished teaching a short course to begin his third year which had been a really bad experience for him: "I just came off a really bad [course] where everything just sucked, and there could still be a bit of that lingering this term, so, you know, I would like to reflect again on my teaching." Roger said that he would use the word "jaded" now to describe himself – and would use the same word for his colleagues – and so he wanted me to facilitate his reflections again.

METHODOLOGY

I will now briefly point out the theoretical framework I used to oversee the research conducted with Roger.

Data Collection

Qualitative research procedures were used in the collection and analysis of the data in the case study outlined in this book (Glesne & Peshkin, 1992). Data were collected over a four-year period with weekly meetings during the academic terms of the first year and follow-up meetings during the second year; and similar weekly meetings during the academic terms of the third year and follow-up meetings during the fourth year. Roger agreed to commit himself as much as possible to attend all the meetings, and attend interviews before, during and after the reflective period. There were thirteen, two-hour (average) group meetings in total in each of the first and third years. There were also, follow-up interviews (all recorded and transcribed) throughout the first four years, and at the end of the reflective process, in order to clarify previous insights gained. All discussions and interviews were audio-recorded and transcribed. In addition, throughout the period of reflection, Roger committed to writing regularly in a teacher journal. Roger agreed he could write about anything, and whenever he wanted, but he also agreed to write at least one entry after any "event" was experienced; an "event" was to include a class observation and/or discussion, and a meeting and/or any critical incident.

At Roger's request, I was the facilitator throughout the whole reflective process. In this role, I entered his professional world as he reflected on his practice during these two years and then presented these reflections to the wider community. With their permission I recorded, transcribed and interpreted the discussions, interviews and teacher journals in a bid to unwrap, "the shroud of silence in which our practice is wrapped" (Brookfield, 1995: 136). Throughout the reflection process I attempted to keep Roger's anxiety levels as low as possible by building an atmosphere of openness and trust. Although I followed the framework for reflecting on practice (Farrell, 2015), during the reflection process (see below for more details on the framework) there were no boundaries set regarding the topics for each discussion and Roger decided himself what he wanted to talk about. I shared my perceptions openly with him as a participant-observer where appropriate; however, I did not reflect as much on my own teaching. Rather, I attempted to manage the process so that he could feel he had space in which to reflect on his own practice.

Data Analysis

Because of the sheer volume of data gathered during both the first and the third years, analysis was ongoing and recursive all during the period of data collection (Glesne & Peshkin, 1992; Lincoln & Guba, 1985; Merriam, 2009). For coding of the data, the Farrell's (2015) framework for reflecting on practice was employed. This framework arose out of my previous work and is called the *framework for reflecting on practice* (Farrell, 2015). This framework acknowledges the inner life of teachers and not only focuses on the intellectual, cognitive and meta-cognitive aspects of practice that many of the other approaches focus on, but it also includes the spiritual, moral and emotional non-cognitive aspects of reflection (Farrell, 2015). As Wright (2010) points out, reflective practice must not only focus on classroom teaching behaviors, but also a teacher's previous learning and life experiences, or their inner lives, so that the teacher can become more self-aware in order to be better able to understand, interpret and even reshape their professional practice. However, I did not use it as a prescription but rather as a guide to help us get started while at the same time remaining open to what the teachers wanted to continue, change or invent new items as we went along during the period of reflection. As it turned out, we followed most of the framework outlined below.

This framework has five interconnected levels: *philosophy*, *principles*, *theory*, *practice*, and *beyond practice*.

The first stage of the framework, *philosophy*, examines the *teacher-as-person* because a teacher's basic philosophy begins developing from birth. This stage can be considered a "window to the roots of a teacher's practice because a philosophy of practice means each observable behavior has a reason that guides it even if it is implicit" (Farrell, 2019: 84). Self-knowledge is an essential first step for teachers in working through the framework, but it is often overlooked in earlier literature on reflective practice. Teachers can obtain self-knowledge by exploring, examining and reflecting on their background – from where they have evolved – such as heritage, ethnicity, religion, socioeconomic background, family and personal values that have combined to influence who they are now as language teachers. Reflecting on one's philosophy of practice can not only help teachers flesh out what has shaped them as human beings, and how they think their past experiences may have shaped the construction and development of their basic philosophy, but can also help them move onto the next stage: reflecting on their principles.

The second stage, *principles*, encompasses a teacher's reflections of beliefs – about teaching and learning English – with respect to speakers of other languages. All teachers hold beliefs about their work, students, subject matter, and their roles and responsibilities. Teachers' practices and their classroom instructional decisions are often formulated and implemented (for the most part subconsciously) on the basis of their underlying beliefs because these are the driving forces (along with philosophy reflected on at stage one) behind many of their classroom actions. Thus, reflecting on principles of teaching and learning enables teachers to uncover their beliefs and gain a deeper awareness of their teaching practice.

The third stage requires teachers to reflect on *theory*. It is theory that underlies their practice, from how they plan their lessons, to how they choose activities, techniques, and methods. Teachers can also examine critical incidents, or any unplanned events that happen during a class, outside a class, or during a teacher's career that is vividly remembered. All language teachers have theories – both "official" theories we learn in teacher education courses, and "unofficial" theories we gain with teaching experience. However, not all teachers may be fully aware of these theories, and especially their "unofficial" theories that are sometimes called "theories-in-use". Reflections at this stage/level in the framework include considering all aspects of a teacher's planning and the different activities and methods teachers choose (or may want to choose) as they attempt to put theory into practice.

The fourth stage, *practice*, provides an opportunity for language teachers to explore what they do in their classroom and to closely examine connections between their philosophy, principles and theory with the more visible actions, and thus note any discrepancy between thought and action. At this stage/level in the framework, teachers can reflect while they are teaching a lesson (reflection-*in*-action), after they teach a lesson (reflection-*on*-action) or before they teach a lesson (reflection-*for*-action).

The final stage, *beyond practice* or *critical reflection*, explores the moral, political, emotional, ethical, and community/social issues that impact teachers' practices both inside and outside the classroom. Beyond practice here means that language teachers reflect beyond their methods, and if they "work" or not, to other issues that they must also deal with on a daily basis, such as community and political issues that can impact who they are as teachers and what they do inside and outside their classrooms. Reflections at this stage can assist teachers in becoming more aware of the many political agendas and economic interests that can (and do) shape how we define language teaching and learning. They can become more aware of the impact of their lessons on their community (this also includes the virtual community) and the impact of that community on their practice. In addition, at this critical reflection stage, I have now added more emphasis on how researchers, teachers, and teacher educators can specifically access, explore, and reflect more precisely on teacher emotions by examining teachers' affective language through the lens of the Appraisal Framework (Martin, 2000; Martin and White, 2005; White, 2000). A central component of the Appraisal Framework is exploration of language for expressing attitude that consists of three subsystems: *affect, judgement* and *appreciation* (White, 2000), with *affect* referring to the language used for expressing emotions. I believe that this will better "emotionalize" (Holmes, 2010) the concept of reflective practice so we can better account for the emotional aspects of professional experiences, and how emotions contribute to the making of, and reflections on, professional language teaching practices (Brookfield, 1995).

In order to establish the trustworthiness (a qualitative measurement similar to reliability and validity) of the findings, I (along with a research assistant) assessed the quality of the data by checking for its "credibility" (Lincoln & Guba, 1985: 300). Lincoln and Guba, (1985: 301) suggest that "credible findings will be produced" by "the investment of sufficient time to achieve certain purposes: learning the culture, testing for misinformation introduced by distortions either of the self or the respondents, and building trust." As the present study took place over a four-year period, this constitutes prolonged engagement and thus "sufficient time." The technique of triangulation was also utilized to ensure the findings were credible. During data triangulation, a piece of evidence was compared and crosschecked with other kinds of evidence. Then, at the end of the data collection period for both years, I scanned it all once more for accurate interpretation of patterns and themes and commenced writing this book (Lincoln & Guba, 1985).

MOVING FORWARD

Surviving The Induction Years of Language Teaching: The Importance of Reflective Practice is written in a clear and accessible style and assumes no previous background in teacher education. Each chapter includes **Reflective Breaks** and tasks that prepare the reader to reflect on or apply the strategies or procedures discussed in the chapter. Teachers can gather as a group and reflect on the various topics the teachers discussed and consider the importance of these topics for their context. They can use these topics as a means of generating reflection into their own particular settings and then compare their findings with those reported on in this book.

OUTLINE OF THE BOOK

Chapter 1: Setting the Scene, is an introductory chapter that details not only the lived experiences of one novice ESL teacher during his first year of teaching, but also returns to investigate the lived experiences of this same novice ESL teacher in his third year (on his request) during his third year of teaching. The chapter outlines and describes the research approach taken to gather the data over a four-year period and how the data was analyzed and interpreted. The chapter also summarizes the contents of the other chapters in the book.

Chapter 2: The Induction Years, outlines and discusses the transition from the teacher education program to the first year of teaching and, after that, to the third year of teaching. This is followed by a discussion of how novice language teachers can engage in reflective practice during these years.

Chapter 3: Reflecting on Philosophy in the First Year, outlines and discusses the topics related to philosophy that Roger reflected on during his first year. Chapter 4: Reflecting on Principles in the First Year, outlines and discusses the topics related to principles that the novice ESL teacher reflected on during his first year. Chapter 5: Reflecting on Theory in the First Year, outlines and discusses the topics related to theory that he reflected on during his first year. Chapter 6: Reflecting on Practice in the First Year, outlines and discusses the topics related to classroom practice during his first year. Chapter 7: Reflecting Beyond Practice in the First Year, outlines and discusses how Roger critically reflected on his work both inside and outside the classroom during his first year. Chapter 8: Analyzing the First Year, includes an exploration of what he has realized about himself as a teacher such as his insights and includes self-reflexive questions about his practice. It also includes awareness professional growth over the year and his future professional goals, including questions he has about his future as an ESL teacher.

Chapter 9: Reflecting on Philosophy in the Third Year, outlines and discusses the topics related to philosophy that Roger reflected on during his third year. Chapter 10: Reflecting on Principles in the Third Year, outlines and discusses the topics related to principles that Roger reflected on during his third year. Chapter 11: Reflecting on Theory in the Third Year, outlines and discusses the topics related to theory that Roger reflected on during his third year. Chapter 12: Reflecting on Practice in the Third Year, outlines and discusses the topics related to classroom practice during his third year. Chapter 13: Reflecting Beyond Practice in the Third Year, outlines and discusses how Roger critically reflected on his work both inside and outside the classroom during his third year. Chapter 14: Analyzing the Third Year, includes an exploration of what he has realized about himself as a teacher such as his insights and includes self-reflexive questions about his practice.

Chapter 15: Professional Development Through Reflective Practice reviews the key patterns that emerged from the analysis of the first- and third-year experiences of the novice teacher. The chapter provides an overall appraisal of the impact of these experiences on the development of this teacher and the importance of reflective practice as Roger reflects on reflective practice. The chapter also outlines how language teachers can engage in reflective practice as part of the overall, career-long professional development program.

HOW TO USE THIS BOOK

Surviving The Induction Years of Language Teaching: The Importance of Reflective Practice is intended to be a companion for all novice/early career language teachers because it provides commentary and guidance directly related to the lived experiences of one novice ESL teacher during his first and third years of teaching. This book is also for teacher educators, and program administrators and supervisors who are responsible for providing professional development opportunities for novice ESL teachers. The book is also suitable for those taking graduate courses in TESOL (Cert, MA) who are interested in the field of language teacher education. The book is written in a clear and accessible style and assumes no previous background in teacher education.

CONCLUSION

This first chapter sets the scene for the whole book by introducing readers to the idea of reflecting on the first and third years of teaching English as a second language. The reason for this focus, as mentioned above, is the staggering number of novice teachers who drop out in these important early years. The scene is set to highlight the importance of reflection during this time for teachers, and points to a framework for reflecting on practice as a means to operationalize such reflections, with particular focus on one ESL teacher, Roger, whose reflections take up most of the contents of this book. I use his reflections as a backdrop to explain some of the important issues novice ESL teachers face during these years, and how engaging in reflective practice can help them better navigate their survival and ensure they thrive as ESL teachers. Roger is one such ESL teacher who could have fallen through the cracks, as readers will see, especially during the crucial third year of teaching. The next chapter outlines and discusses some of the major issues novice teachers face during their induction years as they transition from their teacher education programs. I hope you enjoy the remainder of the contents of this book.

Chapter 2

The Induction Years

INTRODUCTION

The induction years, as Farrell (2012: 437) notes, include novice teachers "who have completed their language teacher education programme and have commenced teaching English in an educational institution." For the purposes of this book, this novice period includes the first three years of teaching and especially the third year of teaching. These are also called the induction years for teachers, and they are especially important when it comes to settling into their profession or, indeed, deciding if this is not the profession for them. This chapter outlines and discusses the move from trainee to novice, mapping the transition from teacher education programs. The chapter then outlines and discusses the main issues related to teaching in the first year, as well as in the remaining early career years up to the third year. As mentioned in the introduction, understanding issues related to teaching in these early career years is important for teacher educators, teachers and administrators because research has indicated that, within these induction years, nearly 50% of all novice teachers leave the teaching profession (Ingersoll, 2015).

TRANSITIONING FROM TEACHER EDUCATION PROGRAM

When pre-service teachers (sometimes called trainee teachers or learner teachers) enter a teacher education program they do so in order to acquire the skills they will need to carry out their profession of teaching, be it the teaching of a content subject like science or of English as a second language. After graduation from these programs they are considered "qualified" by many (especially by administrators) because they have successfully completed the requirements of that program. As a result, most people (including the novice teachers themselves) think they have gained knowledge about various aspects of teaching and learning. The "qualified"

ESL teacher, now called a novice teacher, is deemed ready to begin his or her career in a real school and classroom with real students – in this particular context teaching English to speakers of other languages. Thus, the novice teacher will begin his or her transition from trainee to novice teacher most likely with great anticipation of a smooth entry into the profession as a "qualified" ESL teacher.

Many novice teachers arrive at their new school probably a bit nervous but excited and enthusiastic about their future career. More experienced teachers in that school setting may refer to this enthusiasm by calling them "spark-plug go-getters" (Kaufmann & Ring, 2011: 52) because they are very eager to commence teaching so that they can begin to implement what they learned in their teacher education programs and practicum experiences. Indeed, most administrators, and teacher educators consider these "qualified" teachers ready to teach because they have graduated from a recognized teacher education program and thus have acquired the necessary skills to be able to teach from their very first day on the job. After all, the logic goes, why wouldn't they, as they have been prepared for this day over the past certain number of hours (usually 200 hours) in their teacher education program. The main impression is that teaching in the first year is a straightforward and easy process: all the novice teachers have to do is put into practice all the theories and methods they learned during their teacher education program. These should work and must be useful; otherwise why include them in the teacher education program? Indeed, now that they know the subject and the methods, they can teach. However, many mentor teachers and more experienced teachers know that this is not the case as it is much more complicated when a trainee teacher transitions into a novice teacher during that first year. Indeed, for many novice teachers that first day and first month can be a real shock and many quickly realize that they may not have been prepared adequately to teach in real classrooms by their teacher education program. Indeed, Freeman (1994) cautioned language educators and novice teachers alike long ago that most of what is presented in language teacher education programs may be washed away by the first-year experiences of becoming a novice teacher, a point also confirmed later in research studies by Farrell (2017). Some find fault with the contents of teacher education programs as not being relevant and too academic, and that school induction programs (including appointing mentor teachers) also do not help novice teachers during their first days, and months (Farrell, 2016, 2017). Indeed, research suggests that both teacher education programs and schools alike could be taken to task regarding the challenges novice teachers must endure (Farrell, 2012). What is clear is that novice teachers are far from the finished product as they make the transition from learning to teach in their teacher education programs to teaching on their first day, month and year in real classrooms. I now outline some of the challenges faced by novice teachers in their first year of teaching.

THE FIRST YEAR

For the novice teacher, the first year of teaching has been called an unpredictable and idiosyncratic activity (Johnson, 1992), and as such can be an anxiety provoking experience for many novice teachers. One reason for this may be because when novice teachers graduate from their teacher education programs, they must balance precariously between learning to teach (i.e. furthering what was started during the teacher education program) while also attempting to establish their identity of becoming an authentic teacher who is also accepted within an established school culture where, as Calderhead (1992: 6) has noted, "the novice becomes socialized into professional culture with certain goals, shared values and standards of conduct." This process of learning to teach is in fact, a "long-term, complex, and developmental process that is the result of participation in the social practices and contexts that are associated with language learning and teaching" (Freeman & Johnson, 1998: 402).

When a novice language teacher enters the classroom to teach for the first time (i.e.., the "lived practices" noted above), he or she has already accumulated an array of tacitly held prior assumptions, beliefs and knowledge about teaching and learning from their own time as a student in the education system. Consequently, we must not forget that learning to teach in the first year is a complex process because it is also influenced by issues in that novice teacher's life that have occurred long before he or she stepped into their classroom. These influences include their years of previous schooling as students themselves, and the influence or impact of the teacher education program they have graduated from. Thus, the transition from learner teacher to novice teacher in the first year is not so simple as many would believe (see above). In fact, the first year of teaching is challenging because novice teachers' prior assumptions, beliefs and attitudes that were built up during their trainee years learning to teach are often "buffeted and challenged as they learn about teaching" (Loughran, Brown, & Doecke, 2001: 9).

Some of these challenges and concerns have been identified by Fuller and Brown (1975) and they maintain that, for many, there is a sequence of stages they go through in their first year. The process begins when the novice enters the classroom first and is concerned, if not all-consumed, by the need to survive this process. This is then followed by a period where the novice feels he or she is beginning to master some of these challenges as he or she has the perception of gaining more control over teaching. The novice teacher then is faced with what they call an either/or dichotomy of development – either he or she decides to enter a period of a state of resistance to change or he or she decides to stay open to adapting and/or changing their teaching. Fuller and Brown's (1975) process of learning to teach in the first year is a "one-size-fits-all" model where they suggest that in the early survival stages, novice teachers are most concerned about their own survival as a teacher, rather than their students' learning. One reason for this is the reality shock they experience when they enter their real classrooms and their early notions of what it means to be a teacher are abruptly, and unpleasantly replaced by their need to survive the impending chaos of their new world. Suddenly they alone must control a large class as well as deliver the content of their lessons and this can be an overwhelming experience for many. Then as the first year continues, Fuller and Brown (1975) argue, the novice teachers become more settled and begin to notice their overall context that includes concern about their students' learning and the impact of their teaching on learning.

Although Fuller and Brown (1975) describe the process of learning to teach in the first year as a "one-size-fits-all" model, research has affirmed that many first-year teachers actually pass through such stages of development. For example, research by Kagan (1992) reviewed 40 "learning-to-teach" studies, and affirmed Fuller and Brown (1975) stages of development; but others (e.g., Bullough & Baughman, 1993) caution against the idea that teachers actually move smoothly and neatly through each stage. Indeed, because learning to teach is an idiosyncratic experience for most novice teachers, it is probably the case that the above stages are idealistic in nature for many because each context is so different. What many educators do agree on is that, regardless of individual learning to teach experiences and the context in which this happens, all novice teachers will face some challenges and as such will require some kind of assistance if they are to survive this first year.

Some schools (but not all, see Farrell, 2016 for example) attempt to provide such assistance with the implementation of induction programs that include the appointment of mentor teachers to help the novice adjust in the first year. Research has indicated that novice teachers who are mentored tend to be more effective and confident teachers in their early years, since they learn from guided practice rather than depending on trial-and-error efforts alone. In language teaching Malderez and Bodoczky (1999: 4) describe five different roles that mentors could play in order to provide on-site support and assistance to novice teachers during their first year of teaching: (1) Models (who inspire and demonstrate); (2) Acculturators (who show them the ropes); (3) Sponsors (who introduce them to the "right people"); (4) Supporters; and (5) Educators.

However, research has also cautioned that the mere appointment of a mentor is no guarantee the novice teacher will be successfully socialized into the school (Farrell, 2003). Farrell's (2003) case study of the socialization and development of one English language teacher into the profession, for example, revealed that even though a mentor was officially appointed by the school to the novice teacher, there was no further contact between novice and mentor beyond the first introduction on the first day. Indeed, when novice teachers are considered "mentored" like above, the consequences can be catastrophic as Mandel (2006) discovered where the "mentored" teacher could not endure the pressure and finally quit teaching altogether.

The first year of teaching involves the novice teacher realizing that their initial vision (imagined, for the most part) may not match their present reality or lived experiences and the result of this is often a mad dash for survival that can result in the development of a "swim-or-sink" (Varah et al., 1986) mentality that results in high stress levels and, in some extreme cases, leaving the profession. Unfortunately, teacher preparation programs still do not recognize the needs of their learner teachers battling to survive in this first year because their real conditions are not covered with these teacher education programs (see Farrell, 2022 for more on this). In addition, more novice ESL teachers are reporting that they feel that they were not sufficiently prepared for the demands of these real classrooms in real school settings, because what they learned in their TESOL teacher education program was too theoretical. In addition, there is recent evidence from research studies that TESOL teachers are struggling when trying to implement what they have learned in their TESOL teacher education once they begin teaching in their first years (e.g., Farrell, 2017, 2021; Wright, 2010). However, as Farrell (2021) points out, the "elephant in the room" that the profession is reluctant to face is that the contents of these teacher education programs may not be relevant to the everyday needs of learner language teachers. Farrell (2021) has thus suggested that reflective practice should be a key element in language teacher education programs, especially as it can act as a bridge between theory and practice for learner language teachers, where they can reflect on, evaluate, and adapt their own practice. The contents of this book is also one such example of the power of reflection for early career teachers in their first three years. As Cirocki, Madyarov, and Baecher (2019: 2) point out: "Teacher learning is an ongoing, reflective and constructive process. It begins during university degree programs, or certificate courses, and continues in and outside the classroom throughout teachers' careers." Thus, TESOL teacher education is a process that begins in the TESOL teacher education program that includes practice teaching, and continues through the early career years,

BEYOND THE FIRST YEAR

The above discussion of the first year of teaching outlines how the transition experienced during this first year as the novices "battle" to survive "in the trenches" is a complex process, which can have long-lasting effects on their future careers (Bezzina, 2006). Indeed, the teaching profession is now infamous for the low "survival" rates for novice teachers, or more crudely stated: it is "the profession that eats its young" (Halford, 1998: 34). For many early career teachers, their initial expectations of what they perceive the education profession to be, and the realities they then face in a real classroom, can be so different and deflating that they quickly begin to realize that teaching is a far more complex career than they had first imagined during their teacher training and even their first year (Melnick & Meister, 2008).

For teachers in their first three years as novices, Vonk (1989) identified two developmental phases that many undergo: the "threshold" phase and the "growing into the profession" phase. The "threshold" phase is where novice teachers transition from the teacher education program into full time teaching during their first year. The "growing into the profession" phase occurs during the following years – when teachers begin to focus more on their teaching skills and competencies – and culminates with colleagues accepting the novice as a real teacher, usually at the end of the fifth year. First year teachers require help and support, and so too do early career teachers, because research has indicated that it is the best and the brightest among the early career teachers who appear to be most vulnerable and likely to fall through the cracks and, ultimately, leave the profession at the end of the third year (Smith & Ingersoll, 2004).

Unfortunately, in many schools there may be little sympathy among the more experienced teacher colleagues for the plight of early career teachers because they "often feel that they have paid their dues and that new teachers must do the same. They may view surviving the first three years of teaching as a badge of honor" (Renard, 2003: 63–64). Yet novice teachers in their second and third years also need and want help from within the staffroom. As Johnson (2006: 45) put it, "New teachers yearn for professional colleagues who can help them acclimate to their school's unique culture, help them solve the complicated, daily dilemmas of classroom teaching and guide their ongoing learning." Just as with first year teachers, mentors should be kept in place for novice teachers well into their third year (Farrell, 2021).

During the second year of teaching, research has indicated that although many novice teachers still feel passionate about teaching and the profession, a lot depends on what kind of school they find themselves in and if the school and community have committed teachers who are willing to mentor novice teachers (Lindqvist et al., 2014). Teachers in their second year need guidance and support and this comes mainly from the principal or whoever is in charge. Mentoring at this stage requires someone the novice can trust and who knows how to guide a novice teacher rather than just telling or lecturing the novice. Many novice teachers in their second year are still very enthusiastic about teaching and what they have learned in their teacher education programs but need open minded colleagues willing to listen to them rather than conservative colleagues looking out for themselves (Lindqvist et al., 2014). During the second year, novice teachers begin to experience certain aspects of teaching that they may not have anticipated – such as lots of paperwork, planning and preparation and marking – that can weigh them down because many of them will have entered teaching to be dynamic in the classroom only. It is at this stage they also get to know more about the nature, function and operations of the schools and institutions in which they work.

Those novice teachers that stay in their third year – that is, those that have received support and encouragement – are most likely to still feel optimistic about their career choice and are probably ready to experience (and even expect) new challenges. However, others may still feel dissatisfied about their career choice because of perceived difficulties within their teaching lives. The latter discontentment can occur in contexts where novice teachers are not encouraged to collaborate and where school leadership is not apparent or modelled to novice teachers and are thus not inducted into a supportive environment. As Perryman and Calvert (2019: 16) note, "I do not think it is the children/behavior that drives teachers away from the profession – it is the lack of support and trust from management that ultimately is directed from the state – pressure of constant tests, assessments and targets. Teachers needed to be trusted more." Most research points to the establishment of relationships (or the lack of such relationships) that is most appealing and motivating for novice teachers in their third year, and that makes the most difference beyond the actual classroom teaching. Whilst in the third year most novice teachers still enjoy teaching in the classroom because they find it rewarding and a positive experience, if the school environment is negative and they have an excessive workload, they will find this stressful and may soon lose the motivation to go into the classroom. As Perryman and Calvert (2019: 12) relay the reflections of one such teacher, "I thought it [workload] would be a challenge but didn't realize just how challenging that was going to be," with the result that this teacher intends to leave at the end of her third year of teaching.

REFLECTIVE PRACTICE IN THE INDUCTION YEARS

How then can novice ESL teachers prepare for these "transition traumas" in their first years given that many language teacher education programs are lagging behind in providing learner teachers with the means to smoothly transition to a career as a teacher? (Farrell, 2016, 2017; 2021). For example, the theory/practice gap is pointed out as a perennial problem that still persists in many TESOL teacher education programs. In addition, many novice ESL teachers are reporting more and more that their initial expectations of being able to apply what they have learned in these programs are being quickly overcome by their new classroom reality as well as the various organizational and institutional responsibilities that leave no room for application of their newly gained knowledge (Artigliere & Baecher, 2017). This all leads to low levels of satisfaction for novice ESL teachers in their second and third years of teaching and some even decide that they have had enough and leave the profession (Redding & Henry, 2018).

Hence, novice teachers in these induction years (years 1 to 3) can also help themselves more by engaging in their own reflective practice activities. They can and should also do this with the aid of the school appointed mentor, or as Feiman-Nemser (2001: 18) calls it "educative mentoring." Here the mentor encourages the novice teacher to engage in reflective practice, and research indicates that such collaborations can result in reduced rates of early career teacher attrition. Reflective practice generally means that novice language teachers gather evidence by systematically examining their philosophy, principles, beliefs, and theory – as well as their actual practices – while also critically reflecting beyond practice (Farrell, 2015)

Engaging in such evidence-based reflective practice enables novice language teachers to articulate to themselves (and peers as well as mentors and supervisors) what they do, how they do it, why they do it, and in such a manner gauge the impact on their students' learning. Novice language teachers, therefore, can make informed decisions about their practice based on what they learned in their teacher education programs as well as what they experience in real classrooms with real students in their induction years.

The first question – what novice teachers actually do in each lesson – is very important because what teachers think they do and what they actually do in the classroom is not always the same (Farrell, 2022). In order to answer this question novice teachers must *look* at what they do now in their teaching. Thus, they must gather evidence about what they do (not what they think they do), and this can be from a variety of sources such as from self-reflection, their students' reflections, and their colleagues' (peers, mentors and supervisors) reflections. Novice teachers can make use of reflective tools such as teaching journals, audio and/or video recordings of themselves teaching.

Teaching journals are a good way to begin self-reflection as they provide novice teachers with a written record of various aspects of their practice both inside and outside the classroom. Writing has a built-in reflective mechanism because novice teachers must stop to think about what to write, and they can see their thoughts and reflections in writing after they have finished. Such reflective writing can include written accounts of thoughts, classroom observations (see below), assumptions, beliefs, attitudes, and experiences about their practice both inside and outside the classroom (Farrell, 2013a, b). Of course, there are different modes of writing for reflection, including handwritten or typed journals, or online writing in blogs, chats and forums. When teachers write regularly in a teaching journal, they can accumulate information that on later review, interpretation, and reflection can assist them in gaining a deeper understanding of their work (Farrell, 2007, 2018a,b). Thus, by writing regularly, novice language teachers can better identify and address critical issues that may appear in their practice, and as a result provide more learning opportunities for their students.

Novice language teachers can also record (audio and/or video) their lessons as an aid to self-reflection. The most important type of concrete classroom communication data a teacher should collect is a recording of the communications and a record of this recording in the form of a written classroom transcript. If we rely on our memory of classroom communications and events, we may miss some important data because we all have selective memories.

> **Reflective Break**
> Audio or video record your class. Now play the tape and try to answer the following questions:
>
> - What did you notice first about the recording?
> - Did you focus on your voice (and physical appearance if you used video)?
> - Did you notice your pronunciation?
> - What did you notice about your students?
> - Are you comfortable with the speed at which you heard yourself speak?
> - If your students did not respond, what did you do?
> - How much wait-time did you allow in which your students could think before answering your questions?
> - How did you check on your students' understanding?
> - What kind of reinforcement did you give and how often?

Once the classroom communication data has been collected, the teacher then needs to transcribe the recording. It may not be necessary to transcribe the entire recording; teachers can decide what aspect of the classroom communications they are interested in knowing more about. For example, teachers may only be interested in reflecting on the impact of their verbal instructions in their classes, so all they need to do is listen to and transcribe those parts of the tape that show the teacher giving instructions and then the turns immediately after this (for about five minutes) to see what impact these instructions have had on their students' learning. Other topics could include the type and frequency of teacher (and student) questions, how tasks are set up in their classes, or the type of language in use in group discussions (if teachers of English language learners wish to focus on this aspect of classroom communication). After transcribing classroom communication, the teacher can analyze and interpret the data. After making interpretations about the communications that exist in their classes, teachers can decide if they want to make any variations in the patterns that they have discovered. In this way, teachers can take more responsibility for the decisions they make about their classes. Teachers can also share the transcribed data with their mentors, peers and even their students.

When language teachers record (audio and/or video) their lessons, they can have a more accurate depiction of what is actually happening during the lesson, rather than what they think is happening. When in full flight of teaching, it is very difficult for most teachers, and especially novice teachers, to be able to realize and reflect on everything that is happening at once in their surroundings. Therefore, play back and listen (and see ifthe lesson is videoed) how much is happening during each lesson is important.

Although I outlined and discussed self-reflection for novice teachers above, I believe that collaborative reflections are more in line with what Dewey (1933) encouraged many years ago. When novice teachers self-reflect, a good starting point, they can obtain more insight about their practice. However, they may also be selective about what they are noticing and may avoid aspects of their practice that may seem uncomfortable for them. Thus, obtaining even more feedback from their colleagues through peer, mentor, and/or supervisor in a collaborative manner may yield even more information about their practice (for more on collaborations, see below).

For example, novice language teachers can engage in lesson study where they collaborate with other peers to plan and teach various lessons. Lesson study is non-evaluative and grounded in everyday classroom practices. In lesson study teams of teachers (who can be all novices or a mixture of novice and experienced teachers) usually co-plan a lesson and, after the lesson, the team (the teacher, observers, and any invited outsiders) gather together to discuss their observations. After the group discussions, the team revisits the lesson based on the feedback they received, and a revised lesson is then delivered either to the same class or to a different group of students. A second review is held that focuses on the overall effectiveness of the lesson. The lesson study cycle ends with the team publishing a report, which includes lesson plans, observed student behavior, teacher reflections, and a summary of the group discussions.

Associated with the above outlined lesson study above is collaborative classroom observations and reflections where novice language teachers invite peers, mentors, supervisors to join them to observe them teach. Of course, there should be general agreement amongst all parties on the process: the exact observation procedures and type of instruments (quantitative, qualitative, or both) to be used during this session, and the arrangement of a schedule for the observations. Participants can, for example, decide to take a general approach to collecting data by using such instruments as written ethnography and/or they can make an audio and/or video recording of their lesson (Richards & Farrell, 2011). Teachers can also take a more detailed approach by using some form of category instrument to collect data such as checklists (Richards & Farrell, 2005) or even a particular category instrument such as SCORE (Seating Chart Observation Record) (Richards & Farrell, 2011). For example, Richards and Farrell (2011) reported on a short series of classroom observations where a facilitator for a novice ESL teacher used a seating chart observation record or SCORE as a category instrument to collect hard evidence and discovered that such a non-inferential classroom observation instrument was more beneficial to novice ESL teachers than more open-ended instruments because it enabled the teacher to move from a descriptive reflective phase to a more critical stance on her practice. The instrument allowed the teacher to see that there was convergence between her stated beliefs and her actual classroom practices.

Engaging in reflective practice for novice language teachers is powerful, especially if they feel isolated in these first three important years of teaching. By engaging in reflective practice, they can begin to uncover their philosophy (who they are), principles (what they believe), theory (how they plan) and practice (what they do) and critically reflect beyond practice (why they do it). The remaining chapters of this book outline and discuss the reflections of Roger – one particular novice ESL teacher in Canada during his first year and then during his third year with the aid of a facilitator (this author). This case-based, qualitative research can be challenged as being only focused on the lived experiences of one ESL teacher, and thus considered narrow and overly unique. In fact, all of my research *with* language teachers over the past 40 years has been case-based and challenged in a similar manner and even considered as lacking rigor, perhaps because of my own research bias. I always answer the same: that too much rigor can lead to "rigor mortis" especially in more statistical-based research methods where the person-as-teacher is lost, as well as the context in which he or she teaches. I outlined in the previous chapter how I implement trustworthiness, which also addresses the rigor question (Lincoln & Guba, 1985). By presenting Roger's case I hope, too, that researchers who normally work within the quantitative paradigm may (re)consider the rigid nature of predetermined data that is not present in the approach taken in this book. In fact, the data is generated during the process of reflection and, as such, coding is immediate and ongoing throughout the process. The time invested in this data collection (of four years in total) enabled me to develop a positive rapport with Roger so that he trusted me enough to allow me to enter his professional world as a novice ESL teacher. I now, with Roger's permission, invite you, the reader, also to enter Roger's professional world as I outline his reflections on his philosophy, principles, theory, practice and critical reflections beyond practice in his first year and then in his third year.

CONCLUSION

This chapter has outlined and discussed issues related to teaching in the induction years that include the transition from trainee to novice teacher, the first year of teaching and the remaining early career years to the end of the third year. The chapter points out that although novice ESL teachers may survive their first year "transition traumas", this does not mean they are out of the woods and settled into their teaching careers. Unless they have adequate support from school appointed mentors, and/or supervisors, research has indicated that the "traumas" will continue in the second and third (early career) years of teaching. Indeed, being an early career ESL teacher is a difficult job requiring much responsibility with an abundance of expectations from many different sectors, including students, colleagues and administrators. The chapter highlights the benefits of engaging in systematic reflective practice, both alone and/or with peers, mentors and supervisors. In so doing, novice language teachers can help themselves better survive any challenges they may encounter as they transition into a rewarding career as a language teacher. What follows is a detailed case-study of the lived experiences of a novice ESL teacher in Canada, Roger, during his first year and then his third year of teaching through the mediational tool of reflective practice: specifically, the framework for reflecting on practice that was introduced in Chapter 1.

Chapter 3

Reflecting on Philosophy in the First Year

INTRODUCTION

This chapter introduces you to Roger's philosophy which is the first stage of the framework introduced in Chapter 1. This first stage of reflection examines Roger's "teacher-as-person" and suggests that professional practice, both inside and outside the classroom, is invariably guided by his basic philosophy that has been developed since birth. Thus, in order to be able to reflect on our basic philosophy, we need to obtain self-knowledge and we can access this by exploring, examining and reflecting on our background – from where we have evolved – such as our heritage, ethnicity, religion, socioeconomic background, family and personal values that have combined to influence who we are as language teachers. As such, teachers talk or write about their own lives and how they think their past experiences may have shaped the construction and development of their basic philosophy of practice. I first present Roger's early experiences through the "Tree of Life" (Farrell, 2021) without divulging any personal information that can reveal his personal details and this is followed by Roger's professional role identity discussion.

ROGER'S EARLY EXPERIENCES

Although I briefly introduced "who" Roger is in Chapter 1, this section will provide more details about him and how his early life experiences have influenced and possibly shaped who he is as a teacher in his first year. According to Farrell (2019), the "Tree of Life" represents a teacher's chronological development of their personal early experiences growing up, and is divided into *roots*, *trunk* and *limbs* as follows: the "roots" provide the foundations of what has shaped early years such as family values, heritage, ethnicity, religion, and socioeconomic backgrounds. The "trunk" captures experiences from early school years all the way to high school years and university years; in other words, educational experiences as a student. The "limbs" represent all professional experiences as a teacher. In this section I present Roger's "roots" and "trunk".

Roots

- Born in [a country outside Canada].
- Immigrated to Canada when 3½ years old.
- I have two younger sisters.
- My family was very conservative Christian and strongly adhered to the Christian faith; I was raised to be respectful and to follow rules, in a sense; now I'm not as conservative as my family is, but still hold on to the basic principles of the Christian faith; I've learned to be tolerant of others and to be respectful of people from different backgrounds; honesty, integrity, a strong work ethic, and patience are qualities that I've developed as a result of my faith.
- I went to school at 4 years old and this is how I learned English, though I have no recollection of it; I apparently learned English very quickly and fitted into my group of peers very easily.
- My parents worked very hard to adapt to Canadian culture and had to work a lot to get by; my mom was mainly a stay-at-home mom and took care of other kids during the day; my dad worked at a few different jobs during my childhood; both my parents were a big part of my life as a child, and I think I may have subconsciously observed how they integrated into Canadian culture and learned English.
- My family and I went back to [their country of birth] frequently and had family from [their country of birth] visit us often; we mainly spoke [country of birth language] at home for the first five or six years that we lived in Canada and slowly switched to English as us children became older.
- I continued to learn/use [country of birth language] by visiting and interacting with my extended family and reading [country of birth language] comic books.
- I didn't ever feel negative about the [country of birth] language or culture, but just slowly stopped using it as I got older; now I can still speak [country of birth language], but it takes a little bit for it to become fluent again.
- I still don't completely consider myself Canadian and still feel a connection to the [country of birth] culture and language.

Trunk

- Family trips back to [his country of birth] and having family visit us from [his country of birth] greatly impacted my view of language as a tool of communication and I think I fostered an appreciation of second languages and their unique function as another way to communicate with people; I noticed that being able to speak more than one language opened doors that monolingual people could never access.
- Teachers who impacted me during my school years:

  - I had several grade schoolteachers who I noticed had a real passion for teaching and I could see their joy when teaching us; this was a quality that I noticed very quickly made a big difference in how "good" a teacher was. I noticed that my teachers who were full of passion cared more about their students, cared more about how they taught (they were more interactive and valued input from students), and they cared to know more about their students' personal lives and interests. In my eyes, this made them better teachers and I think it influenced how I am as a teacher as well as I always make a point to find out more about my students interests and personal lives and try to incorporate that into my lessons.

  - I also had a grade schoolteacher who very obviously ostracized the "bad" students in the class and made examples out of them. I always felt bad for my peers who were treated this way and thought that it wasn't a good way for a teacher to deal with students who were not behaving the way they wanted them to. I think students with learning problems or attention problems have root causes for them, and those should be identified and dealt with rather than just not caring about the students.

- Teachers who impacted me during high school:

  - My favourite teachers were once again the ones who genuinely cared about their students and who cared to know them on a personal level. I had a few high school teachers who I was close with and was able to connect with them in different ways, not just academically. They cared about my hobbies and interests and wanted to help me become the best student that I could be. Once again, this is something that influenced my own teacher values as I see a great importance in connecting with students at a social level too, to a certain extent obviously.

  - I had a teacher in grade 9 who gave marks based on what she thought of you. If she liked you, she gave you better grades. I hated this, even though she liked me. I didn't see how it was fair.

> ▸ During high school (and university) I worked at a tree nursery during the summers and on weekends and worked with Mexican migrant workers. Upon reflection, I have come to realize that working with these guys also impacted how I view second language learners. I became quite close to some of these guys and even spent time with them outside of work and learned about the tremendous sacrifices they made to come work in Canada and of course to deal with communicating in English. Because of my experiences with them, I learned to value what foreigners have to offer and that everyone who learns a second language in a different country makes sacrifices of varying proportions. At the tree nursery I also had a boss who made a large impact on who I am today. He realized that I had leadership qualities and helped me develop those by giving me increased responsibilities the longer I worked for him, to the point where I was the one running the operation when he was on holidays in the summer. He taught me what it takes to be a leader, but he also had some qualities that showed me how not to treat those who are under my leadership. He was often very emotional and had a short fuse. He also didn't take the time to completely understand a situation before reacting. These were qualities that I didn't see as good ones for someone in a leadership position, including a teacher. So, when I teach, I'm often very patient and take the time to evaluate a situation before reacting. Also, I don't let my emotions take a hold of me, especially in the classroom.

Limbs

- I studied Applied Linguistics for my BA undergraduate years. Then I entered an MA Applied Linguistics program that focused on Teaching English as a Second Language (TESOL) for my graduate degree.
- I began teaching in a university language program after graduation. At the time of my reflections with Tom I had been teaching there for three years.

Reflective Break
- Comment on Roger's journey so far.
- How do you think his early experiences with multiple languages in his home has influenced him as a teacher today?
- How do you think his past teachers have influenced him as a teacher today?
- Have you been influenced by any of your past teachers?
- Fill in your Tree of Life in Figure 3.1 (below)

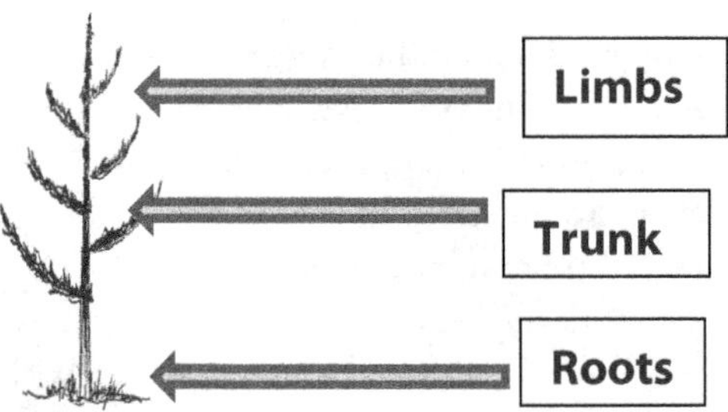

Figure 3.1 Your Tree of Life (from Farrell, 2019)

After drawing your "Tree of Life" you can begin to "see" particular prior experiences and events (both positive and negative) that occurred as being significant for your development as a person and, later, as a teacher. Teachers can thus begin to identify and synthesize various life events such as their early childhood experiences; experiences as a student in primary school; experiences as a student in high school; experiences as a student in college or university; any informal learning experiences; perhaps "best"/"worst" language learning experiences; "best"/"worst" courses/teachers; influential teachers as role models; "best"/"worst" teaching experiences. When teachers note all of these and more, they can begin to write up their story in order to uncover past influences that have shaped them in their current position as a teacher.

ROGER'S FIRST YEAR PROFESSIONAL IDENTITY DEVELOPMENT

The previous section outlined Roger's early life and points to several interesting experiences that may have impacted his reason to enter teaching (mostly positive experiences with most of his grade schoolteachers) and the field of second language studies as well (initially using English as a second language as well as being an immigrant, and his studies of Applied Linguistics during his undergraduate and graduate life). Also, as noted above, Roger began his teaching career right after graduating from his MA program and the section that follows outlines and discusses his philosophy through his professional development during his first year.

For the purposes of this book, the concept of "professional identity" refers to teachers' knowledge of themselves as teachers and answers the question "Who am I as a teacher?" and "What kind of teacher do I want to be?" In addition, professional identity development really takes place as a result of the interaction between personal philosophies and professional practice. Some scholars even suggest that, within an educational context, identity development is all about giving meaning to these changes. Language teachers in their first year are required to perform many different roles, as they learn how to collaborate with colleagues, in order to be able to participate in a school community. Thus, this chapter attempts to outline and discuss Roger's professional role identity as he began his teaching in a university language center during his first year on the job.

The following top five professional identity roles for Roger in his first year as a language teacher were identified in order of their frequency:

1   Pedagogical & Language Expert
2   Novice/Learner
3   Individual
4   Student-centered Facilitator
5   Didactic

Pedagogical & Language Expert

The most frequent professional role identity that Roger identifies either explicitly or implicitly throughout his first year is that of the role of pedagogical expert. This includes his sense of confidence in his knowledge and training as well as his qualifications as a language teacher as he transitions into his first full year as a language teacher. This role also includes his stated confidence in how he can measure student knowledge of their needs with learning English as a second language and his knowledge of all things related to teaching English as a second language.

From the very beginning of the first semester, Roger makes several references to his confidence in his "qualifications" as a language teacher that he suggests makes him a pedagogical and language expert as he embarks on his teaching career. During his first week, Roger says that he suddenly realizes that his students "look at you as if you're that teacher" and that he feels at that time that "I did not need that title of teacher." He says that he told them to call him by his first name and not use the term "teacher" as this is too new for him. Then, after his first week on the job, Roger says that he really felt like he was a teacher because he has experience in that role; he remarks: "I've actually given lessons. I have students do work that I've assigned. I have my own classroom. I definitely feel like a teacher now."

Roger notes in the very first week of his first-year teaching that he feels "more qualified to teach the way I feel comfortable with, versus someone saying, 'this is how you do it, just follow these steps, it's simpler.'" When Roger began his first week of teaching, and started to get to know the type of classes he would be covering this semester, he says that although his masters degree program was useful to teach him about "diversity in language teaching" he straight away noticed that his classes had students from one country as a majority and so he was excited to use his knowledge to teach this group. In fact, Roger says that he was very excited to start his teaching career because of his qualifications; Roger continues, "when I stepped into the classroom that first day it was exciting because I'm loaded, so to speak, with this new knowledge and yeah, it's exciting to see if I learned a lot about classroom management, classroom control, teaching methods, and so on, from the masters program." Roger states that he was proud of spending "five years doing a BA and an MA" but gets frustrated when he notes in certain locations (he did not specify) a "Mr. Joe Blow up the street could walk up into an ESL school and say 'hey, I speak English, can I have a job?', and they'll say 'come on in.'" Roger continues:

> I haven't really been personally affected by someone else taking my job who is not as qualified as I am, but I mean I've definitely thought about it before like why is it that ESL teachers like even the fact that why can't I teach ESL in the public-school systems with my MA? Whereas I can teach at the university level, which is a much higher level, right? I do have higher qualifications.

Thus, for Roger, the proper qualifications to teach English as a second language allows him to call himself a pedagogical and language expert and his master's degree gives him more respect than "Joe Blow"; Roger continues,

> I feel with an MA you feel that you'll be more respected because you have this especially in the academic world where it's all about, hey what's your qualification, or whatever. I just kind of know that people higher up say well this guy's just got a BA you know, where as he has an MA he might know a thing or two about it.

Roger separates himself from other teachers he feels that may not have such qualifications or expertise and notes, for example, that "anytime there's an issue like plagiarism or something like that, I always have the resources to be able to back up why it's wrong, why I caught it, why I gave them a zero and so on." Roger continues about the topic of plagiarism and his confidence that he has the "resources and the knowledge to back up what I do." Roger says that because of his MA training he is aware of how students may try to plagiarize and that he will pick this up immediately if they try it in his classes:

> I've been trained to do this kind of stuff. It's pretty easy to pick it out, I mean, there's maybe one or two students who, if they plagiarized, I wouldn't notice because they have really good writing style, and

whatever, but for the majority of them, it's like this complex sentence,
like wow or this whole paragraph with these complex words.

Roger notes that he is so confident in his pedagogical and language expertise that
he intends to put a lot of effort into teaching and focusing on issues that he feels he
is good at (such as pointing out plagiarism above) because if he did not do this, he
"would almost be cheating myself and my potential students by not teaching something that I'm good at." He feels to teach "the easiest things and take the easiest
path" would be a waste of his five years of BA and MA training and so this makes
him a confident teacher going into his first semester. As Roger says, "okay now I'm
qualified, I know how to do this. My MA definitely gave me the confidence that
now I'm equipped to do this, and my opinions are actually valuable for even my new
colleagues to hear." Thus, even during his first weeks on the job Roger repeats his
confidence not only in his qualifications to teach English as a second language, but
also his feeling of being "very competent to teach those skills."

As the first semester progresses, Roger says that he is especially pleased with his
knowledge of academic writing and his expertise in how to teach this, because he
has noticed many of his students are supposed to enter regular university classes
but do not have a competent knowledge of grammar. Roger notes that because they
are entering university classes, they will be lost because, "there's nobody there that's
going to say, 'well here's a grammar mistake, there's a grammar mistake' and at that
point if they aren't self-aware of how important grammar is and how to make sure
that your grammar is consistent throughout your paper, then nobody is going to tell
them." So, Roger says that he will try to get them "to have this ability to self-correct
their own work" so that they will not lose marks. Roger pities them "because they
have difficulties writing a simple sentence without grammar mistakes."

One more issue arising for Roger during his first year is that because most of the
students are from the same country, they are continuously speaking their L1 during
class time and that this is against school policy and his policy. So, he always tries to
keep the students from speaking any language other than English in the classroom.
Roger notes that "even just minutes after I tell the entire class that one of my biggest goals in my speaking class particularly is to speak English all the time in class.
And then a few minutes later they're chatting off in [their L1] again and this seems
to be in all of my classes." This frustrates Roger a lot so he tries to "eliminate" their
L1 or, at the very least, "keep it to a minimum." He says that his students are here to
learn English and so they should not be speaking their L1 and he even gives extra
homework to "repeat offenders."

Roger's role of pedagogical and language expert continues throughout the first
semester and his second semester as he gains more experience and thus feels more
comfortable as a teacher. Roger says he feels more confident and "more natural" as a

teacher than during the first semester. He attributes a lot of his growing confidence also to the fact that he has been teaching a "good class" and this may have helped him a lot as well. Roger says that he has been very confident in these roles (pedagogical and language expert) throughout his first year because of what he learned in his MA program and that he feels teaching is "something that I'm meant to do." Roger continues, "I'm confident I'm teaching this the way that I want to teach it and that the students are actually learning and benefitting from it."

At the end of his first year of teaching Roger notes that he is happy with the way he "looked as a teacher and how I like my body language as a teacher" even though everything has been very new for him during this year. Roger says that he feels he was meant to do this as a career and that it is "something that I'm actually good at." Roger notes that he is happy with his career choice as a teacher and that after his first-year experiences as a teacher, he realizes that it is "the right job, it's something that suits me personally, too."

> **Reflective Break**
> - What is your understanding of teacher as "pedagogical and language expert"?
> - What do you think of Roger's experiences of this role in his first year?

Novice

The second most frequent role identity Roger mentions is his realization that although he may have considered himself as a pedagogical expert in terms of his qualifications, he is also a novice teacher. From the very beginning Roger acknowledges that he sees himself as a novice teacher relative to teachers with "more experience" or "a lot more experience"; he remarks, "I don't have that much experience, but you know, marking, teaching writing, teaching other skills and the like." This is especially true for his first semester teaching as he also acknowledges that he has only had experience teaching writing and speaking and that he spends too much time marking papers. He says, "one of my other colleagues, who's also a first-time writing teacher, she was saying she was spending like an hour marking each one like me." However, Roger also says he was not mentored by any experienced teacher and that there was no induction program in the school he was teaching in that first year.

Roger says that, as a novice teacher, he still has much to learn even though he feels "very qualified" and has the pedagogical and language knowledge (see above) to deliver all his courses. Roger remarks that he remembers "a quote that said, 'a good teacher always learns,' I've definitely learned a lot being a teacher this term and need to learn more." After his first semester teaching, Roger recalls his own past experience as a student and figures he could look at issues he encountered during this semester "from that angle." Roger says that from his experience as a student, he knows "the loopholes, I know where you can get away with things and where you can't right? I mean that in itself gives me a bit of an insider." So, he says that he can use this "insider knowledge" more the second semester of his first year. Roger remarkes,

> now I'm the teacher and watching my students. I know what it's like to be a student and to be you know bored, tired, whatever, but there's still going to be a final exam on materials that are covered going to be covered from here until then. In order for you to do well on that you need to be here.

Roger notes that the institution could have helped him more during his first days and weeks with an "orientation" of some kind as he had none. Roger realizes that an orientation "would be a pretty significant thing. And also, just saying, this is how things work here, feel free to use your own teaching methods, or even just hooking us up with a mentor teacher. Someone who's been teaching for 5, 10 years."

Even though Roger admits that he was still a novice teacher throughout his first year, he also says that he realized that the school he was teaching in has some "problems that need to be changed" (such as no orientation or induction program for novice teachers as noted above) and that he is "affected by some of them." He says that as a novice he was disappointed that there was no induction program or mentor he could go too because "everyone seemed too busy with us novice teachers", so he just talked to one or two more experienced colleagues when he had pressing questions. He says this is very important for novice teachers to seek out more experienced teachers to run things by:

> I would recommend talking to another teacher who's had a lot more experience who's taught the same classes you have because I mean you're starting off and you really don't have a clue how to do quite a few things, so just hearing someone else's way of doing things can maybe help you, you know, just have something … like by hearing someone else's way it's a way that you can do things for the time being until you figure out your own style, your own practices.

That said, at the end of his first year teaching he says that he has learned a lot about himself as a teacher and that he feels competent as a teacher. Roger remarks, "from the skills that I've been teaching I feel now that I'm very qualified, very competent to teach those skills just because I've seen the final results, I've seen how it works, but I am still a novice teacher I'd say."

Individual

The next professional identity role that Roger identifies with either implicitly or explicitly is that of "Roger as an individual" where he notes that "every teacher is different and has different ways, styles, methods, preferences, and choices in regard to how they go about teaching; values freedom in following one's own way, discovering what works best for that person." Perhaps this role is connected to his role as a novice but without much institutional support to develop, so he has to survive as an individual from the very first day on the job. For example, even though Roger says that he does not get nervous easily, but he did somewhat on his first day when he walked into his first class and there were only five students, but he was told he would have twenty-five and he did not know what to do or who to approach for advice.

Roger says that he realized that he would be left alone to survive but this was not a problem for him because he felt qualified to do what he liked anyway as an individual. Roger remarks, "I kind of want to have my own personal stamp on what I do. For me, I don't know, I feel like I'm more qualified if I'm able to do it the way that I feel comfortable with versus someone saying, 'this is how you do it, just follow these steps, it's simpler.'" Roger linked this notion of doing things by himself to his education and his personality; he continues, "I've had all this education and I have always just been the type of person that likes to figure out things on my own and see what happens."

So, Roger is not unhappy about being left alone during his first year as a teacher as he notes "It kind of gives me the freedom to, you know, develop the course the way that I think seems fit and I can kind of put my stamp on things, my way of doing things on it." That said he also wishes that he could have had a chance to talk to more teachers with experience teaching the courses he was assigned to during his first year. Roger remarks that "it would be good to have a weekly meeting, or bi-weekly meeting, or even a monthly meeting with the same instructors who teach the same course, just kind of get together and say, hey how are your regular classes going? What are you doing? What are you finding? You know, what's working for you? What isn't working?" This way, he says, he could compare what he was doing with other approaches to consider if their way was better or not for him. Roger reflects that "by hearing someone else's way it's a way that you can do things for the time being until you figure out your own style, your own practices." For example, he says, he tried not to prepare too much ahead of a class so that he is "more natural as a teacher." However, one time during his first semester he provided the incorrect material for his class, and he realized this as he was trying to explain it to his class. So, although this is his "personal choice, a personal style not to prepare too much so you're more natural", he also knows this is "risky" as he feels challenged to think on the spot as occurred during that class. Thus, he says, it would have been nice if he had regular discussions with other teachers so he could compare such experiences.

> **Reflective Break**
> - What is your understanding of teacher as "individual"?
> - What do you think of Roger's experiences of this role in his first year?

Student-centered Facilitator

Another professional role Roger explicitly identifies is the "student-centered teacher" who desires to help students, and does more work for their benefit. Roger says that for him, "everything is about the students, not the teacher." Roger notes that, "compared to other teachers, I go less by the book. I think I'm more interactive with my students I think I'm more of a student-centered teacher than a teacher-centered teacher." Roger also relates this to his idea of being a facilitator where he does not want to force his students to learn or push them too hard but wants it to be voluntary and exploratory as he guides or facilitates their learning.

Throughout the first semester, Roger notes that he tells them almost every class, "any questions, talk to me, email me, ask me, I'm here to help." In fact, over and over again when discussing his students, Roger says that he is there to help and support them all the time because he realizes that they have some struggles to deal with learning English as a second language, "in a new country, a new culture, a new learning style, a new system of learning and so on." Thus, he wants to connect with them "on a personal level" about whatever they want to talk about. Roger talks about one such topic beyond learning English – when one student asked him for advice about getting an oil change. Roger relates this example as follows,

> Like even this week a student asked me, where can I get an oil change? And you just start talking to them and then, oh man, even just something like as common and simple as I need an oil change, I think that is an important thing too, is connecting with them on a different level than only academic.

Thus, he speaks of trying to "mould" himself "toward certain types of classes" and to remain flexible in the way he teaches them and be willing to try new approaches in order to help his students and develop what he calls "a student-centered classroom" during his first semester. As Roger notes, during his first semester, "something that

I found myself doing a lot throughout the term, is asking my students like what do you want? Or what do you think about this? Kind of having their input in. So, I think as part of my teacher, like the way that I see myself as a teacher is one who's student centered and flexible." Roger contrasts this approach to a teacher-centered classroom where "it was all about me and you know how much I'm teaching and how much work I'm doing, obviously I wouldn't give a test or anything. I would just tell them do some extra practice and figure it out yourself type thing. But I figure, like my approach is more I want to help the students. It's all about them."

Roger's description of his student-centered approach changes somewhat after his second semester teaching in his first year. Although he recognizes that perhaps he could do more to help his students, he also realizes that if his students do not understand something, they must take some responsibility for this; it is "not the teacher's problem that after spending a significant amount of time on something that the students still don't understand it." Roger begins to realize the limitations of his offer to provide help to his students in a student-centered classroom but that he still does not want to force them to come to him for help. He continues: "A lot of it is their responsibility where you know, I offer them help, I tell them, look you can come talk to me, I can help you, and I think they should come see me, but I mean I obviously can't force them to come see me."

Roger does not want to force his students to answer any questions because he thinks this should be a voluntary process, he notices "the same four or five students who always participated" and now he says that he must work on getting more to participate. As he remarks, "I don't want to make anyone feel like they have to answer questions, but I don't know, that's kind of a fine line sometimes, is how much you want to push them, right?" Roger says that towards the end of the second semester of his first year his teaching was probably shaped by the personality of his classes as one class had most students from one country but the other was more diverse. He notes:

> Because a lot of the way that you teach depends on the personality of your classes and I mean the fact that one of my classes was 95% [from one particular country] made it a very different class than other classes. It's a lot quieter, it's a lot more not as exciting in a sense, as let's say a class where there's you know, 50% [different country] students, just because of their personalities, right?

Roger noticed then that he "models" himself towards the way the students in a particular class "want me to be" so that he can facilitate their learning. However, during the second semester of his first year teaching he also seems to struggle with this role as a student-centered facilitator with the need to maintain a degree of authority or power over his students to get them to do particular tasks. For example, Roger mentions a few times that he needs to be a bit more of a "hard-ass" teacher because he does not want to make everything too easy for them and that they probably respect such a teacher more:

> I want to accommodate some of their requests too, but within reason, right? I want them to work hard and sure they don't like it at that time, but after the fact, they'll realize okay, wow that was good that I learned that much stuff, and you know, my teacher pushed me because now I have to learn how to push myself.

Roger wonders at the end of this second semester of his first year as a teacher how he can reconcile his role as a student-centered facilitator guiding his students to learn, with the issue of how much control he should use to get them to learn without being too controlling. Roger summarizes this as follows: "I kind of want to have a more casual way of acting with them but then at the same time I don't want to lose the power that I have over them."

Reflective Break
- What is your understanding of teacher as "student-centered facilitator"?
- What do you think of Roger's experiences of this role in his first year?

Didactic

Another professional identity role that emerges for Roger during his first year as a teacher is that of being "didactic", or moralistic to his students. Perhaps this role is a lead in from the above acknowledged dilemma of trying to balance facilitation with some control – another role that Roger identifies is that of acting as a parent for his students, and this happens more during the second semester of his first-year teaching. As a "parent" Roger acknowledges students are "adults" and are responsible for their own learning, and so he denies being their "babysitter", yet he realizes that he now struggles with how to respond to their "acting like children." He says that he thinks his particular group of students, because they are from a particular region of the world, may be less mature for their age and so may require more guidance: "I'm not here to babysit them. They should be paying attention, if they don't pay attention, they're not going to learn it and if they don't learn, then well they're not going to do well. I don't want to tell them, hey wake up, wake up, wake up. I don't know if that's my, well it's my problem, but I mean it's more their problem." In fact, although he has not mentioned this to his students directly, he feels that they act like children at times and that he gets frustrated with this:

What I really wanted to tell them was, look you guys are really acting like kids right now. You're playing with pieces of paper, you're you
know, goofing off, you're not paying attention, just hyper like a child
would be."

This is a role where Roger finds himself telling his students about what is "right
and wrong" (such as plagiarism); what is, or should be, appropriate behavior in a
multi-cultural environment, as well as appropriate behavior in an academic setting;
and how to acculturate to the local cultural and academic setting. For example, one
of these classroom rules also connected to school rules is that the students have to
speak English (the target language) at all times and so Roger feels that he has a moral obligation to enforce this rule. Over and over again in both semesters of his first
year of teaching, Roger says that he had to continuously remind his students not
to use their L1 during class time, but they continued to use this regardless. Roger
says that this irritated him during the second semester; he relays, "What irritates
me about it is that I've told them use English in this class. That's one of the classroom rules, in fact that's the number one classroom rule. I don't have many rules but
speaking English in my class." When asked why he wanted to enforce such a rule,
Roger says that it was wrong (morally) for students just to continue using their L1
when students and himself are from other language (L1) backgrounds that are different and thus may not be able to understand what they are saying. In fact, Roger
says that the whole class may be missing out on getting some useful information
from these students because of this lack of understanding. He notes, "there are people from other cultural backgrounds, and other language backgrounds, including
me, who don't understand what they say, and perhaps they're saying something useful and if they would've said it in English, someone else could have benefited from
that." Roger also suggests that he "feared" some of these students who use their L1
continuously may also be engaged in "idle chatter" not related to classroom tasks,
and he can tell such discussions, he says, by "their body language."

Another issue related both to his own classroom rules, and the school rules is
the issue of plagiarism that Roger feels the need to enforce. Roger has a passionate
objection to plagiarism saying, "it's wrong, it's lying, it's an offense", but he worries
that some of his students do not feel the same way about this for whatever reason.
He notes that some students copy other students' presentations and he is worried
that they don't really "realize that the average student in a regular university class
would be offended by this, and that they shouldn't use it." He says that he would always mention this after a presentation that he knew was plagiarized and that "after
this happened, after every presentation, as a class we talk about it." Roger says that
when they are doing a presentation they should consider the audience and "if you
know your audience don't like these types of things, you probably shouldn't use it.

And yes, you have freedom of speech and freedom to do these sort things, but it doesn't happen in this place in academic world." He mentions that if students persist they could be expelled from the university for plagiarism. Indeed, if challenged about his "accusations" of plagiarism, he says "[I] always have the resources to be able to back up why it's wrong, why I caught it, why I gave them a zero and so on."

For Roger, this didactic professional identity role is interwoven with his desire to present a multicultural approach to his lessons and he tries to point out to his student that if you are from a monoculture, adapting to a more multicultural classroom may take some effort on their behalf. He explicitly tells all his classes about this multicultural approach and that "part of being in a multicultural classroom is that people won't always cater towards your beliefs or your opinions." He also says that he has pointed out to the students that part of being in a university is to hear different opinions and to consider "what is appropriate and what is not." For example, in his writing classes, although there is a note written on the syllabus about plagiarism and Roger talks about this on the opening day, inevitably the students first written assignment has "many examples of plagiarism" and, as he says, "the first thing we do once I hand them back is like scold them or whatever, lecture them about how wrong this is." Overall, Roger feels that he has a moral responsibility to inform his students about the above issues as it is helpful for his students' adaptations to a new environment: "you have a lot of cultural backgrounds that interact differently, that learn differently, and a big part of learning is that you know how your students learn best."

> **Reflective Break**
> - What is your understanding of teacher as "didactic"?
> - What do you think of Roger's experiences of this role in his first year?

CONCLUSION

This chapter began with a background to Roger's early life experiences which noted that he was an immigrant and English as a second language speaker in his early life in Canada. These early experiences may have influenced him to take up his later university studies both undergraduate and graduate in Applied Linguistics where he studied second language development and teaching. The chapter then examines Roger's first year of teaching and presents his identity development with five main roles discussed in order of frequency: *Pedagogical and Language Expert*; *Novice and Learner*; *Individual*; *Student-centered Facilitator*; and *Didactic*. These roles suggest that Roger was confident in his qualifications as a language expert and his ability to teach but he recognized that he was a novice teacher with no experience. In addition, the institution in which he was teaching offered no professional develop-ment at entry or during his first year – that he was an individual there – which he noted suited his personality. The final two roles were that of student-centered facil-itator and didactic which suggest a certain amount of tension between his wish to bring students into their learning and at the same time making them take responsi-bility for their learning. All of these role identities suggest that Roger was trying to establish himself as an ESL teacher throughout his first year, to find a balance be-tween his personal ideals, his students' reactions and the requirements of his insti-tution. This is the first introduction to Roger's process of becoming an ESL teacher through analysis of his philosophy. The chapter that follows introduces Roger's first year principles of teaching and learning.

Chapter 4

Reflecting on First Year Principles

INTRODUCTION

This chapter introduces you to Roger's principles, which is the second stage of the framework introduced in chapter 1. This second stage of reflection examines Roger's deeply held assumptions, beliefs, and conceptions of language teaching and learning. These assumptions, beliefs, and conceptions can originate from a number of sources, such as a teacher's experiences as a student and what has or has not worked in previous lessons (Richards & Lockhart, 1994), and considering these sources while reflecting on principles of teaching and learning thus enables teachers to uncover their beliefs and their transferability to practice (which will be explored more in Chapter 6). In order to understand how teachers handle their work it is necessary to understand the beliefs and principles from which they operate. Farrell (2019) states that "teachers may struggle to articulate and externalize these tacitly held assumptions and beliefs" (p.17); however, by doing so, teachers are better able to identify their strengths and areas for improvement, and modify these beliefs when necessary. Teachers' principles are, for the most part, reflected in their beliefs which are complex and cover a range of issues such as beliefs about their students, themselves as teachers, teaching and learning English as a second/foreign language, and many more issues related to how teachers conceptualize their work (Burns, 1992).

The sources of such beliefs can offer a window into their meaning and, as Richards and Lockhart (1994) posit, they can be derived from experience, school practice, personality, educational theory, reading and other sources. As Richards (1998) points out, all these beliefs form a structured set of principles and act as a filter through which teachers make instructional judgements and decisions and, as such, should be examined.

Reflective Break
- What are your beliefs about teaching and learning English as a second/foreign language?

ROGER'S FIRST YEAR PRINCIPLES

One problem with examining teachers' principles in terms of their beliefs is that they often remain hidden to, or tacitly held by, the teacher and so must be brought to the level of awareness by being articulated in some way. When teachers are given a chance to articulate their beliefs about teaching and learning, they soon discover that their beliefs are far from simple. The most frequent beliefs that emerged from the data were Roger's beliefs about the use of L1 in his classes, teaching and learning writing, teaching and learning grammar, making his lessons challenging, collaboration with colleagues and his overall beliefs about ESL teachers.

L1 Use in Classes

At the very beginning of his first year of teaching Roger said that he believed that when his students were speaking their L1 during his lessons, that it was an indication that they were not paying attention to his teaching and so he would try to stop them. Roger said, "I know that they're not really paying attention to their work, necessarily, if they're speaking in [their L1], so I mean I think I have several methods that I will end up using to try to eliminate that." When asked about how he would "eliminate" Roger said that he heard about a technique of filling out squares on the white/blackboard each time students use their L1 in class and when the squares are full, he would give the entire class homework. Roger explained,

> Well, for example, something that I've heard about and that does work effectively with some groups is every time someone speaks [their L1], you fill in a square that you draw on the board, so you have three squares and after three of those squares have been filled in, then the entire class has homework that night. Each time one or two students are speaking in [their L1] I'll fill in a square. After three, the entire class will have homework that night. So, the purpose of that is to try and get them to work together as a group to stop people from speaking in [their L1] and use English instead. And I know it's not fair to those who don't speak [the same L1] because there are a lot of [the main L1] students, who always speak English, but perhaps that'll kind of make those [majority L1] speakers feel bad.

In addition, Roger said that he heard about a different method of asking the speaker of the L1 to leave. Roger remarked, "Well, another method, and this is after, you know, I've kind of picked out the people who are always speaking [their L1], just ask them to leave, very politely."

After the first few weeks teaching, Roger noted that he modified the above ideas to suit the classes he was teaching and decided not to give extra homework to the group because he decided that for some of his students it "is so natural to just turn around and speak in [their L1]." So instead, he decided to quietly watch who is always speaking their L1 and to tell them to stop or they "are going to have to pay me a dollar." He then said he would use any money for a class party at the end of the term. He said that he wanted to enforce the speak in English only during his lessons because it was a class rule that they all agreed to in the beginning and that he was "irritated" when they continued to speak their L1. Roger said,

> I don't have many rules, but speaking English in my class is, in my opinion, very important because there are people from other cultural backgrounds, and other language backgrounds, including me, who don't understand what they say, and perhaps they're saying something useful and if they would've said it in English, someone else could have benefited from that.

Reflective Break
- What are your beliefs about the use of L1 in your classes?
- What do you think of Roger's beliefs about the use of L1 in his classes?

Teaching Writing

In terms of his beliefs about teaching and learning writing, and continuing on from the use of L1 in his lessons, interestingly enough Roger said he does not get annoyed when the students use L1 in these classes. Roger said, "I don't think it quite bothers me as much in writing class, but I hear them whispering [their L1] here and there, and if it's a problem, then you know, I'll say 'if I keep hearing [their L1], you'll have some homework' or something, right? Because sometimes it's hard to pinpoint and say, 'it was you,' or 'it was you' because they're all kind of huddled."

In terms of the content focus should be in his writing classes, Roger noted that although the school wanted his classes to complete three of four major essays throughout the term, he did not think that this was viable because it would not benefit his students. Roger remarked,

> I would rather just focus on one major essay and focus on each step. I mean, obviously with a North American writing style it's very linear, you know, you start with choosing your topic, your thesis, outline, whatever, so what I want to do with this writing class is give them the

steps to writing an academic paper and it's pretty much like a format anyway. You just follow the steps and you write a half decent paper.

Roger said that writing four or five essays over the course of a single term would be possible but, he said, "to me that would be useless." He said that he would rather spend more time focusing on one thing "just writing one essay so that, rather than scrambling through the whole process, you focus on the steps that are needed to finish it." Roger then relayed his beliefs about teaching writing: starting with what he called "tiny things" and then moving on to "bigger things" when they have "the smaller things down pat." For Roger, the "bigger things" are things like writing an entire composition and the "smaller things" are "simple things like a sentence has a subject and predicate and you know subject verb agreements, even simple things like using articles and when to use them, when not to use them." For Roger, the actual teaching of writing would include lots of time for the students to practice writing not just "knowing what they should do." As Roger explained, "one thing that I really am trying to focus on in my writing class is to focus for at least two or three days on one thing and have them practice and practice a lot."

> **Reflective Break**
> - What are your beliefs about teaching and learning writing?
> - What do you think of Roger's beliefs about teaching and learning writing?

Teaching Grammar

In terms of his beliefs about teaching and learning grammar, Roger said he believes that knowledge of grammar is very important and that his students should master grammar rules, especially for his writing lessons (see above). However, he said his beliefs were not yet solid as he has a dilemma regarding how much focus he should place on grammar. Roger said, "writing and grammar are so closely connected that you can't ignore it but at the same time you can't really focus on the grammar too much, so it's kind of like a struggle, like how much do you focus on it, but how much do you just brush it to the side?" He noted that for his writing classes his main focus is content, but if the students make grammar errors he takes marks away from the overall grade. Roger said, "I told them that I'm like taking away marks for grammar and I'm doing this so that they realize that when they're writing something, they also have to focus on the grammar, they can't just write whatever they think and just focus on content, you also have to think about grammar." Roger said that he has a specific technique of dealing with "grammar mistakes":

if, for example, the auxiliary verb was in the wrong place, I'd take an arrow, move it to where it should be or if they use a gerund instead of an infinitive or something I'd cross out: "Cross out that –ing and fill it in." So, it's not like I would just leave them hanging with like "Oh there's a grammar mistake in this sentence, please fix it." I would fix it for them because at this point, they're not going to revise it so I might as well show them.

The reason, he said, that he points out the exact grammar mistake any student makes is because he is preparing them for university classes where a professor will not point out such mistakes. Roger goes on to explain the realities of university: "There's nobody there that's going to say, 'well here's a grammar mistake, there's a grammar mistake' and at that point if they aren't self-aware of how important grammar is and how to make sure that your grammar is consistent throughout your paper, then nobody is going to tell them."

> **Reflective Break**
> - What are your beliefs about teaching and learning grammar?
> - What do you think of Roger's beliefs about teaching and learning grammar?

Making Classes Challenging

Another of Roger's beliefs, especially at the beginning of his first year, was his idea of making his classes and lessons challenging for his students. This was especially when he was teaching university bound students when he said, "I don't want to make the speaking class easy for them because I know from what their level is to what they're going to be exposed to in university there's still a big gap so I might as well make it challenging, so hopefully it'll be challenging enough for everybody." Thus, he said he will be a "hard-ass" if necessary, continuing, "I don't want to make everything easy for them." In another class he wanted to make sure the students knew about plagiarism and its problem within the Canadian university system and that it is wrong although the students from different countries outside Canada may not realize it. Roger said, "that's something that I really pointed out that plagiarism is actually wrong, it's lying, it's an offense. It's like you can get kicked out of university for it." Roger said that after he mentioned this although some of his students realized it was wrong, others did not seem to think so. Roger remarked, "I think some of them were like oh ok, well yeah, this is a really serious thing, but some others were like oh well maybe I just skirt classes and try and hand in something like that."

Thus, Roger said, he decided to make his classes more challenging from then on, midway through his first semester teaching, with specific lessons that would focus on the issue of plagiarism and show them how and why it was wrong. Roger noted, "I always have the resources to be able to back up why it's [plagiarism] wrong, why I caught it, why I gave them a zero and so on." Roger said he marked all writing with this issue of plagiarism in mind but that he would always explain to each student how he found it, and why it was wrong to plagiarize. Roger said, "you have to explain why, because they won't learn otherwise." At this mid-point in his first semester Roger also worried that such a belief might cause come conflict in his class and the result might hinder his teaching. Roger said, "once you start handing out negative things as a result to this the whole classroom culture can become negative. Which is what I really want to avoid."

Roger said his above stated beliefs about making classes challenging are because his particular students will go into university classes all held through the medium of English, or English for academic purposes (EAP) and so he must prepare them for this transition. Roger noted, "the way that I approach it is: it's an EAP class, so I'm preparing them for university and that's what I've told them too. I'm saying 'your next step is real university classes, so I'm not going to make things easy for you here. I'm not going to make them hard either, but I'm going to actually prepare you for the next step.'" Roger said that he believed this was a fair way to approach his teaching.

> **Reflective Break**
> - What are your beliefs about making his classes challenging?
> - What do you think of Roger's beliefs about making his classes challenging?

Collaboration with Colleagues

As a novice teacher, Roger says he was eager for communication and collaboration with some of his more experienced colleagues. He also worried that there was no formal orientation program during his first weeks, and this threw him off somewhat as he believed he would have lots of collaboration before he started. Roger said, "there really isn't any kind of formal introduction or training session or even just, you know, this is how things work here type thing. There's nothing. There's no instructor's manual or, you know, rules of how we do things. It's just more assumed that you'll find out what's happening by asking around." So he was puzzled somewhat about what to do about this initial belief and realized, early on, that those who were in a position of responsibility in the school may not be the best people to ask as they are not in the classroom, so he said that he wants to collaborate with his "fellow co-instructors." Thus, he attempted to seek out some instructors that teach the specific skills he was teaching. He said, "the nice thing about this program is that it's divided into skills" and he will use this but in an interconnected way. Roger continued, "the way I see it is like obviously grammar and writing are quite closely interconnected, but since my class is writing, I'm focusing more on the writing aspect than the grammar, but I will be communicating to the grammar teacher like 'I don't know whether you've noticed this in your class too, but these are some grammar points that they have issues with.'" Roger also said he believed there were other ways he could use to collaborate – for example, when making lesson plans. Roger remarked, "one instructor is working together with me, like we're making lesson plans together and kind of helping one another out. We both contribute equally."

However, although he said he enjoyed the freedom of teaching the way he wanted, Roger also said that he felt that he needed more guidance from the institution during this first semester and wished they collaborated more. Roger remarked,

> On one hand it's nice because it kind of gives me the freedom to, you know, do things the way I want to do them and it's not like the [person in charge of] writing is telling me, ok, this week you're doing this, this week you have to do that. But on the other hand, perhaps it would be good to have, you know, a weekly meeting or biweekly meeting, or even a monthly meeting with all the same instructors who teach the same course, just kind of get together and say, hey how are your regular classes going? What are you doing? What are you finding? You know, what's working for you? What isn't working?

After a few weeks teaching, Roger said that he realized that many of the different levels (students were assigned different level classes according to their English proficiency entry level tests) were interrelated regardless of the skill that was emphasized, and he said he believed that it made even more sense to have more collaboration among the instructors in each level. Roger said that he noted this especially for the higher level class he was teaching when he said, "a lot of the things that they do in the classes are interrelated, like one of the presentations in my speaking class is based on the essay that they write in the writing classes so then you have to communicate with that teacher as well." However, Roger said, a lot of this collaboration was not happening during his first year of teaching.

Reflective Break
- What are your beliefs about collaboration with colleagues?
- What do you think of Roger's beliefs about collaboration with colleagues?

ESL Teachers

From his very first day on the job, when he walked into his classroom, Roger said he felt like a real ESL teacher and this feeling stayed during the first few weeks of his first semester. He said,

> I've taught classes now, I've actually given lessons. I have students do work that I've assigned, and I've assigned homework. I definitely feel like a teacher now. I have my own classroom now that I'm in charge of. I can control what happens in this classroom. I can say, "we're going to do this today, we're going to do that today" and the students will have to do it (laughs). I'm excited, really, yeah definitely.

However, towards the end of his first year, this excitement waned somewhat and his beliefs about ESL teachers and the teaching profession took a bit of a nosedive – especially when he mentioned, in a discussion towards the end of his first year, that ESL teachers were second-class citizens in the eyes of many especially when teaching English overseas. Roger noted that he has all his qualifications but, at the end of his first year, he wondered about a "career" especially if he wanted to go teach in a country where English was not used as a first language. Roger remarked, "Second-class citizens. ... jobs overseas, like 'you can speak English, oh you can teach it too', you know? ... Well, that would never happen for like a primary or a secondary school teacher, where it's like 'oh you don't have your qualifications, then go get them or else you're not teaching'." He said that many people do not really respect ESL teachers in Canada with similar ideas of "you speak it, you can teach it". Roger continued, "I think it's more the fact that ESL teachers aren't necessarily respected as much as any other type of teacher, like the primary, secondary school teacher." He also questioned "why ESL teachers are among the lowest paid teachers" in Canada. So Roger worried that ESL teaching may be "a dead end job after a couple years... it's hard to pay your bills." However, he decided not to say anything as he wanted to get a position the next term; Roger continued, "it's difficult to voice your opinion and you just totally keep quiet because you don't want to jeopardize your job neither, because for all you know, you might have said something wrong and you won't get a job next term."

Reflective Break
- What are your beliefs about ESL teachers?
- What do you think of Roger's beliefs about ESL teachers?

SOURCES OF ROGER'S FIRST YEAR PRINCIPLES

After articulating beliefs, teachers should then examine the sources of these beliefs, which have been built up over a teacher's career. For example, Shi and Cumming's (1995: 104) study of the beliefs and practice of five experienced language teachers discovered that, even though they had been educated in the same institution and by the same methods, the knowledge guiding their instruction is largely based on personal beliefs – "founded on years of previous experience, reflection, and information."

One or more of the following sources of beliefs can be considered and used either individually or in combination (adapted from Richards & Lockhart, 1994):

- *Teachers' past experience as students.* For example, if a teacher has learned a second language successfully and comfortably by memorizing vocabulary lists, then there is a good chance that the same teacher will have his or her students memorize vocabulary lists too.
- *Experience of what works best in their classes.* This may be the main source of beliefs about teaching for many second language teachers and, as such, many practicing teachers may not want to break an established, and perceived successful, routine.
- *Established practice within a school.* These practices can be difficult to change because the school has always used this method, or that teachers would have to complete a particular unit in a specific time period.
- *Personality factors of teachers.* This can be an important source of beliefs as some teachers really enjoy conducting role-play or group work in their classes while others are more comfortable conducting traditional teacher-fronted lessons.
- *Educationally based or research-based principles.* This can also be a source of teachers' beliefs in that a teacher may draw on his or her understanding of research in second language reading to support use of predicting style exercises in reading classes.
- *Method based sources of beliefs.* This suggests that teachers support and implement a particular method in their classes – as, for example, when a teacher decides to use total physical response (TPR) to teach beginning second language learners, he or she is following a method of suspending early production of language for the learner.

When examining the sources of Roger's beliefs, Kindsvatter, Willen and Ishler's (1988) categories were used for analysis of all the data. The following top six categories for Roger in his first year as a language teacher were identified in order of their frequency as follows:

1   Approach or Method
2   Personality Factors
3   Educationally-based or Research-based Practice
4   Own Experience as a Teacher
5   Experience of what Works Best
6   Established Practice

These results indicate that Roger was influenced a lot by his academic background in applied linguistics, and his master's degree in teaching English to other speakers (TESOL), in that he has acquired a lot of knowledge about different theoretical approaches to teaching as well as many different methods; and, as such, he was eager to try these out during his first year. In addition, as his first year commenced, he believed his personality traits also impacted his beliefs about his teaching in addition to his continued review of research on particular topics that came up during the year. As the year was coming to an end his beliefs were beginning to become more impacted with his own experiences as a teacher, and of what worked and did not work best in his lessons. His beliefs were less impacted from what was expected by the various administrators in his institution as he circumvented many of these.

Reflective Break
- What are the main sources of your beliefs? Do they come from your teaching experience, school practice, your personality, some education theories you like, your reading or other sources?
- What do you think about the sources of Roger's beliefs?

CONCLUSION

This chapter has outlined and discussed Roger's principles about teaching and learning English as a second language – as well as the sources of his principles – in his first year as an ESL teacher. The results have been presented mostly in terms of his stated beliefs as well as any he implied throughout his first year of teaching. The results indicate that Roger's most frequent beliefs were related to his students' use of L1 in his classes, teaching and learning writing, teaching and learning grammar, making his lessons challenging, collaboration with colleagues and his overall beliefs about ESL teachers. The chapter has also examined the sources of his beliefs and six categories for Roger in his first year as a language teacher identified in order of their frequency as follows: his approaches and methods, his personality, what the research suggests, his own experiences as a teacher so far, his experiences of what works best for him up to now and what the school or institution has already established as accepted practices. What emerged from these was an excited first year teacher who considered himself ready and very qualified (academically) to begin his teaching career. What is also clear is Roger is also just beginning to articulate his beliefs to himself and they are still very much in the formation stage as one would expect in his first year as an ESL teacher. The results will be discussed more in depth in Chapter 8, which analyzes Roger's first year experiences. The next chapter examines Roger's theory during his first year of teaching.

Chapter 5

Reflecting on Theory in The First Year

INTRODUCTION

This chapter introduces you to Roger's theory in his first year of teaching. Theory explores and examines the different choices a teacher makes about particular skills taught (or they think should be taught) or, in other words, how they want to put their theories into practice as they teach. Influenced by their reflections on their philosophy (Chapter 3), and their principles (Chapter 4), teachers now actively begin to construct their theory of practice. All language teachers have theories, both "official" theories we learn in teacher education courses and "unofficial" theories we gain with teaching experience. However, not all teachers may be fully aware of these theories, and especially their "unofficial" theories that are sometimes called "theories-in-use". Reflections at this stage in the framework include considering all aspects of a teacher's planning, and the different activities and methods teachers choose (or may want to choose) as they attempt to put theory into practice. As teachers reflect on their approaches and methods at this level, they will also reflect on the specific teaching techniques they choose to use (or may want to choose) in their lessons. In order to reflect on these, teachers will need to describe specific classroom techniques, activities and routines that they are using, or intend to use, when carrying out their lessons. Another means of accessing theory is to explore and examine critical incidents (any unplanned or unanticipated event that occurs during a classroom lesson and is clearly remembered) because they can be a guide to a teacher's theory building. This chapter covers Roger's first year planning and critical incidents.

Reflective Break
- Do you plan extensively? (e.g., do you write detailed lesson plans? If yes, what do you usually write? If no, why don't you write an extensive plan?)

- How do you plan the content you will teach? Is it from the textbook and or syllabus?
- How do you plan and sequence activities?
- How do you plan your method and approach to teaching a particular lesson?
- Do you ever go into a lesson without planning?

ROGER'S PLANNING IN THE FIRST YEAR

Roger noted that the program in which he was starting his teaching career highlighted the cultural diversity in the classroom, and that this was considered to be a good thing for learning English as a second language. Roger also remarked that his master's program had taught that classes with students from various cultures have many benefits for those involved. This prepared him for such diversity and, as a result, influenced the way he planned his lessons and class activities.

Roger said that the amount of preparation at the beginning of the term was somewhat "overwhelming at times as everything is thrown at you at once from all directions." This was something of a reality check coming straight after his teacher education program. The biggest immediate issue, he said, was trying to adjust to this hectic existence and balance life, work and family relationships all at the same time. As Roger noted, "this is the first September in 19 years that I am not returning to school as a student; now I'm returning as a teacher and sometimes it feels like there is no difference in terms of workload between starting a semester as a student or a teacher. Both parties need to prepare, organize, and get back into the swing of things as the semester begins."

As this particular semester began, however, he noticed that some of this preparation did not help him fully with lesson and activity planning – one issue being the use of students' native language (their L1) and the use of the target language (the L2 – English in this case) in the classroom. Indeed, Roger said that he was beginning to realize that some of the discussions in his master's program were "from a researcher's point of view such as, 'Well, you know the L1 is okay in the classroom if it's used to help learning too.'" Roger noted that many of these comments were for teaching in "ideal conditions" but not necessarily practical for novice teachers such as himself trying to figure out what to do in the "real conditions" he was faced with in the classroom. For Roger, the students that he was teaching were in an English for academic purposes (EAP) program and, as such, they needed to practice specific English skills in order to survive in a university class/lecture context. He realized that their use of L1 in his lessons would be detrimental to their progress in English development, and he began to wonder how he could design his lessons around this reality. So, Roger started his planning in earnest and began to consider details in particular skills related to English development. Although he had some form of central syllabus – the same syllabus given to each instructor – he noted that one cannot just follow it, because each lesson is different. Roger realized that he must modify the syllabus accordingly, with tests adapted for suitability for specific classes.

These early attempts at classroom planning, which had sounded so simple when he was a graduate student, proved to be a challenge now that he was a teacher with real students. This was particularly the case with regard to the focus on grammar in writing classes. Roger said that the MA program did "not touch on grammar in writing class." Whilst they talked about feedback and error correction, it was only in generic terms, with some broad-brush ideas around the types of things to focus on. Grammar was simply something that "you should give feedback on in a writing class", and there were no specifics around the idea that one cannot negotiate meaning in writing as one can in speaking. Roger continued, in writing there can be "no negotiation of meaning if it does not make sense, whereas in speaking you can negotiate meaning. If you say something that has grammar errors and it doesn't make sense you can try and like figure out: 'what do you actually mean', but in writing I think grammar is doubly important because, there's not that ability to negotiate meaning."

This meant he was faced with a particular dilemma when it came to teaching writing from the first draft onwards. Roger noted, for example, that in his master's program he had learned about language theories that state: "on first drafts focus on content alone because that's the most important thing," rather than on any grammar issues. Roger, however, was preparing his students to enter university directly after graduation where they would have to be careful of grammar errors from the very beginning of the writing process. Roger remarked, "in university they write first drafts but very rarely, so this will mean that on their second, on their final drafts or whatever draft it is, they're handing in a paper that's full of grammar errors and in university they will definitely lose marks based on that." Roger said that he was worried about this – that his MA program had not prepared him for it – and so he was learning to adjust his planning and his teaching accordingly. Roger continued,

> so, what I'm trying to do here to a certain extent is to try and get them to have this ability where they, well hopefully and maybe even ideally, where when they're writing on their own, they kind of self-correct their own work and realize that well, sure I'm writing all these nice things but if there's a grammar mistake then they will be losing marks on that.

Roger noted that his lesson planning was really to his own specifications: what he thinks is important to cover in each lesson. Roger continued, "I want to have my own personal stamp on what I do. I feel like I'm more qualified if I'm able to do it the way that I feel comfortable with versus someone saying, 'this is how you do it, just follow these steps.'" Roger said that he has his own way now to teach writing: "the way that I kind of look at teaching writing specifically, is that you know, you start with the tiny things, you slowly get bigger, and bigger, and bigger, and eventually once you get to the bigger things, they should have the smaller things down pat." He said that he does not care about their spelling but that grammar will be important for them in a university setting. When further explaining this Roger said that "the bigger thing is writing an entire composition" and, as such, the students would have to learn the structure of an essay. Then "the smaller things" for Roger are "simple things like a sentence has a subject and predicate and subject-verb agreements." So he said that he would plan for his students to spend more time practicing all these rather than him lecturing them on what they are. Roger said he would specifically build in these practice sessions into his writing classes because he feared they did not have enough practice in the beginning levels of the institute in which he was teaching. Roger continued:

> You can't just expect them to, within one or two classes, completely understand how to use something like articles so maybe the pace of some classes or some teachers are too quick to focusing more on covering the material versus making sure students understand the basics. I mean, I could make them write four or five essays throughout the whole term, but to me that would be useless. I would rather spend time taking more time focusing on one thing and then the next, and just writing one essay or maybe two essays so that, rather than scrambling through the whole process you focus on the steps that are needed to finish it.

With that in mind, Roger designed the course around one major essay for the term making sure the students got the details of one rather than giving them three or four essays as other teachers who had this class before him had done. He said that giving lots of essays really does not benefit the students, saying that he wanted "to focus on each step of one essay so they get it correct." For this he noted that in English writing the requirement is for a linear type of writing style that he said starts "with choosing your topic, your thesis, and outline." By following such steps he said that this will help his students write an academic paper; as Roger remarked: "just follow the steps and you write a half decent paper."

In addition to his own personal planning, Roger wondered if he would be able to get some ideas from his colleagues but this proved difficult for him. He noted that the institute was rather top down and directives were sent rather than negotiated. He said that although there was a "lot of interaction between teachers, it is not always academic in nature but it is friendly." Roger said that he thinks the lack of sharing of teaching ideas is related to the nature of the institute he is working in and that they do not provide for any training or professional development that could be used to collaborate with other teachers. Roger remarked, "There is no formal introduction [when he arrived the first day/week], no training session, no instructor's guide or manual or rules. There's nothing." Roger said that it is "assumed that you'll find out what's happening." Roger said that he felt a little lost at times as he tried to figure out what to do. The only staff meetings that he attends deal with general things happening in the program. Roger continued, "How to deal with a general problem or something like that, but for each specific course there is nothing and we are pretty much left alone." On the other hand, Roger noted that such "freedom" was positive as he said, "it's not like there's someone that's kind of hounding me, so to speak, on what I'm doing."

Thus, Roger said that he was not as clear as he thought he would be when planning each of his lessons given that he was prepared with language theories but now he "is in the real world" and things are somewhat different when teaching "real students". That said, Roger said that such dilemmas as above have caused him to think more about planning his lessons carefully. Roger noted, "I'm planning a lot. Every class that I have, which before I go into the class, obviously I have it prepped." However, he also said that he was not planning minute by minute in great detail because he said such an approach doesn't seem natural." Roger remarked, "Obviously you can't just have this, a really good schedule structured for a course, you go in there and you follow to a T. What if something else happens, something that is more meaningful than what you have? Then why not go off." In fact, Roger discovered that he would be challenged to plan for all his students because of individual learning styles and different personalities while at the same time trying to keep all students motivated. Roger realized that his MA was more idealistic when compared to his actual classroom experiences in real time. Roger said,

> I know that in my MA classes we spent a lot of time discussing different learning styles and personalities and how we can reach out to all kinds of students, but once you are actually in a classroom full of students with different personalities, you really start to think, wow, this is actually not as simple as it seemed when we discussed it in class. I think I do a pretty good job of using different kinds of activities that are focused on different ways of learning (e.g. doing work in groups vs. individually; using either PPT, the white board, or nothing when teaching; using examples from the textbook or generating examples from students' suggestions). However, there is still always a (nagging) notion that one or more students left that class feeling like they've learned nothing or just simply bored. I guess that is just normal and can't be avoided!

Reflective Break
- How do you plan your writing classes?
- Do you have a specific plan in mind for all writing classes or do you plan it according to the group you are teaching?
- How to you treat grammar in a writing class?
- How many essays do you have your students complete in a semester (12 weeks)?

ROGER'S CRITICAL INCIDENTS FIRST YEAR

I now outline and discuss some critical incidents Roger experienced during his first-year teaching. During the first semester of his first year Roger said that he wanted to always give "very clear and explicit instructions" in each lesson – and especially when giving an assignment or a test. In one lesson during mid-semester he decided to give what he called a "surprise in-class assignment" and proceeded to explain each section of the assignment in what he thought were "clear and explicit words." He had thought that they all understood his directions as nobody had any questions at that time, but many had questions once they started the assignment. So he decided to explain the entire assignment in the following class and the same thing happened with no questions from anybody, yet they still did not understand the assignment properly, which was evident from their answers. After that, Roger said he was "a bit frustrated" and so he decided that he would have "each student read all the instructions before they start any writing and tell them that any questions they have must be answered before they start writing." Roger hoped this would avoid any distractions and stop the need to explain the assignment "over and over again." However, this same issue was to develop into a critical incident for Roger in the weeks that follow. I outline this critical incident in Roger's own words in the section that follows.

Critical Incident I: APA References
I was teaching APA referencing to my students, which really should have been a review for the majority of them. I figured I would spend an entire class period on referencing books and journal articles as these are the two types of sources students are using for their research essays. I spend a good 20 minutes going into every detail of how to reference a book using APA formatting and told my students to closely take notes on what I'm teaching as it will help them pay attention and retain the information so they can go back to it later (one thing to note is that students all have a copy of an APA style guide booklet that very clearly gives examples and steps for referencing). After I receive acknowledgement from the class that they are clear with referencing books, I move on to

journal articles and go over every last detail of how to properly reference journal articles. Once again, the class demonstrated that they were familiar with the material and ready to do some practice. I left that class thinking that my students should be comfortable with referencing now, especially since they have their style guide as backup. In fact, I was happy with this lesson and thought it was well worth the time to spend an entire class on this small, yet important part of academic writing.

Fast-forward several days later. Students are submitting their references to me online using the *dropbox* so I can check that they are using appropriate references for their essays and that they are using proper APA guidelines. After I download them all, I open them up to start marking them. I was shocked to find that a good 80% of the students did not follow APA guidelines and seemed to have no clue how to reference. Also, many students did not follow the guidelines of using a minimum of 3 journals and 2 books for their essay as many of them used only books, others used online articles, others used magazines, and some used sources from the 1960s. I thought I had clearly laid out all the guidelines the previous week in addition to giving my students a handout with all the specific requirements for the essay. I was so incredibly frustrated after marking those assignments, especially after having a class average of 40% for that assignment. I felt that as a teacher I had spent the right amount of time on teaching this material to the class and that there really was not much else I could do.

Roger's Response

It seemed to me that many students were just lazy and did not care about the specific details of academic writing or that maybe they could not take this work seriously. So, to increase their motivation and show the importance of following guidelines, I had an in-class assignment where a large part of the assignment dealt with referencing. I told the students that each reference question was worth one point and that for each error they would lose one point. Many of them were shocked by this but seemed to suddenly realize that they needed to learn how to use the APA. The best part of it is that they are allowed to use their style guides for assignments and tests, so they really shouldn't have any excuse not to do well on this part. After administering, collecting, and grading the assignment, I was pleased to see that most students did well on the referencing section and that maybe all they needed was a little bit of extra motivation in order for them to put their full effort into learning. For the most part, the majority of the students finally seemed to understand the APA, however, there still are a few that just don't seem to understand the concept of referencing as I just had a student ask me this week to explain what an in-text and end-of-text reference is. This is so frustrating to sometimes feel that you can say or teach something so many times and still find students who seem to be absolutely clueless about something they should have grasped by now!

Reflective Break
- What is your understanding of the critical incident above?
- What would you have done?
- What do you think of Roger's response?
- Do you think it was successful?
- Why do you think a few students still do not follow?

Although Roger seemed to have gotten some understanding of how to "encourage" his students to engage in the classes with more enthusiasm and rigor – given that they would probably fail because they did not get sufficient points that he had instituted – he still encountered other incidents within the first semester that caused him more surprises. The next incident is related to the previous incident, and I outline it in the following section in Roger's own words again.

Critical Incident II: Cheating/Plagiarizing
The next thing, which is linked to referencing (see Critical Incident I outlined above), is related to giving back marks and students' reactions to this. In lieu of the lack of understanding of APA referencing (see above), I gave students a homework assignment which offered them a chance to practice using the APA and get a mark for it. Of course, there were several students who clearly still did not understand the concept of using the APA and they failed the assignment miserably. It is very easy to give those marks as the students clearly did not follow the guidelines and therefore don't deserve a decent mark. What is not easy to do, however, is give students zeros when they submitted copies of the assignment that were identical to some of their classmates. As I was marking, I found three sets of identical submissions. A group of three students, all of whom would otherwise have done really well on the assignment, had the exact same errors… errors that weren't common. I gave these students zeros and called them out on cheating. I did the same to two other sets of students who submitted copies of the same work that was absolutely terrible anyway. WOW, did they ever have a reaction to this! Everything was blown out of proportion and students accused me of wanting to fail them (in the course!) and that this was not fair as they clearly did not do the work together and this just happens to be a coincidence. After I explained very clearly to them how there was no chance, they all could have had these exact same errors, they finally said, "well, we worked together and compared some of our work to see if we are doing it correctly". At

this point, I explained to them that in university, and in the [language institute], that handing in copies of work which you did with another student is not ok, especially if you hand in identical work. I explained to them that you need to acknowledge that you worked together with someone on an assignment and that usually you need to check with the instructor that it is ok that you hand in collaborative work. But under no circumstances do you hand in identical copies of an assignment. In fact, in university that is considered cheating and an automatic zero and therefore, they will also receive zeros. I still showed them the grade they would have gotten and some feedback so they can learn from it, but ultimately, they would receive a zero. The students were still upset, but after my explanation seemed to understand what they had done and admitted that perhaps this would be an example to everyone that you cannot hand in identical work. I felt happy that I could resolve this issue, but on the other hand I felt a bit bad that I had to give them zeros, even though they would have done well. I know that I need to have a firm grip on my students and be firm with my decisions, especially since I'm preparing them for university classes where there is very little sympathy. Sometimes as a teacher you feel like you're a bit cruel, but then again, who wants to be a pushover?!

Then in another class I had the same problem but worse as half the students plagiarized their first drafts. No paraphrase, reference, or quote. I was nearly ready to stop marking these essays after the tenth or eleventh essay, I was so frustrated. Did these students really not understand the concept of incorporating other people's work into their own essays without simply copying and pasting?! I was so frustrated that I decided to stop manually copying and pasting what I believed to be plagiarized work into Google, then I loaded all the essays on to Turnitin.com and simply gave anyone who plagiarized in any way a zero. This means that a student who had an essay that was 58% plagiarized (yes, that was a real number) and a student who plagiarized one sentence both received a big, fat, 0%. Some students who plagiarized got feedback (they were lucky enough that I marked their essays before I became frustrated) while others didn't. I simply attached an originality report from Turnitin.com to their essays and told them to fix the plagiarized portions of their essays. All 12 of the students who did not plagiarize received detailed feedback, simply as a reward for not plagiarizing. Yes, this might be harsh and maybe the students who plagiarized need feedback the most, but I was so angry and upset that I really didn't want to give them feedback. I just told them to come see me if they wanted any extra help. I didn't want to waste my own time marking and giving feedback on an essay full of plagiarized work since they didn't care to spend the time to properly write their essays. This was definitely the most stress and frustration I've had all term and as a novice instructor. All that time spent over the term on how to avoid plagiarizing, and this happens.

The day I gave the results and feedback back to the students (last Friday) I was a bit nervous as I knew that some of my students who received a zero potentially could freak out and I really didn't want to deal with it as I knew I was upset too about the results. However, I was quite surprised to see how my class dealt with this problem. I first gave back the results to the students who didn't plagiarize and told them they were free to go. No one left, but that was fine. Then I explained to the class that everyone who did not get back a mark got a zero due to plagiarism. So far no reactions… some appeared shocked, others appeared confused, and others had that look that said, 'crap, my teacher noticed…' I explained to them how serious of an offence this is, especially in credited university classes, and many of them seemed shocked to hear how big of a deal it really is, even though I had told them the same thing at the beginning of the term. Then I told them what their problems were in terms of how they plagiarized and how to fix it. I opened up the website www.plagiarism.org and went through some of the details on plagiarism with them. Yet, no student complained or caused a scene as I thought some would. Most seemed to understand now that you really can't just copy and paste a few paragraphs from an article into your essay and reference it. Some even said, "but, I had a reference… why is this plagiarism?" I was shocked that those hours we spent on paraphrasing and referencing really did not have any effect on certain students. I explained to them that this draft is only worth 3% of their final grade and that it wouldn't really affect their final grade. However, their final drafts are worth 10% and a zero on that would be devastating to their final grade. So, get your butts in gear, fix the problem, and you should be fine. I also told them that I would put their essays on Turnitin.com again and if there was any plagiarism, they would receive a zero again. I also offered to help them with their essays, to check it for plagiarizing before they submit the final draft, and any thing else they need help with. So, I offered them many solutions and chances to get help, yet only a few have stepped up, so I am curious to see their final drafts.

Reflective Break

- What is your understanding of the development of the first critical incident into another critical incident where some of the students according to Roger, were cheating and then into another different incident where half the class were plagiarizing?
- Do you agree with Roger's way of dealing with them all?

- Have you even encountered students who "cheat" and/or "plagiarized"? If yes, what did you do (if anything)? If no, what would you do?

The third major critical incident that Roger was confronted with during his first year was related to the topics that are raised by students, his in particular. In this case, the topic was related to a person's body image. I present this critical incident in his own words.

Critical Incident III: Student Controversial Topic

Another critical incident occurred this week and I'm a bit uncertain of how I handled the situation. This time it was in my level 5 speaking class (which by the way is an amazing class that has a great bunch of students who always do everything to the best of their abilities. I have very little to say about this class so far because we've been doing a lot of presentations and they all have been going really smoothly). For the last week we've been doing discussion speeches (essentially shortened seminar presentations) focusing on journal articles selected by the coordinator and chosen by students in groups of 3 or 4. All of the presentations from last week ranged from ok to nearly perfect, so I was very happy about them so far. This last group was a group of three (all of the others were groups of 4 so I purposely had the group of three go last so they had a chance to see a few as a bit of an advantage). This group consisted of three [from the same country] males and they were presenting on a journal article discussing weight control behavior and perceptions of weight. I initially was hesitant to include this journal article but ended up thinking that it would be fine. Was I ever wrong. The focus of the majority of their presentation was ok, but the visual aids they used didn't really aid them and were an obvious distraction to the audience. There visual aids included pictures of nearly nude models, a video of a woman's "weight loss journey", and other examples that were less than appropriate. I let them finish their presentation as none of these visual aids were highly offensive in nature (I would have stopped it otherwise!) and saw this as an opportunity to learn about, and discuss, what not to do in a presentation. The presentation itself was not great and the audience and the presenters seemed to be aware of this. One thing that we've been doing in that class is discussing the positives and negatives of each presentation after it's finished. During this discussion, several students voiced their opinion about the visual aids and how inappropriate they were. Points that came up were that these are not academic in nature, there are people from cultures where these types of pictures and videos are offensive, there is no place for these pictures in any presentation, and that as nice as these people looked, these pictures did not act as aids. One thing that was mentioned was that the relationship between weight perceptions and sex appeal are very closely linked and that maybe it was appropriate to show one of these pictures to briefly address this topic. But not the point they did. I felt that as a class we had a good discussion and that this issue somewhat resolved itself. However, there were still some students who were a bit upset about having seen these things. But that raised the issue of what university life is like. There are going to be things in university that you see or hear about that you do not agree with. But you still need to have an open mind towards these things and accept they exist; you don't need to agree with them though. I wish I would have raised that issue, but I didn't think about it until after class. Did I do the right thing by letting these students present what they did? I still think so, but it definitely caught me and other people off guard and caused a bit of an uncomfortable situation.

Reflective Break
- What is your understanding of the issue of body image?
- Do you agree with Roger's way of dealing with them all?
- Have you even encountered students who bring up controversial topics? If yes, what were the topics and what did you do (if anything)?

CONCLUSION

This chapter outlined and discussed Roger's theory that included his approach to planning and his experience of various critical incidents that also give him greater self-awareness about teacher-learning complexities regardless of what he plans his lessons around. In terms of his planning, the chapter described, for example, how Roger discovered from the very beginning of his first year that his MA teacher preparation courses did not prepare him for the reality of what he would face in real classrooms with real students and how he would plan for a focus or no focus on grammar in his writing classes as well as how to deal with his overall freedom of designing his own lesson plans rather than following a centrally designed syllabus. In addition, the chapter outlined and discussed three critical incidents that Roger was faced with in this first year: APA formatting, plagiarizing, and controversial topics all made him realize that there are no simple solutions in teaching. The next chapter introduces Roger's actual classroom practices in his first year of teaching.

Chapter 6

Reflecting on Practice in the First Year

INTRODUCTION

Up to now, I have presented Roger's reflections on his philosophy, principles and theory, or the "hidden" aspect of teaching, during his first year of teaching. In this chapter I present Roger's actual practices during his first-year teaching. These include his visible actions during observed lessons as well as what he said he attempted to accomplish during his actual teaching as well as his students' reactions (or non-reactions) in these lessons. Teachers have several different methods of examining their practice. For example, teachers can engage in classroom observations (self-monitoring, and/or critical friendship with an observer), and they can record (audio and/or video) their lessons and later transcribe the recordings for more accurate recount of what occurred. Teachers can also be interviewed – about what they did while teaching – after a lesson or many lessons. In Roger's case we engage in all of these aspects (although he did not do much self-monitoring when I was observing his lessons) to gather information about his actual teaching practices. I now present Roger's perceptions of what he did while teaching during his first year.

ROGER'S ACTUAL TEACHING FIRST YEAR

Roger said that before he goes into each class he teaches, he has already done a lot of planning (see also Chapter 5). However, he said also that he is ready if something happens that he has not anticipated and he does not worry about changing his plan on the spot:

> I'm planning a lot. Every class that I have, which before I go into the class, obviously I have it prepped. But not to the point that I say "okay now I'm doing this, then this, then this" because to me that doesn't

seem natural. Obviously, you can't just have this, a really good schedule structured for a course, you go in there and you follow to a T. What if something else happens, something that is more meaningful than what you have? Then why not go off?

From this point on I present his actual teaching of a grammar class. Before this class Roger reflected on how he has been grappling somewhat with how to approach teaching this skill. Roger noted that until this point in his first semester he had "tried both inductive and deductive approaches to teaching grammar, but I don't know if I actually spend enough time 'teaching' my students." He said that he wondered about the "teaching part" of the grammar class in that he knows he relayed the new grammar structures to the students in these lessons and had them practice them afterwards in various activities, but he now wondered about the type of language he himself used during these lessons especially related to the lower level proficiency class he was teaching at that time. Roger said, "I think I might have some issues with the language I use when I'm teaching. I have been used to teaching [high proficiency] students so far and now I'm teaching two [lower proficiency] classes and I feel like I'm not simplifying my language enough for the level or slowing down enough for them." He said he wondered about this because he thinks he got used to speaking "at the rate of a native speaker and use larger words" with the high proficiency students, but he wondered if his lower proficiency students could follow with his fast speaking rate and unfamiliar vocabulary use. Thus, Roger said that he was interested in having me observe his teaching for this and many other reasons as he was interested in exploring and reflecting on what he was actually doing in his grammar classes especially. I now outline my observation of a one-hour class I observed.

Roger's Grammar Lesson

For this observed grammar class Roger said that he focused on teaching the structures of noun clauses beginning with *wh- words* and *if/whether*. The previous day he said that he had gone over noun clauses beginning with *that*. This class was one of two or three days focusing on noun clauses. Roger said that since this is the first time that they are really going over this, the students are not expected to be able to explain it, etc. but instead be familiar with it and be able to identify it. The students have low-intermediate knowledge of grammar but, according to Roger, some are more knowledgeable than others. In this particular class, other language skills included speaking, writing, reading and listening are also covered but with an emphasis on the grammatical structure of noun clauses. The process of combining noun clauses with main clauses, identifying noun clauses, and special uses of noun clauses were identified and focused on according to Roger. Roger said that he would structure his teaching as follows: after students listened and learned, they complete exercises checking their comprehension of noun clauses. These exercises include filling in the blanks, changing questions into noun clauses, and writing their own sentences with noun clauses. Evaluation includes taking up the answers and discussing any differences in answers. Pedagogical materials used in this class included the whiteboard and textbook (along with personal examples). The proxemics of the classroom was the following: students were arranged in a U-shaped pattern with a few desks in the middle of the U (Figure 6.1).

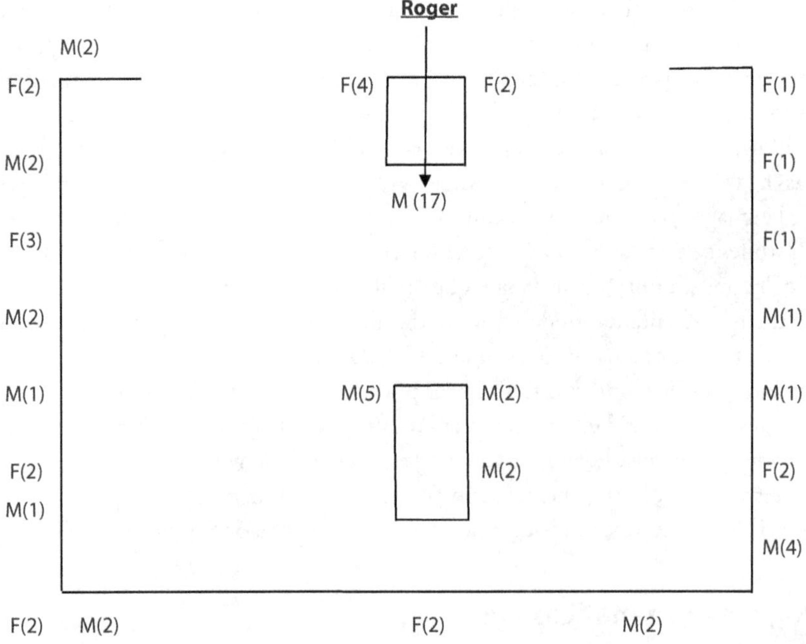

Note: F(2) = female student two interactions with teacher; M(1) = male student one interaction with teacher. The long arrow shows the directional flow of the questions and answers between the teacher and the students who participated the most. The lesson was videotaped and later transcribed. I first provide a detailed transcript of the lesson and Roger's reflections on this in the post-lesson reflections that we had, as well as his reflections on watching the video of his lesson.

Figure 6.1 Roger's Class Map

Transcription ESL class

1   R: (indistinguishable phrase) Yeah, yeah, ok. And these types of noun clauses. Well, I'll just write them on the board again. Ok. (pause) And just a quick summary, ok?, you always have a main clause and a noun clause. (Indistinguishable clause [maybe, there's rummaging around, so it's hard to tell]). Ah but, ok, there were different types of noun clauses right? So, noun clauses that begin with (UC: that). Actually, wrong category, ok? so, (pause) There are three categories. Ok? Ones we talked about yesterday, that are noun clauses that begin with that. Ok? These were facts. Right? Today we are going to be looking at two, two different types of noun clauses, ah, the first one are wh- noun clauses. K? These begin with wh- words. K? And we are also going to be looking at if and whether noun clauses, ok, so ones that being with this. So, these are yes/no type questions. Ok? And these are open questions. So, we say yes/no are closed questions, closed questions. K? So, we'll start off with wh-, on page 331. Ok? Ah, you can see that it gives you a few examples here. K? So the main clause and the noun clause. And let me just erase this to use this again. So, let's pretend that Rainie has a question. K? (pause) Alright, so, Rainie wants to know something. Ok? So, she wants to know a lot of things. So, let's... what are some things that she wants to know? Why is snow cold? K?

2   That's, let's, let's just pretend that that's one question. Ok? When is (pause) when is this class over? Ok? And once again you probably want to keep taking a few notes. Ok? Ah, (pause) ok, where is Roger from? I don't know, not China, not Saudi Arabia, I'll tell you that. Ok? Ah, (pause) and the last thing, what is the answer? K? Here we have our wh- words. Ok? Now, you can see here that all of these have wh- word and then the verb. Ok? But, we want to connect this main clause with these noun clauses. Or, we're going to be making noun clauses. So, how do you think we can do that? First of all, the noun clause can replace what?

3   S: (UC: the verb?)

4   R: No, the noun clause can replace a...

5   S: Noun

6   R: Noun, right? Ok, now where's a noun in this main clause here that we can replace?

7   S: Something

8   R: Something. Ok? So, we want to take each one of these and replace something with that. Ok, so we'll go over to this side here. So, Rainie (pause). So, let's start with number 1, Rainie wants to know,

9   Rainie: (CT: that, why snow is cold.)

10   R: Ok, so you said why,

11   Rainie: (CT: snow is cold)

12   R: So, I'm going with the original answer that I heard, Ok? Why is snow cold? Alright, this was what I heard. Ok? Now, is this correct?

13   Rainie: (CT: No)

14   R: No

15   Rainie: No

16   R: What is incorrect? What is the problem?

17   Rainie: (CT: mumbling) There is a statement and question.

18   R: Yes, that's the first problem. Ok? Rainie has a question, but when I use it in the main clause like this it's a statement. So that's the first thing we have to fix, (CT: indistinguishable phrase) is no question mark, with a period. There is one more thing that's wrong with this.

19   Rainie: Why and is.

20   R: Why and is.

21   Rainie: No, no, is and snow.

22   R: Ah, is and snow. So, what about those two?

23   Rainie: Ah, change them.

24   R: Change them. (pause) So Rainie wants to know why snow is cold. Does that sound correct to you?

25   Rainie: (CT: yeah)

26   R: Yes, ok? and that is correct. So that's one thing that you need to know when you're making noun clauses using wh- words. Ok? The noun clause does not follow the structure of a question. Ok? Questions, the verb always comes before the subject. Ok? However, when you're making a noun clause with a wh- word, ok, such as why, we need to invert. Ok? We need to switch the subject and the verb. Ok? So, in this case we need to say Rainie wants to know why snow is cold. Ok? This is not a question even though you see a question word, even though you see why, k, it's not a question, it's a statement. Ok? Let's try it with number two. So, Rainie wants to know, ok, let's just pretend I wrote that.

27   Rainie: (CT: when the class is over)

28   R: Right, so Rainie wants to know when this class is over. Ok? And that's yeah, that's exactly it. What about that one? Number three.

29   R: (CT: Rainie wants to know where is Roger...)

30   R: Yes, where Roger is from. Alright? And the same thing with the last one, what the answer is. Ok? So, I think you seem to understand that. So, that's the first thing that you need to know about noun clauses that are based on, you know, questions. Ok? You, you have to invert, you have to switch the verb and the, and the subject. Ok? Um, alright, however, ok? That is only if,

the main clause here is a statement. Ok? Um, now, the main clause can also be a question. Ok? So for example, I can start off (pause) can you tell me? Ok? If my main clause is can you tell me, ok? It is now a question. Ok? So, when I add my noun clauses to this, ok? It will look like this (pause). Ok? Everything stays the same. Ok? The subject and the verb are also inverted, but, now I have the question mark. Ok? So, can you see the difference between these two sentences? Rainie wants to know why snow is cold. Or, can you tell me why snow is cold? Ok? One, in the first one here the main clause is simply a statement. Ok? Wants to know, that's the statement. Can you tell me, however, in that case the main clause is a question. Ok? Um, so we need to remember that, ok, what type of punctuation do I need to have at the end of my sentence. Is the main clause a statement, or is it a question? Ok? Um, now, another reason we can use these types of questions, ok? Is also to be polite. Ok? Um, so, using main clauses that are questions like this with noun clauses, ok? Is a form of being polite. Ok? If I have this (pause) Ok? I have two questions here. Can you tell me when the bus leaves, and when does the bus leave? Ok? Which one do you think is the most formal way to ask a question? Which one is the polite way to ask a question?

31   S: (CT: the first one)

32   R: The first one. Ok? There's nothing wrong with asking the question when does the bus leave? Ok? But, if for example, you're in the bus station and you have no idea when your bus leaves and you see a nice old lady sitting there and you think she knows the answer, ok? You wouldn't ask her, hey, when does the bus leave? Ok? You, you could ask her that, but it wouldn't be very polite. Ok? And instead, we can use these type of structures, ok? Can you tell me when the bus leaves, please? Ok? And that makes it sound more polite. Ok? So we can use noun clauses with main clauses that are questions to ask questions in a more polite way. Ok? In a more formal way. So, any questions about these types of clauses? Clauses that begin with wh-, very similar to clauses that begin with that. Ok? But the main thing, well first of all there's two things that you need to think about. What are they? So, when I make noun, when I make sentences using noun clauses beginning with questions, what is, what are the two things I need to think about?

33   S: The verb and the noun.

34   R: Yes, so where is the verb in the sentence, ok? Remember to (UC: put that there) ok? Remember to move it. The second thing...

35   S: (CT: a question.)

36   R: Is it a question? Ok? Good. Alright, so let's do some practice with this and then after that we will move onto the next thing. Ok? So turn to page 332 in your books. (pause) We are going to be doing activity four. Ok?

Now, activity four says that it's a listen to some questions, ok? Ah, unfortunately, we don't have the CD to this book, ok? So we can't listen to it. However, what you're going to be doing is your going to be making up questions. Ok? So, for example number two, I'd like to know... Ok? And then it's up to you to decide what you would like to know. Ok? But make sure that you use, noun clauses that begin with question words, with wh-. Ok? (students work independently)

37   R: Alright seems like most people are finished this exercise. So, before we move on to the next one, let's quickly take this up. So, does anybody want to volunteer their question, or their answer for number two? Ally?

38   Ally: I'd like to know when the company first got started.

39   R: I'd like to know when the company first got started. You must have had the answers to this book. Yes. Ok? That is a correct way of using this. Ok? I'd like to know when the company first got started. Ok? So, we're using a wh- word, the verb is after the subject. Ok? Good. What about number three? (UC: Tasha.)

40   Tasha: Um, can you tell me who the head is?

41   R: Who the head is? You must've also had the answers in your book. Yes, that's exactly what the (UC: sticky) said. You're good. Yes, so can you tell me where the head of the department is? Ok? Number four? Lu?

42   Lu: Can you tell me when you (UC: will leave school)?

43   R: Can you tell me when...

44   Lu: When you will leave school.

45   R: When you will miss school?

46   Lu: leave

47   R: Leave. Yes, can you tell me when we will leave school. Yes, ok? Excellent. Sherlock, number five.

48   Lu: I wonder how I get your (UC: heart)

49   Lu: (CT: laughs)

50   R: I wonder how I get your...

51   Lu: (CT: heart)

52   R: Heart? O, so romantic.

53   Lu: (CT: laughs)

54   R: I wonder how I get your heart. (CT: laughs) Ok? Ah, yeah, so how and how many those are also question words that you can use to start off these types of noun clauses. Number six. Can you tell me...Allen.

55   Allen: Can you tell me what the boss's name is?

56   R: Yeah, can you tell me what the boss's name is? Perfect, ok? Number seven. Kelly.

57   Kelly: um, I would like to know whether it is necessary to work overtime, everyday?

58   R: I would like to know...

59   Kelly: whether

60   R: whether? Ah, so you are already skipping ahead. Yes, you can say that, whether we have to work overtime. Yeah, ok. And number eight, one more volunteer. (UC: Reisle)

61   Reisle: Can you tell me when you get your car?

62   R: Can you tell me when you get your car. Yup. That's exactly right. Good. Alright. And one more thing related to this ok? Exercise six on page 333. Ok? Ah, so imagine that tomorrow you have a job interview, ok? And you're asking your friend to help you to prepare, and your friend already had her interview with the same boss. Things like these are the questions that he will ask you. Ok? So, what you're going to do is, you're going to fill in the blanks ok? Using the questions that are below. So, for example, number one. They, they will probably ask... Ok? The question here is, what is your job, what is your current job title? So, you will say, they will probably ask what your current job title is. Ok? (Students work independently)

63   R: (UC: [talks quietly])

64   R: Alright, wow, you guys are the fastest workers I've ever seen.

65   S: (CT: chuckles)

66   R: You always finish in like ten seconds. Alright.

67   S: (CT: chuckles)

68   R: Let's quickly take this up, before we move on to the next one. Ok, so the question number two, they will want to know...

69   S: (CT: indistinguishable phrase)

70   R: K, how about we just raise our hand and one person can answer and then we can agree. So, who has the answer?

71   S: They, they will want to know what your job duties are.

72   R: Yes, they will want to know what your job duties are. Everyone agree with that?

73   S: (CT: yes)

74   R: Ok good. Number three, they will ask... Lu.

75   Lu: what qualification you have

76   R: what qualifications...

77   Lu: you have.

78   R: you have.

79   Lu: (indistinguishable phrase)

80   R: Uhum, that's a good question. So first of all is it correct if I say, they will ask what qualifications you have? Is that correct? Everyone agree?

81   S: (CT: no)

82   R: No, why not?

83   S: Because it's a question and if you say uh what question uh what qualify what qualifications do you have... (CT: no)

84   R: Yes, in the sentence, they will ask what qualifications do you have, do you think that's correct?

85   S: (CT: no)

86   R: So, what did you have for an answer then?

87   S: Uh what uh, they will ask what uh, qualification you have.

88   R: You have. Ok. Yes. And now back to (UC: [CT: laughing] finals questions it was the same, I don't really know what that one was about, uh but anyway, back to finals questions) why don't we use the word do? Ok? Because when we make a question, ok? I can't just say what qualifications you have? Ok? I have to insert auxiliary verb in this case do, to make it a question. Ok? But, when you take a question and you make it back into a statement, ok? You take out that auxiliary verb that you added in before. Ok? So in this case, you take out the word do, ok? So we have, they will ask what qualifications you have. Ok? Does that make sense?

89   S: (indistinguishable phrase)

90   R: In this case, any helping verbs like do, ok? Any verbs like that, yes, we take them out because they're part of the question, but they're not part of the statement, ok?

91   S: But they said uh if, if you, if he uh adds uh do...

92   R: Yes

93   S: it,

94   R: Yes

95   S: it becomes uh question

96   R: a question, yes exactly. Ok. Alright, let's, let's try number four, they will want to know... Mo

97   S: Who your pr...

98   R: previous

99   S: employ employer is.

100   R: Is? Was. Ok? Who your previous employer was. Ok? Because you're not working for him anymore. So therefore, it's past, ok? Number five, they will ask...

101   S: Who you, was employer

102   R: Pardon me? For number four?

103   S: Yeah, they want to know who your employer is?

104   R: who your previous employer was. Ok?

105   S: So here we have was?

106 R: Yes, because was, because was is the main verb in the sentence, ok? But, if you go back to number three, ok, what qualifications do you have? Ok? Have is the main verb, do is the auxiliary verb that we add in to make a question, right? So when we make it back into a statement we take that out. Ah number seven, they will ask...

107 S: (CT: Number five)

108 R: Ok. I'm in a hurry today, number five, they will ask...

109 S: They will ask how long you worked for your last job

110 R: Yes, ok? They will ask how long you've worked in your last job. Ok? And once again, or sorry, how long, yeah, how long you worked. It's past tense, right? So, yeah, once again in this case, we take out did. Ok? Number six, they will want to know... Song

111 Song: why you leave your last job.

112 S: (CT: leave. left)

113 R: Why you left.

114 S: (CT: left)

115 R: Ok? So, here you can see they are asking you why did you leave your last job. Ok? So right now that's a present situation, but, they will want to know why you left. Ok? So that's, it's changing tenses a, a bit there but we talked a bit about that yesterday so, ah, number seven, they will ask... Wendy

116 Wendy: They will ask what your salary was.

117 R: There, yes, they will ask what your salary was. Good, and number eight, they will want to know...

118 S: (CT: why you want the job)

119 R: Why you want the job. Alright, good. Seems like you, that you understand this. Ok? Any questions right now about these types of noun clauses? No? Alright, ah what time do we have? Ok, still have enough time here. Alright so, the last thing about noun clauses, ok? Are noun clauses that begin with if and whether, ok? And these are yes or no type questions that we take, ok? Ah, so, if you look at these questions, ok? Will we have class tomorrow? Yes or no, ok? Is the snowstorm going to be bad? I don't know, yes or no. Are the weathermen always right? Do I have to swim to school tomorrow, ok? If you start asking me that, if there's this much snow, do I need to swim? Uh, no you stay home. Ok? And, did we lunch together yesterday or on Monday? Ok? That's for you grandmother who's old, can't remember things. Ok? Did we eat lunch yesterday, or on Monday? I don't remember, I don't know, but... Anyway, these are the, the questions that we have, ok? But, we can add these types of questions into main clauses again. Ok? Ah, so it's kind of the same thing as with noun clauses that begin with wh-, ok? There are a few of the same rules here. Ah, but before we do that, ok, I said

that noun clauses that begin with if or whether, and you might be wondering when do we use if and when do we use, use whether, ok? The quick answer is you can use them both in the same situations, ok? They mean the same thing in that case, but, whether is usually considered more formal. Ok? More polite, whereas if is considered more informal. Ok? So you can use them, you know, in the same ways, there's not a rule saying in this case use whether, and in this case use if. Ok? But you can use them interchangeably is the word, which means it doesn't matter which one you use. Ok? So, let's start here. Now, imagine that I am asking this to my friend, what situation would that be? Informal. Right? So, let's use if. Ok, so I am wondering if...

120   S: we have class tomorrow. We have class tomorrow.

121   R: Ok, so I heard this, I am wondering if we have class tomorrow. Yeah. Ok? That's perfectly fine. Ok? And in this case we have class tomorrow. Ok? Will we have class tomorrow was the original question. Ok? but once again, ok? Will is an auxiliary that we add in to make the question. Right? I, I can't just say we have class tomorrow? Ok? We need to add in will we have class tomorrow, but, when we're taking that question and making it back into a statement we can add it to our main clause, we take that out again. So I, so I can say, I am wondering if we have class tomorrow. Ok? Is this a question or a sente..., or a statement?

122   S: (CT: statement)

123   R: Statement. Ok? Alright, let's pretend that I am talking to my professor. K? Very, very formal situation. They're very scary people, those professors. So, I'm just kidding. So, let's use whether. K? So I want to know, is the snowstorm going to be bad? Ok? But imagine this is a statement now. So I am adding this question into the main clause, I wonder, Ok? Whether...

124   S: (CT: the storm, is going to be bad)

125   R: Snowstorm

126   S: (CT: is going to be bad)

127   R: Ok? So, yeah that's perfectly correct. I wonder whether the snowstorm is going to be bad. Question or statement?

128   S: (CT: statement)

129   R: Statement, ok? Are the weathermen always right? I wonder that all the time, because they always seem to be wrong. So, I don't know.

130   S: (UC: if weathermen are always right.)

131   R: Ok, if, whether, it doesn't matter, weathermen (CT: are always right.) Yeah, good. Now, ah, when we're making these, we can add another word in here and it means the, it has the same meaning, but I can say I don't know if the weathermen are always right, or not. Ok? you can add or not at the

end of these sentences, just to add some emphasis. Ok? It, there's not really any different meaning between this, ok? Or I can say, I don't know if the weathermen are always right or not, or I can say, I don't know whether the weatherman are always correct or always right or not. Ok? So that's something that we can add onto our sentences, with these types of noun clauses. Ok? I can also say (pause) I, ok I can also say I don't know whether or not I have to swim to school tomorrow. Ok? So we can take this or not and move it right after whether. Ok? However, I cannot say, I cannot say I don't know if or not I have to swim. Ok? Or not can only go after whether, not if. Ok? But, I can say I don't know if the weathermen are always right or not. Ok? So if you are going to use or not with if, it's at the end of the sentence. But if you're using it with whether, it can be immediately after whether, or at the end of the sentence. Now, another thing that you need to remember, or that you need to look out for when you're making these types of sentences is verb tense. Ok? So this question here, did we eat lunch together yesterday or on Monday? Ok? What am I referring to, or what is the time period that I am referring to? Something in the past. Right? It was either yesterday or Monday. Ok? Ah, actually today is Tuesday so, it should be yesterday or Sunday. Ok? But anyway, ah so let's add this here. Ok? So, I don't remember, if...

132 S: (CT: we eat)

133 R: we...

134 S: (O: eat lunch)

135 R: eat?

136 S: (CT: ate)

137 R: Ate, yes. Ok? Since it is something that happened in the past, the verb tense needs to show that. Ok? So, I don't remember if we ate lunch (pause) together yesterday or Monday. Ok? So I, I could also add that on if I wanted to, I don't remember if we ate lunch together yesterday or Monday or not. Does that sound correct?

138 S: (CT: yes, no)

139 R: No. Ok? And let me tell you why it is not correct. Ok? In this case, we have three options. Did we eat lunch together yesterday or Monday or not? Ok? When you have these types of sentences you only leave the listener or the reader ok? Two options. Ok? I cannot say I don't remember if we ate lunch together yesterday or Monday or not. Ok? It's one or the other. Ok? So, in that case, it's incorrect. Ok? Any questions about these types of noun clauses? No? Ok. Alright, so just to finish off we have a little five minutes left. Ah, on page 335 in your books. (pause) So once again, this is supposed to be a listening activity but you can make it into your own creative activity.

Ok? Ah, so here we have a situation. Alice is thinking of having a birthday party at a restaurant and she's asking her friend Todd about the restaurant. Ok? So pretend you are Todd and that you are going to give her some answers. Ok?

140 S: Roger

141 R: Yes

142 S: (Indistinguishable – quietly asks R a question)

143 R: (indistinguishable – quietly answers)

144 R: Yes, Yes that was my mistake. So Sherlock pointed out something that was my mistake. Ok? The sentence here, I am wondering if we have class tomorrow. Ok?

145 Sherlock: We will

146 R: Yes, ok? The tense in here is, we will have class tomorrow. Ok? I hope that didn't confuse anybody, and if it did, come talk to me after class. Thanks Sherlock.

147 R: Alright so, I notice most people are not finished yet so please finish this for homework. Ok? Ah, and we'll take it up tomorrow next class. Right? Ah, so actually it's fine because today another teacher was leaving and he said, I hope I don't see you tomorrow. Ok? And we both laughed because that's pretty much the only time you can say that to somebody and, you know, that's polite and it's socially acceptable to say I hope I don't see you tomorrow, because there's a snowstorm. Right? So you already know about that one.

148 S: (CT: indistinguishable phrase)

149 R: Yeah, you know what, whether or not there's a snowstorm, people won't be around, I don't think. Anyway if I don't see you, enjoy your new year.

150 S: (CT: thank-you)

151 R: And some of you I will probably see, what? Friday?

152 S: Yeah

153 R: Yeah

154 S: No, next, next (CT: Monday)

155 R: Next Monday

156 S: Yeah

Note: R: Roger; S: Student or students; CT: cross talk (everything that is in CT will be inside brackets); UC: Unclear (everything that is UC [i.e. a guess was made to what was said] will be inside brackets) indistinguishable phrase: not even a guess is possible as to what the speaker is saying.

ROGER REFLECTS

As the above transcript (we also videotaped the class and Roger also watched the video and sometimes comments on this below as well) shows, there were a total of 157 turns (some of these can be debatable and readers may want to add or remove some of the turns) in a 50-minute lesson. Teachers can gain this knowledge by capturing the oral communications that occur in their classrooms, and the only valuable way of accomplishing this is to record the class using an audio recorder/or video recorder (with audio) and then to transcribe what was said to produce a lesson transcript. Of course, reviewing audio and video recordings can add to this knowledge by revealing the prosodic features of the teacher's voice, such as stress and intonation, which are not visible in a transcript – not to mention all the nonverbal information provided by facial expressions and body language are also valuable.

We met after this class to discuss the transcript and any other reflections Roger may have had after reading the transcript of the lesson. I would like to point out that I (this author) was not in a supervisory role; rather, I was his facilitator and mirror when it came to his reflections. In other words, I facilitated his reflections but did not take part in the class. After reading the transcript and reflecting on it, Roger began to reflect on its contents and his class. Roger said he was pleased overall with how his class went and how he notes his students performed. Roger said,

> The students performed really well in this class. They seemed to understand the material completely and the concept of noun clauses and their forms and functions. The problem of taking out auxiliary verbs when making noun clauses came up but was explained and fixed. A notable achievement was that pretty much the entire class seemed comfortable using noun clauses.

He judged it overall to be a "successful class" because he said that he felt he had spent enough time explaining noun clauses to the students and that he also gave enough examples to check their comprehension. Additionally, after completing their exercises and giving answers, it seemed as if the students were able to identify and comprehend the uses of noun clauses.

Roger then began to reflect on particular turns within the transcript and attempted to explain his thinking at that time. For example, he chose the segment from the transcript between turns 8 to 34 as a highlight for him to comment on. Roger said that he chose that segment because he found it interesting to see how he teaches new information to his students. Roger remarked, "the first parts of grammar classes are supposed to involve 'exploration' of new concepts and I think I did a good job with that by trying to find answers as a class, rather than me just giving them answers." Thus, Roger said he was happy to have his students explore new concepts before finding out how they work so that the class as a whole can have a better understanding of them. He noted that he used "real-life, real-time input from his students" to accomplish this because this helps them relate better to the material he is trying to teach. Roger continued, "It also allows me to show them what not to do sometimes, depending on if I get an incorrect answer from the class." Roger explained that his overall structure of teaching when he introduces a new concept is to explore it first with his class and then provide more detailed instruction, which is good for the students because he said it is "a student centric way of teaching."

Roger then chose the segment from the transcript between turns 123 to 131. He said that he highlighted this segment for two reasons: first, he was interested to see how he was giving instructions to his students while teaching and second, he wanted to find an example of where he used real-time and real-life examples to illustrate particular points. Roger wanted to see, through the transcript, if he was giving clear instructions for his students to follow. He said he noted in this segment that he frequently used the filler "ok", and he judged that he was using this "too much." He said when he watched the video of this segment and his class overall, he "started to get annoyed" and vowed to stop using this filler from then on as it did not reflect what he wanted his students to get from him. Roger said that he noticed that he tends to ask for student input a lot when he teaches, and "even when I'm teaching new information." He wondered about this and considered that his "presenter side" wants him to "keep the audience involved." However, he also noted that he wants to consider his "teacher side" in that he may be realizing that his students can learn better if they are involved and actively thinking about new concepts. Roger continued, "so I was happy to find that even when I'm teaching new information, I use the students' responses to guide where I'm going with things."

The second main point of interest from that segment is that the examples he used and the situations that he created were mostly based on current, real-time events/occurrences. For example, Roger noted that the day the observer was in his class he used "my professor" in examples. The following day, there was supposed to be a snowstorm, so all the examples he used dealt with the topic of snow. So, Roger said he believes that using such real-life examples that "have context and meaning to the students helps them focus on the new things being taught."

In terms of watching the video of the class, overall, Roger said he was happy with what he saw and especially because he said he "looked like a teacher and how my body language and so on. That was something I wanted to look at too." Roger also said that the video shows him that he feels and looks more comfortable teaching grammar than the other skills. He said he was also happy overall after watching the video because his students seemed to be mostly paying attention and were interested in the lesson. More specifically, after watching the video, he said he was happy with the number of questions that he asked because he "thinks the best way to keep your students interested is probably to ask them questions to see what they know about this, and using examples that students create, is helpful." Roger also said that when he asks questions, he does not force anyone to answer them. However, he noted that the same four or five students were answering his questions so this may be something he should focus on in the future when he is teaching but he did not know how to really go about this. Roger continued, "I don't want to make anyone feel like they have to answer questions, but I don't know, that's kind of a fine line sometimes, is how much you want to push them, right?"

> **Reflective Break**
> - What did you notice first when you read Roger's transcript?
> - What do you think of Roger's reflections on his transcript?
> - What do you think about Roger's reflections on the video of his teaching?

CONCLUSION

This chapter outlined and discussed Roger's actual classroom practice during his first year, with a detailed example of a recording of one of his lessons. I focused on one lesson only because of the level of detail it provides as outlined in the transcript of the entire lesson as well as Roger's reflections on both the transcript of this lesson and its video recording. The major aspects of the transcript that Roger chose to focus on included his interest in how he teaches new information to his students, how he gives instructions and how he uses real-life examples when teaching grammar. On reviewing the video, Roger reflected on his use of questions and how he identified as a teacher. Overall, Roger was happy with how the lesson went and felt it was successful. The chapter that follows outlines Roger's reflections beyond practice.

Chapter 7

Reflecting Beyond First Year Practice

INTRODUCTION

The final stage/level of the framework entails teachers reflecting beyond practice. This fifth stage/level of the framework takes on a sociocultural dimension to teaching and learning. This is called critical reflection and entails exploring and examining the moral, political and social issues that impact a teacher's practice both inside and outside the classroom. Critical reflection moves the teacher beyond practice and links practice more closely to the broader socio-political as well as affective/moral issues that impact practice. Such a critical focus on reflections also includes teachers examining the moral aspect of practice and the moral values and judgments that impact practice as well as their own emotions before, during and after practice. It is this latter aspect of critical reflection that will be covered in detail, regarding Roger's emotions during his first year of teaching. For the most part, the language teaching professional has somewhat neglected this aspect of teachers' well-being in terms of their personal and emotional investment as they transition from trainee to novice teacher. Research in general education suggests that it is important to pay attention to teachers' emotional investment because, as Callahan (1988: 12) points out, they "constitute reflexive personal signals, or 'vital signs' informing us of inner processes" of teachers' emotions.

Teachers can specifically access, explore, and reflect more precisely on teacher emotions by examining their affective language through the lens of the appraisal theory of emotion (White, 2000). A central component of the Appraisal Framework is exploration of language for expressing attitude that consists of three sub-systems: *affect*, *judgement* and *appreciation* (White, 2000), with *affect* referring to the language used for expressing emotions. Affect is defined here as "a feeling encompassing a variety of moods and emotional states that help form the emotional makeup of an individual (Robbins et al., 2017: 261). I analyzed Roger's reflections for affective language using White's (2000) approach, which includes examining the data for *adverbials*: "happily", "angrily", "fearfully", "proudly"; *attributes*: "I'm sad". "He's <u>frightened</u> of spiders"; *nominals*: "His <u>fear</u> was obvious to all"; and *verbs*: "This pleases me". "I hate chocolate". Thus, by applying the above categories of affect to the linguistic expressions which appeared in Roger's reflections during his first year, a deeper scrutiny of his use of affective language was possible as presented below.

ROGER'S EXPRESSED EMOTIONS FIRST YEAR

From the very first meeting we had during his first year of teaching, a scan of all the data collected during Roger's first year of teaching show that for the most part his experience of teaching involved positive emotions that included his four main feelings such as "confident" (the most prevalent emotion expressed by Roger throughout his first year), "curious", "enjoyment", and "excitement".

Excitement

Roger expressed his "excitement" about his new career and that he was "confident" in his qualifications and ability to do it, although he also said he was "nervous" starting out as a novice teacher in his own "real classroom, teaching real students" for the first time. From the very first day on the job Roger said he felt extreme excitement to the point he could not sleep the night before. Roger continued,

> I was excited. It was the first time after my masters, really, that I stepped into the classroom and to me that was exciting because it's, I'm loaded, so to speak, with this new knowledge and yeah, it's exciting to see if I learned a lot about classroom management, classroom control, teaching methods, and so on, from the masters program.

Roger reported that after his first week in the classroom he felt even more excitement because of the actual experience of teaching real students:

> I've taught classes now; I've actually given lessons. I have students do work that I've assigned, I've assigned homework, you know? It's, I definitely feel like a teacher now. I have my own classroom now that I'm in charge of. I can control what happens in this classroom. I can say, "we're going to do this today, we're going to do that today" and the students will have to do it (laughs). I'm excited, really, yeah definitely.

Enjoyment

Roger also expressed his "enjoyment" with his career throughout his first year of teaching. For example, early in his first year he expressed his enjoyment with giving presentations and that he will enjoy seeing his students giving presentations. He also said that he will enjoy learning how to teach during this first year. After a few weeks teaching, Roger noted that he 'enjoyed' teaching speaking classes more than writing classes because of the workload difference as well as how one is more interactive than the other. Roger mentioned that teaching writing involves a lot of marking he must do after the class, but not teaching speaking as he only marks presentations while they are occurring. Roger continued, "I prefer teaching speaking because it's just more interactive and you see a lot of progression." That said he also noted that he enjoys teaching writing as well because he can see how they develop their academic writing skills. Roger remarked, "I enjoy teaching that too because you also see them learn the steps of academic writing. But writing seems to be a little bit more complicated, you know, the whole APA thing, the whole academic English, whereas teaching a speaking class they just present." In fact, when he is teaching writing, Roger said that he is always 'curious' about what his students would produce in their writing after his instruction and indeed, in each of the classes he was teaching.

Curiosity

This curiosity can be grouped with the excitement he felt above attempting to put into practice some of the knowledge he gained from his graduate courses. For example, Roger said that he wanted to try to get them to write complete first drafts rather than fragments of a draft. So he said, "I'm kind of curious to see their first drafts, which are due, which is really their rough drafts, but I'm trying to get them to write as complete of a draft as they can." Because his students were studying English for academic purposes (EAP), Roger wanted them to pay special attention to in-text referencing and use of references as this would be a main requirement for them when they enter university, their true purpose for taking his classes. Roger remarked, "I'm curious to see their use of in-text referencing, when to use references and whether they include their reference page or if it's in proper format, and so on." Roger said his level of curiosity increased as the term progressed with this particular course because he said they rarely ask him any questions in class or send him any emails requiring assistance. As Roger said, "I tell them almost every class, any questions, talk to me, email me, ask me, I'm here to help." His curiosity remained throughout his first year with his expressions of wonderment about how his students would fare in their mid-term and final exams after his instructing them.

Reflective Break
- Why do you think Roger had a strong feeling of curiosity during his first-year teaching?
- Did you have a similar feeling? If yes, why? If not, why not?
- How do you think Roger kept up this feeling of curiosity during his first-year teaching?

Confident

Roger also expressed throughout his first-year teaching that he felt confident not only that he was well qualified to be a teacher but also that he was able to be successful in his first year. In fact, Roger said that overall, he is a confident person and for teaching he is more than capable of dealing with any controversy that may come up because he said that he has "the knowledge to back up what I do." Roger said that because he has just qualified with his master's degree, this experience as a student helps him understand the "system" better so he can better help his students navigate it. Roger remarked, "from being a student myself, I know the loopholes, I know where you can get away with things and where you can't, right? I mean, that in itself gives me a bit of an inside view to help them more." Regarding his background training to help prepare him for his first year, Roger said that he is confident that he has enough knowledge to get him through. Roger remarked, "I think overall my MA definitely gave me the confidence that now I'm equipped to do this."

For example, Roger said that the courses he took during both his BA and MA courses gave him the knowledge to be able to talk about materials the institution uses as well as how to "handle" different cultural backgrounds that are in most language classrooms. He said that although he has heard that most novice teachers are shocked when they first walk into a diverse classroom, he was not because of his training. Regarding the different skills he was asked to teach in his first year, Roger also said that he felt "very qualified, very competent to teach those skills just because I've seen the final results, I've seen how it works." Roger noted that he now feels more like a teacher and would now describe his "identity as a teacher" after this first year of teaching. Roger gave specific examples of why he identifies as a teacher and compares himself to other teachers he has peripherally observed during his first year and noticed some differences related to use of the textbook, interactivity with students in a teacher-centered versus student-centered approach to teaching. Roger remarked:

> I would say that I think, compared to other teachers, I go less by the book. I think I'm more interactive with my students. I think I'm more of a student-centered teacher than a teacher-centered teacher, I mean, a lot of the things I did this past term didn't necessarily make my life easier. But, you know, I thought there are extra things I could do that I think might help my students learn something better. As a teacher, I am not only concerned with, "how does this affect me?", but "how does it affect my students?"

Roger also said that during his second semester of his first year teaching the institution chose him (or, as Roger said, he was "assigned") as a mentor teacher for trainee teachers to observe him teach. Roger said he was happy with this "assignment" especially because the other teachers who were chosen were all much more experienced than he was. Roger said that "it was kind of cool that I was put on that list, considered to be able to mentor someone at this point, but it might have something to do with it [the course he was teaching] that I'm comfortable with it, I'm confident with it." Indeed, as the term progressed, Roger said that he was becoming even more confident in his identity as a teacher; and one more example of this was his successful completion of mid-term examinations that he had to create himself, as he noted that his students "did very, very well." Roger said that he had no prior training making any examinations so he wondered how it would all turn out. Roger said he was very happy with the result and said that he, "definitely gained some confidence in creating tests and exams with this."

At the end of his first semester teaching during his first year, Roger admitted that he realizes that after this experience teaching, he still has a lot to learn, and he knows that each class he meets will have its own personality that may take some adjusting to, because it's different to what he has just experienced. Roger continued,

> A lot of the way that you teach depends on the personality of your classes. The fact that one of my classes was 95% [the same ethnicity] made it a very different class than other classes that I hear about. It's a lot quieter, as let's say a class where there's, you know, many different ethnic groups, just because of their personalities.

Towards the end of his first year, Roger's confidence was growing even more when he said that after watching video of his teaching, he thinks that he looks "pretty natural" as a teacher, compared with during his first semester. Roger said, "I think that I look pretty natural when watching myself, whereas the first semester I can pretty much say for a fact that I wasn't natural like that." Roger noted that "even comparing myself teaching now to when that video was recorded, I noticed that I feel more comfortable teaching grammar, even from then." Roger said that he has gained more confidence in himself as a teacher from his first semester and he attributes this to the experience he has gained during the year. As Roger noted,

> I think by now I've got enough experience behind me that more or less I know what I'm doing, and I know the processes that are part of teaching and so on. So I don't think I could say 100% full experienced, fully qualified teacher. I think that probably takes a few years. But I would say I'm a well-established teacher by now.

At our last meeting during Roger's first year teaching, he said that the most important feeling he has is his confidence in his ability. Roger continued,

> I know like that I have confidence in what I'm doing, how I'm doing it, what I'm teaching, you know, pretty much confidence in all aspects of handling a class. So that's definitely one thing is confidence. But also, just it's more of a natural thing now. I find I don't have to think as much about what I'm doing or plan it out carefully. Now it's just more of a natural flow.

Reflective Break

- Why do you think Roger felt confident during his first-semester teaching?
- Did you have a similar feeling during your first semester? If yes, why? If not, why not?
- How do you think Roger kept up this feeling of confidence during his first-year teaching?
- Do you think Roger may be overly confident after just one year teaching experience?

When novice teachers express emotions such as the positive emotions Roger has expressed in this chapter, they can gain insight into the inner workings of what it really means to be a teacher in its true, holistic sense. Novice teachers can gain more insight into how they interact with their colleagues, students (both inside and outside the classroom), as well as their preferences for using various activities or avoiding others. In fact, such emotions can influence every facet of a teacher's life and overall well-being.

> **Reflective Break**
> - Can you point to how your emotions (either positive or negative) affect:
>   - your use of English when teaching English;
>   - your interaction with students;
>   - how you respond to unanticipated classroom incidents;
>   - the extent to which you make use of particular methods or activities;
>   - the kind of feedback you provide;
>   - the level of satisfaction regarding your career choice as an ESL/EFL teacher?

CONCLUSION

This chapter outlined and discussed Roger's expressed emotions during his first-year teaching.

The findings reveal the four positive emotions he used with "confident" being the most frequently expressed emotion. The other main emotions he expressed were "curiosity", "excitement", and "enjoyment". Roger's expressed emotions are an important indicator of his overall adjustment to his role and identity as a novice ESL teacher and the fact that they are positive is an indication that he has made a smooth transition from his teacher education program to his first year as a teacher. Such transitions do not always progress so smoothly especially since, by his own admission, he was left alone to "sink or swim", and so it is important for novice teachers to gauge their emotions because they are good indicators of the level of satisfaction the teachers derive from teaching. The chapter that follows gives an overall appraisal of Roger's first year as an ESL teacher.

Chapter 8

Analyzing the First Year

INTRODUCTION

The previous five chapters outlined and discussed Roger's first year reflections on his philosophy (Chapter 3), his principles (Chapter 4), his theory (Chapter 5), his practice (Chapter 6), and his reflections beyond practice (Chapter 7). This chapter summarizes some of the important findings from all of these reflections so that we can portray an overall image of Roger that illustrates his lived experiences during his first year of teaching. The chapter also outlines Roger's own reflections on what he has learned from his first year of teaching.

FIRST YEAR REFLECTING FROM PHILOSOPHY TO BEYOND PRACTICE

In this section I provide a summary of Roger's major reflections on his philosophy, principles, theory, practice and beyond practice during his first year of teaching.

Philosophy

Roger's early positive experiences with education when he was in grade school impacted his decision to enter the field of teaching English to speakers of other languages (TESOL). Indeed, because he is an immigrant to Canada himself, he said that he had empathy for all ESL students and that is why he wanted to enter the TESOL field, after graduating from his MA program, to help ESL students like himself learn to speak and write English.

From the very beginning of his first year, Roger identified himself, and his roles, based mostly on the knowledge he gained in his BA and MA programs and especially his most frequently stated role of *pedagogical expert*. Roger noted that he was confident in his teaching ability before he began teaching because of his knowledge of linguistics and language, and his practice teaching training. Roger said he had complete confidence in deciding what he would teach, how he would teach and how he could gauge his students' needs with learning English as a second language.

Although Roger noted that he was confident in his teaching qualifications and abilities, he also acknowledged he was a *novice* teacher with little experience in real classrooms and so he would have a lot to learn. For this he said that he was looking forward to some guidance or professional development from the institution during his first year, though this did not happen and, in fact, he was left alone to "sink or swim" as he put it.

Related to his role as a novice where he was left alone to survive without any help from the institution he was teaching in, Roger soon recognized another identity role fast developing during his first year – that he was an *individual* trying to survive his first year because of the lack of any guidance. Roger was surprised that he would have to take on this role during his first year as he noted he had never imagined he would be left totally alone to teach even during his first few weeks on the job. On reflection, he said that his strong personality probably helped him embrace this role rather than waiting for anyone to help him. He also reflected that he should have taken the initiative more to ask for help rather than waiting, especially when it came to planning lessons.

Roger said that he always wanted to take on a student-centered role as a teacher as he did not want to be an oppressive teacher dominating each lesson. For this he said he wanted interactive lessons and thus he said he planned for this throughout his first year of teaching. Roger noted that he figured that he was more student-centered and more interactive with his students than the other teachers during his first year. His other major identity role during his first year, however, could be seen to conflict with the student-centered role in that he was observed taking on the role of being "didactic" (this word was not directly stated by Roger but seemed to fit his beliefs), or moralistic to his students as the first year progressed. Roger said that during the first year he felt at times his role was that of a parent, and moral authority, telling his students (who were teenagers or young adults) what was "right" and what was "wrong" within an education setting (e.g., there was an issue with plagiarism), and/or what is or should be appropriate behavior in a multi-cultural environment, and how to acculturate to the local cultural and academic setting.

Reflective Break

- Looking again at the five professional identity roles (*pedagogical expert, novice, individual, student-centered teacher*, and *didactic*) that Roger (either explicitly or implicitly or both) took on during his first year, which of these identity roles would you take on and why?
- Comment on their frequency. Would you rank them similarly? Why, or why not?
- Which identity roles would you not take on and why?
- Do you think any of these roles are opposite (e.g., student-centered teacher and "didactic") to each other considering his experiences?
- Can you think of any identity roles that first year teachers may take on that may clash without their realizing such a possibility?
- List any identity roles you think Roger missed during his first year of teaching.

Principles

Roger's reflections on his principles during his first year brought him closer to considering what he believed about learning and teaching English as a second language. In fact, Roger's principles were guided by his beliefs related to his teaching approaches such as the use of students' L1 in lessons, teaching and learning writing, teaching and learning grammar, and making lessons challenging.

For example, Roger believed strongly, and stated this throughout his first year, that his students should only use English in his classes and there was no place for their first language (L1). In fact, he even developed some methods in his lessons to discourage the use of L1 – such as giving extra homework to the entire class even if only one student used his or her L1 during a lesson. In addition, if particular students continued to use their L1 during lessons he would "fine" them by making them pay one dollar for each time they spoke their L1 and put the money gained towards funds for an end-of-term class party.

Related to his beliefs about learning and teaching English writing as a second language, Roger said his beliefs clashed with those that the institution wanted for such lessons. For example, Roger noted that although the school wanted his students to complete four major essays over the course of one term, he said that he did not believe this was an effective method of teaching writing for his students because they would not learn how to write from the basics. Roger said he believed that his students needed to move from small aspects of the mechanics of writing (such as learning that a sentence has a subject and predicate and subject/verb agreements, and articles) first and then to larger items such as writing a whole essay. In terms of his beliefs about learning and teaching grammar, Roger said that he believes that grammar is very important for his students to know and that in his writing classes (as discussed above) in particular he takes marks off when students make grammar mistakes. He noted the reason for such a strong belief is that he must prepare them for university work where professors will not point out such grammar mistakes.

> **Reflective Break**
> - What do you think about Roger's beliefs regarding his approaches and teaching methods during his first year?
> - What do you think about Roger's belief regarding L1 use in his lessons?
> - What do you think about Roger's beliefs regarding grammar?
> - What are your beliefs about learning and teaching English as a second or foreign language and where do they come from (their source)?

Theory

Roger reflected on his theory during his first year, especially with regard to lesson planning, and realized that although he considered himself a pedagogical expert and ready to teach because of his academic training, the reality of the classroom changed all this. In fact, Roger said that he became acutely aware from the first few weeks teaching that his MA teacher preparation courses did not prepare him for the reality of what he would face in real classrooms with real students and how he would plan his lessons. Although Roger acknowledges that there was a central syllabus given to each instructor, he had to adapt the syllabus but did not really know how to write such lesson plans as he had no training for this in his teacher education program. For example, Roger did not know whether or not he should focus on grammar in his writing classes, and how to plan lessons from the first draft onwards. Roger noted, for example, that there are language theories that he had learned about in his master's program that say that "on first drafts focus on content alone because that's the most important thing," and thus not on any grammar issues. However, Roger said that the program he was teaching was preparing his students to enter university directly after graduation where writing first drafts is not the same as in a language school. Therefore, students will have to be mindful of grammar errors from the very beginning of the writing process they are engaged in. As a result, throughout his first year, Roger struggled with shifting ideas and different plans to solve such a dilemma.

In addition, other dilemmas or critical incidents that Roger faced in this first year included problems with his students adapting to using APA formatting, plagiarizing in his lessons, and his students' use of controversial topics – all of which were difficult for him to deal with. His first major critical incident, regarding the use of the APA referencing system, shocked Roger because, despite a lot of instructional planning and explanation time in class, most of the students did not follow APA guidelines or understand how to use references. Linked to the same writing class was an incident where half the students plagiarized their first drafts. Using evidence from Turnitin.com, Roger gave anyone who plagiarized a zero. Again, he said he was very annoyed with this because he had spent a lot of time planning and teaching lessons about how to avoid plagiarizing. These two incidents, along with one related to how to deal with controversial topics raised by his students, caused Roger not only to articulate what his beliefs were but also challenged him to reflect throughout his first-year teaching on issues that were complex and with no easy answers.

Reflective Break
- How do you plan your lessons?
- Do you have a set syllabus or are you free to plan as you go?
- What critical incidents have you encountered in your first year as a teacher?

Practice

Roger's actual classroom practice during his first year focuses on one lesson only because of the level of detail it provides as outlined in the transcript of the entire lesson as well as Roger's reflections on both the transcript of this lesson and its video recording. Both of us sat and watched the video and Roger reflected on various aspects of what he saw and what he read in the transcript. It is important to point out that I was facilitating his reflections as the observer, but I was not his supervisor, so he was free to comment on whatever *he* found interesting.

The major aspect of the transcript and video that Roger talked about was his interest in reflecting on how he teaches new information to his students about particular grammar items and how they responded. Roger said that he was happy with the way his students seemed to understand the grammar structures he was teaching (noun clauses in this case) as they indicated that they could follow the material all through the lesson as shown in the transcript. He also noted that, towards the end of the lesson, his students were able to use noun clauses without much difficulty and this was an indication that the lesson went very well for him. More specifically, he chose particular segments of the transcript and went through each of them because he saw how his instructions were being received and the students being able to follow them without much difficulty. Roger also noted that he was very happy to see how the real-life examples he used when teaching grammar were very effective for his students' learning. Indeed, when reviewing the video and looking at himself teach, Roger said that it shows that he looks like a teacher and that he is comfortable teaching. He elaborated that he prefers to teach grammar more than any other skill such as listening, speaking, reading or writing. Overall, Roger said he was happy with how the lesson went and felt it was successful after viewing the video and going over the transcript.

Reflective Break

Recordings and transcriptions are the best concrete evidence we teachers can get about our work. We can collect this type of concrete data by placing a tape recorder or video recorder in our classroom.

- Audio or video record your class. Now play the tape and try to answer the following questions:
  - ▶ What did you notice first about the recording?
  - ▶ Did you focus on your voice (and physical appearance if you used video)?
  - ▶ Did you notice your pronunciation?
  - ▶ What did you notice about your students?
  - ▶ Are you comfortable with the speed at which you heard yourself speak?
  - ▶ If your students did not respond, what did you do?
  - ▶ How much wait-time did you allow in which your students could think before answering your questions?
  - ▶ How did you check on your students' understanding?
  - ▶ What kind of reinforcement did you give and how often?

Transcribing the Recording

Once the classroom communication data has been collected, the teacher then needs to transcribe the recording; this can be the most painful part of the whole process because it can take a long time to transcribe a one-hour class. Keep the transcript as simple as possible by numbering each turn (when someone takes a turn to speak) and keep to the original wording as accurately as possible (do not change it to make it more readable). It may not be necessary to transcribe the entire recording; teachers can decide what aspect of the classroom communications they are interested in knowing more about. For example, teachers may only be interested in reflecting on the impact of their verbal instructions in their classes (as Roger noted above), so all they need to do is listen to and transcribe those parts of the tape that show the teacher giving instructions and then the turns immediately after this (for about five minutes) to see what impact these instructions have had on their students' learning. Other topics could include the type and frequency of teacher (and student) questions, how tasks are set up in their classes, or the type of language in use in group discussions (if teachers of English language learners wish to focus on this aspect of classroom communication). So, after you have recorded the lesson:

- Select sets of turns (or episodes) – similar to what Roger did above when he read the transcript – that seem likely to provide the evidence relevant to the question in focus.
- If you have not transcribed the whole lesson, only transcribe that portion of the tape.
- What did you notice throughout your viewing of the lesson?

Beyond Practice

When reflecting beyond practice, I chose to focus on Roger's expressed emotions during his first-year teaching through the use of the Appraisal Framework (see Farrell, 2022 for more on this) which explores the language for expressing attitude such as affect, to refer to language used for expressing emotions. Thus, by applying analysis of affect to the linguistic expressions which appeared in Roger's reflections during his first year, a deeper scrutiny of his use of affective language was possible.

For the most part, Roger seemed to express only positive emotions during his first year of teaching, with the four most frequently found in all the data being his use of "confident", "curious", "excitement", and "enjoyment". Roger expressed his "excitement"about his new career and that he was "confident" in his qualifications and ability to do the job. Roger also expressed his "enjoyment" with his teaching that included giving presentations, as well as watching his students giving them, and being a teacher throughout his first year of teaching. He was really "curious" about being able to put into practice some of the knowledge he had gained from his graduate courses and, although he was successful for the most part with this, he also realized that he was not fully prepared for teaching "real students" in "real classrooms" and as such had to adapt a lot. That said, Roger was supremely "confident" not only that he was well qualified to be a teacher but also that he was able to be successful because he was able to make such adaptations in his first year.

Roger's expressed positive emotions indicate that he has transitioned well from his teacher education program to experiencing a successful first year teaching. He seems satisfied that he has had a successful first year even though he had no real assistance from the institution and, indeed, the administration did little to even follow his progression during this important first year. Novice teachers learning to teach in their first year on the job will experience a range of emotions, because they will meet so many different people all engaged in the process of learning. The fact that Roger had a firm grasp of his subject matter (especially the rules of grammar), gained while a graduate student, contributed to him being confident in his own ability to succeed during his first year as a teacher. His positive expressed emotions indicate that he was sure of his teacher identity at the end of his first year of teaching and he was excited with his students' reactions to his teaching. He also seems to have created conditions in his lessons for his students to experience positive emotions while learning, by encouraging questioning and interaction throughout his first-year teaching.

> **Reflective Break**
> - After reading about Roger's emotions, try to note your emotions while teaching during your first week, first semester and first year, and compare them to Roger's expressed emotions.

ROGER REFLECTS ON THE FIRST YEAR

Roger reflected on his overall experiences during his first year and I present his answers in his own words.

> There are a few issues that impacted me in an important way this term. The first is how students react to instructions, or how much emphasis is placed on instructions. It seems that, no matter if I gave verbal or written instructions, many students would avoid following them and do things their own way, or what they see as the best way of doing something. As a result, many students did not properly accomplish a given task or did not accomplish a task at all! This was very frustrating because it seems to undermine your position as a teacher.
>
> The second issue that impacted me was that of the lack of retention from one proficiency level [in his institution] to the next. It seems that a large number of students that are supposed to be familiar with certain things either forget them overnight or were never taught them properly or at all. For example, in my writing class there were some students who did not know anything about a thesis statement, many didn't know about bibliographies, and there were a few others who didn't know some things that they should have. This makes it difficult for an instructor because now you're forced to spend time on things that you didn't count on and the level of the class varies even more.
>
> The last issue that really impacted me was that I was able to be in complete control of my classroom without anyone really telling me what to do. This felt really good, and it made me feel qualified and "officially" ready to enter the teaching profession. Of course, there were some times that it was a bit overwhelming to plan my lessons without any help but, overall, this freedom to do what I thought best was an important step to become a full-time teacher.

Reflective Break

- What is your opinion of the three main issues Roger chose to focus on?
- Why did he choose two negative impacts and only one positive impact?
- What were the main issues for you during your first year as a teacher and why?

The question of what I have learned during my first year is almost better off being asked as what *haven't* I learned! There were so many things this semester that I learned or became better at: classroom management, time management, how to deal with frustrated students, how to deal with external matters impacting the whole program and institution I work in, how to work together with other instructors, how to work effectively and confidently on my own, how to present material to students for the first time, and how to use my knowledge of academics to teach others. This list is not extensive, but these are the most important and valuable things I have learned.

Reflective Break

- What is your opinion of what Roger said that he learned during his first-year teaching?
- What did you learn during your first year as a teacher?

In terms of what I think I need to learn more about – well, I think I need to learn more about organizing and preparing for a class at the very beginning of the term. It is very difficult to plan out an entire course with only a textbook and this is something that I need to be better at or just need to become more familiar with. I realized that it is very difficult to do a long-term plan and not deviate from it. Instead, it's better to plan from week to week while having a general, long-term plan. Also, all the administrative tasks associated with the beginning of term bogged me down a lot and I need to be better at becoming more efficient that way.

Another thing that I need to learn more about is giving clear, direct instructions, or at least repeating instructions more often. Even at level five, there are some students who still can't get instructions the first time you give them. However, I feel like I'm insulting some students' intelligence by repeating instructions three or four times. So, I need to become better at giving clear instructions the first time or two, so I don't have to over-repeat them.

The last thing I need to get better at is gauging my students' abilities after teaching them something and finding out if I need to spend more time on a specific point. Sometimes I feel like I rushed them through certain things and that they didn't end up learning something well enough. But, of course, after practice and experience, I will become better at these things.

> **Reflective Break**
> - What is your opinion of what Roger said he still needs to learn at the end of his first year?
> - What did you think you still needed to learn at the end of your first year?

The question of how I would describe myself as a teacher after my first year is not the easiest one to answer as it is like looking at yourself in a fuzzy mirror. What is my identity at this point? After one year of full-time teaching, have I become someone different or solidified an identity for myself? I would say that, no, at this point I don't have a solidified identity yet, but rather a half-molded identity. At this point, I would say that I am a student-first, learner-centered, easy-going, novice teacher. I say student-first and learner-centered because every class I teach I try to focus it on what the students need and giving students lots of practice and opportunities to use what they learn. I don't particularly like the classes when I'm lecturing the whole time because I feel like I'm cheating the students of something, but I don't know what. However, I realize that those types of classes are a necessity. I say I'm easygoing because I try not to let the little things bother me too much, such as students speaking in their L1s, cellphones going off, students not doing work, and so on. However, at the same time I realize that small issues can end up becoming big issues. But, I prefer not to let small things bother me so that they become big things. I also say I'm easygoing because when it comes to lesson planning, I feel that I don't always need to be ultra-prepared and prefer going into a class room and doing things on the spot. This doesn't mean I don't prepare; it means I feel comfortable with spontaneity and coming up with things on the spot. This I feel is as much as I can describe my teacher identity for now as it really is just developing and isn't "complete" yet.

Reflective Break

- What is your opinion of how Roger describes himself as a teacher in terms of his professional identity after his first year of teaching?
- How would you describe yourself as a teacher in terms of your professional identity at the end of your first-year teaching?

If I had to give a novice teacher advice based on my experiences this past semester, I would say this:

- Don't let the little things bother you.
- Learn to prepare ahead of time, but don't over-prepare as it makes you less natural in the classroom.
- Deal with student conflicts as soon as it happens and don't change your answer.
- If you are not familiar with something before you teach it, don't worry about it. You have the advantage of being a native speaker over your students and if you read about something, you will be able to teach it.
- Work together with other instructors often since they have experience, they have different opinions and teaching styles than you, and you can learn a lot from them.
- Relax. It's not a competition of any kind and be confident in yourself, even if you feel like you're doing something wrong.

Reflective Break

- What is your opinion of Roger's advice for first-year teachers?
- What would your advice be?

CONCLUSION

This chapter summarized Roger's reflections throughout his first year of teaching as well as his overall analysis of his first year as a teacher. Roger noted that he would not have been able to do so had he not engaged in the reflective process with me and, as a result, he said that he feels "like I've learned a lot about myself and about teaching. The weekly chats allowed me to look at myself from outside the box and reflect deeply on the things I do." The section and chapters that follow rekindle the reflective process when we met to explore his third-year teaching experiences.

Chapter 9

Reflecting on Third Year Philosophy

INTRODUCTION

To recap, the first stage of the framework, *philosophy*, examines the *teacher-as-person* because a teacher's basic philosophy has developed since birth. This stage can be considered a "window to the roots of a teacher's practice because a philosophy of practice means each observable behavior has a reason that guides it even if it is implicit" (Farrell, 2019: 84). By talking about past experiences that may have shaped their philosophy, teachers obtain self-knowledge by reflecting on their background (i.e. heritage, ethnicity, socioeconomic background, family, and personal values) (Farrell, 2015). While teachers can simply write an in-depth autobiography, one way to engage teachers in this stage is through narrative frames where they tell a story of their experience or accounts of their life through prompts (i.e., I became a teacher because...). Narrative frames offer insight into the past "to uncover preconceived theories about teaching and learning" (Taggart & Wilson, 1998, p. 164) as well as help second language teachers answer, "who am I?" through making sense of claims about identity. Philosophy includes the teacher in a personal manner because teaching is multidimensional as it matters who the teacher is. I presented Roger's first year professional role identity in Chapter 3 and, in this chapter, I present his third-year professional role identity.

ROGER'S THIRD YEAR PROFESSIONAL IDENTITY DEVELOPMENT

During Roger's third year he said that he was teaching one extra summer course (hence I write about three semesters during his third year) that was not officially included in the active data collection but nonetheless impacted his teaching and identity development during his third year. This impact (mostly negative) appears in much of the conversation and reflections related to his professional role identity. The following top four professional identity roles for Roger in his third year as a language teacher were identified in order of their frequency as follows:

1   Engager
2   Pedagogical & Language Expert
3   Individual
4   Didactic

Engager

The most frequent professional role identity that Roger recognized, either explicitly or implicitly, throughout his third year is that of the role of engager. For Roger, to be engaging means that he must create more entertaining and exciting lessons that have value; but also his students have to engage – to put some effort into seeing the value of their learning and to take more responsibility for their own learning.

Roger said that during the first semester of his third year he noticed that his classes were not going according to his plans and that he had to do something because he said he could not face another class like the one he had the previous summer semester. Roger said that "as a teacher, you have an ever-evolving audience with one class to the next your students are different and, last semester, I had a class full of duds." Roger said that this class was particularly difficult for him because, "it was like talking to a bunch of rocks." Roger said that after trying to teach them for a number of weeks, he "dreaded" going into each class because they were not willing to interact in any way with him or each other. Roger continued, "it was awful. So, when I went into the classroom after a few weeks of having them, I was not looking forward to it whatsoever because I knew exactly what was coming, which was nothing from them." Roger said that in that previous semester half of the students had actually failed their course and so could not progress to the next level and so, internally, he began to feel pressure as well because he said there is an "expectation that the students will progress to the next level."

Roger worried now that he would face the same difficulties with the language classes he was assigned to teach in the last semester of his third year because the students were "mostly from the same country". He also noted that, although they were supposed to be at a higher level of proficiency in English, they "exhibited the same non-interest as the classes" he had had the previous semester. Roger remarked, "this particular crop of students is really weak. They have very low skill, very low motivation." Roger mentioned that he also had a hard time to get them to stop speaking their L1 to each other, and that when they switched "back to their first language, it didn't really help the interactive part of the classroom."

Thus, in the first few weeks of the third semester of his third year, Roger, noting that his reflections about his negative experiences the previous semester with this facilitator, and the signs early on in the semester that he may have to face similar students with possibly negative effects, decided to try adopting a different attitude and role. Roger said that he would have "to keep on telling myself, you know, this is a different group of students, they are better, and I have to treat them better than I did last term." Roger also decided to take the attitude that his students all want to work, and so he will have to "make them work." However, in order to do this he decided that he "should find interesting things for them to do, and plan interesting things." Roger said that because of his experiences the previous semester, he did not really care too much about changing things and he already had the same attitude this semester when he said, "they have to do this, I don't care how" because he had given up towards the end of that last semester.

Roger realized that as he began this new semester of his third year, he still had the same negative feelings about teaching, and he did not feel like planning anything because he feared the students would not care much. As Roger expressed, "the last five weeks last term has left a lingering effect where the last couple weeks I didn't feel the need to plan carefully and, in much detail, because the students wouldn't have cared either way." Roger said that the previous term he had the feeling that whether he created something he thought was exciting or boring, his students would not have cared either way. So, Roger said that, as the term progressed, he would try to change his approach: as he reflected for action, he realized that for "this term, I find myself thinking that I need to put a little more effort into planning my courses, so that my students enjoy it, right?"

Roger then began to define for himself what this change would mean and that his focus would be making learning fun for his students. Roger said that if his students found that his courses were enjoyable, then they would also become more meaningful for them as well. Roger said that he realized that he wants his lessons to be enjoyable for his students "so that they see meaning in it. Nobody wants to do something that is boring. They don't see value in that." Roger said that he noted his students did not seem to enjoy his lessons and did not see the value in the lessons the previous semester and this was actually stated in his student feedback.

Roger said for him an "enjoyable" lesson is where students ask lots of questions during class, show interest in learning and ask him more questions afterwards; as he said, "attendance, participation, quality work, and questioning. To me those are things that show, hey, I'm interested." Roger said that he wants to "feed that interest so that it becomes even enjoyable for them." Roger gave the example of teaching and learning grammar and how he realizes that learning grammar is not necessarily exciting or enjoyable. He continues, "it's not something that most people find appealing. But it is a necessary thing for someone who's studying academic English. So, for me, enjoyable would be that they're not bored, but even if they find some little bit of excitement in what they learn, where they can realize, hey, I'm learning something. Right? And as a result, their interest level goes up."

When asked how he would gauge their level of enjoyment and engagement, Roger said that he usually examines his students' facial expressions and if he notices that "it's more than a blank stare, that means that they're interested, even if it's just a little bit." Thus, Roger said that he now sees his role as that of entertainer of sorts – to make sure that he helps his students see value in their learning, even if it is grammar – and that he will do this by creating different types of activities that his students will enjoy, while at the same time keeping them "engaged for a long period of time, not just for one day, and I think that's to me something that is exciting too."

Roger said that he also realizes that if he wants to provide fun lessons for his students that "what's fun to me is totally not fun to someone else" and so he tries to explain this to his students so that they will not have any misunderstanding what his lessons are about. Roger also realizes that there are limitations to the type of entertaining and fun lessons he can provide to encourage his students to learn and that his students also must try to engage more. This was also a result of his experiences the previous semester where he said he was "shocked at how little effort these students put into their classes" and, at the time, that he was "at a complete loss as to how can I make these students engage and how can I help them see the value in what they're doing."

Roger said that, on reflection, he probably did not think enough about how he taught the material and how to try to "capture everyone in each lesson to actually engage with the material." He said he found it draining to find ways to keep his students active and motivated and sometimes he felt angry with them as a result. Now he said that he realizes that he should have tried to make his lessons more enjoyable for them with more activities and with a less formal approach. Roger said that he noticed that he had many more slides on PowerPoint that past semester than usual and that these made his class less engaging. So, for this semester Roger said that he would use less slides and he has now "pared my slides down and added things into it where I would go over a few slides and then do some practice together" so he could engage his students more and his classes would be fun and meaningful.

Reflective Break
- What is your understanding of teacher as "engager"?
- What do you think of Roger's experiences of this role in his third year?

Pedagogical & Language Expert

The next most frequent professional role identity that Roger identified, either explicitly or implicitly throughout his third year, is that of pedagogical expert. Similar to the definition of this role as outlined in Chapter 3 that he noted during his first year of teaching, is his sense of confidence in his knowledge as a language expert, and his confidence in how he can measure student knowledge of their needs, but also the further development of his pedagogical expertise from his experiences over the past few years.

During his third year, Roger mentioned that, as a result of his experience of three years of teaching, he has "developed more tools" to help plan his lessons. As Roger stated, "I definitely see myself as more experienced even just in terms of my confidence level. I know that if I do something, or if I do this then x will happen, or it will take me x amount of time to do this type of thing, or, with this type of group of students I need to do this because their personality is more like that." Roger noted that his "repertoire of teaching skills has expanded now" because he has taught the same courses several times over the past few years and, as a result, this allows him to minimize his preparation time but at the same time to "perfect" his courses. For example, Roger said that he uses PowerPoint presentations now a lot in his lessons and he continuously updates them as preparation. Roger remarked, "I often use PowerPoint in my classes and now when I use them, I make them a little better, more streamlined, you know, change things a little bit, so that's, you know, just overall better."

Regarding Roger's knowledge about his students' needs, he said that he still believes that his students are not experts in how to learn English as a second language or how it should be taught, but that he has that level of expertise required to make these decisions. For example, Roger stated, that although his students may "recognize that they need to develop a lot of vocabulary, but they are not experts on how to acquire vocabulary." Roger said that his pedagogical and language expertise is a result of his training and his continued reading of research that informs his practices as well as the new knowledge gained from his experiences teaching over the past few years. Roger said, for example, that "there's lots of research that shows that their [his students'] way of learning vocabulary is not an effective way to learn words, right? So that's what probably most of them are doing ineffectively, just writing down all the words they don't know and trying to memorize."

However, with all his self-professed knowledge both pedagogical and linguistic, Roger noted that the institution in which he was teaching was not always receptive to his new ideas about how to improve overall teaching there. Roger also noted that he was never asked to contribute to curriculum development in the school and that this was detrimental to his development as an ESL teacher. Roger said, "one thing that we never do as teachers is develop curriculum. But how do you grow as a teacher if you don't have an opportunity to do so?" One of the reasons he noted that the school did not include him was perhaps it was encroaching on another colleague's job. Roger stated, "as soon as we do something like curriculum development, we're encroaching on someone else's job description" and that another of his colleagues was told not to engage in curriculum development; he continued, "actually one of my colleagues was told that straight up. That's [curriculum development] not your role." However, Roger said that he had this expertise to share but that they did not want it and so he was frustrated with the school because they did not use his expertise or experience and, indeed, the expertise of his colleagues who were only all too willing to contribute. Roger said that although he was free to "create our own things within the context of our course," he was not allowed to contribute anything "for the greater good of the program." Too often, Roger noted, because the textbook makes up the curriculum, and because students are required to buy them, the teachers are also required to use them. As Roger stated, "textbooks are not cheap and we're expected to use them." However, Roger says that he uses them based on his knowledge and expertise and does not just go from "page 1 to 100 in lockstep fashion" but chooses the content from the book that he thinks "his students need linguistically to succeed."

Towards the end of his third year Roger said that although his training as a teacher has generally contributed to his pedagogical and language expertise, this was impacting him "less and less" as time went on. More often than not, at this stage in his third year, Roger said that his knowledge is now more impacted by "what actually works" for him in his classes. Roger explained this change as follows, "you can learn one way of doing it while you're being trained, but that's specific to what type of student? To what type of classroom? So, right now, our groups of students that we have are different from a typical ESL classroom because they are so much from one culture, and we have to adapt to that to a certain extent." Thus, Roger noted that his teaching experience now contributes a lot to his pedagogical knowledge because he must make so many adjustments to the more theoretical knowledge, he learned in his teacher education program.

Roger said that his training in his undergraduate and MA programs gave him the foundation to work from, or a "starting point" as he noted, but, he said, "from there, you can't always rely on that because things change: your class changes, your style changes over time." In addition, and based on what his students produce in a lesson, Roger said that if they do not use what he is teaching, "then obviously something isn't right and I need to make changes." Now Roger said that he has built up more experiences as a teacher and so he relies more on what worked or "what didn't work" in his lessons to make whatever changes he needs.

Thus, Roger said that in his third year of teaching compared to his first year, his pedagogical and linguistic knowledge is different. Roger said that when he was in his first year of teaching he would plan carefully so that he would "know what you're talking about", but now he said that "it's be more adaptable." Roger said that now he can "recognize what's working in the moment, and if it's not working, be able to change it in the moment. But that you can't do that unless you have some experience or just the guts to go off and try new things."

So, Roger noted that what he learned in his MA program was a lot of research and theories but now he realizes in his third year that he never learned how to apply any of these to his classroom teaching and that this was limiting for him. Roger remarked, "in an MA program you talk a lot about research, but what is an actual in-class application of research?" However, because of his teaching experience of three years, Roger now feels that he has the experience and that he knows what he is doing because of this experience rather than his training.

> **Reflective Break**
> - What is your understanding of teacher as "pedagogical and language expert"?
> - What do you think of Roger's experiences of this role in his third year?

Individual

The next professional identity role that Roger identified with either implicitly or explicitly during his third year was that of an individual. Similar to the definition for the first-year role of individual is where every teacher is different and has different ways, styles, methods, preferences, and choices in regard to how they go about teaching; values freedom in follow one's own way, discovering what works best for that person. One reason Roger embraced his role as that of an individual during his third year was because of the different mixed messages he said that he was receiving from the administration and that he inevitably found himself "subverting the system sometimes." This was the case he said when asked to assess his students in week two of their program "just so that the students feel this is serious." However, Roger noted that they had only covered two or three things and so it is not a good time to do this. Yet, he said he was required to do this; as he remarked "it's more a I have to do it, more than I need to assess what they're learning." So, he said he made his own assessment that required just a little bit of effort for his students as nobody would check it anyway.

Roger said that although he felt somewhat excited to begin his last term during the third year, he noted that, "as soon as the term started all these things came back up where, 'oh by the way you have to do this', or 'by the way this should happen' and the like." Thus, he felt his individualism was constrained again and that the administration was interfering with his teaching. He said that the school is somewhat "unorganized" because they are being given conflicting messages by their coordinators who say, "'do this', but they don't explain how. But it needs to be done in certain way without telling how to do it."

Thus, Roger said that he decides as an individual teacher how he will do whatever directive he is given to do. For example, Roger remarked that one "heavy focus" within the school that term was on developing students' vocabulary and especially acquiring academic words. A directive appeared that teachers should emphasize a word list already developed for each level. As Roger remarked, "there's different sub lists, say there's five sub-lists, and each has fifty words in it. For two weeks at a time, students focus on one of those sub lists, and somehow learn them." Roger said that the students are supposed to find the words on Sakai (an online system the school uses) and then getting the definition for each word and when they go to class regardless of the skill (i.e. reading, writing, speaking or listening), they and the teachers are supposed to "incorporate these words as a part of that activity, so they are learning how to use, them." Roger pointed out that there was no structure about how this should be accomplished. Thus, he had to decide the types of activities he could use and where he could try to bring in some of this vocabulary. Roger then noted that his students did not actually find the words before his classes, and so he worried this was not a good way to teach such vocabulary acquisition. Roger said he improvised his own way of teaching vocabulary even in his grammar classes.

During his third year, Roger said he felt that he was becoming even more of an individual in terms of his role identity because he gave up asking for directions and about the courses he was teaching. Thus, he said that follows his own path and, if someone says he is incorrect, then he said that he will respond at that time. Roger noted that sometimes when the institution insists that he has always done something the same way before, and he does not agree with this, then he will "modify it in my own way." Roger continued, "sometimes it's easier to ask for forgiveness than to ask for permission." Although Roger said that he still tries to ask questions at meetings, inevitably he says that he can predict their answers so he will go his own way regardless. In addition, Roger said that if he is doing something completely different from what everyone else is doing, he will try to explain to them why he is doing it in such a way. As Roger noted, he will try to do it their way, but he said if he "really does not like it, I'll just do my own thing."

Roger gave the following example from his high level of proficiency speaking class, where one of the assignments in that course was that, over the course of the term, the students were supposed to reflect on their assignments and submit a portfolio at the end with all their reflections on what they had learned. Roger said that such an assignment in the speaking class was a written portfolio and amounted to

800 to 1000 words, which he noted "is a lot for an ESL student", and he was also teaching the same students a writing class during that semester. Roger said that he knew these students were working on their major research essays, and in another class that he was not teaching, there was also another written assignment, so Roger observed "it's just a lot of work and I don't think it would be very good quality work. I just don't believe in that."

So, in the end, Roger said that he gave up that writing assignment and replaced it with an interview. Roger remarked, "what I ended up doing was interviewing them instead." Roger said that the coordinator liked the idea when he mentioned what he did, but that all the others were doing something different from him with an institution rubric for a writing portfolio assignment. Roger said he would continue with this interview method for the assignment although the coordinator "was a little bit offended by that." As Roger recounted, "that was one thing I felt strongly about and I didn't want to mark all these written assignments because I had more than enough anyway, and I knew the students absolutely wouldn't be impressed with developing a good portfolio if it was written, so that was one of my modifications." Roger said that not one of his students ever complained about the assignment method although his class was the only one different to the others.

Roger noted that he tried to share things with the coordinators that he trusted, but he observed that "even these people became defensive" when he tried to point out some of the shortcomings of the use of particular activities. Indeed, he noted that some of his "trusted" coordinators even seemed to be "shocked" to hear that his students might have difficulty with that activity. So, rather than blame the activities or materials that the coordinators had chosen because they are deemed to be "good for this type of students, and they should be able to do everything in it", they blamed Roger for not using them "properly." Thus, Roger realized that this was "just another reason why I don't really feel like collaborating or working with people. If the people who are running and supposed to be organizing it don't really know what's going on, then why even bother?" Hence, he said he may as well come up with his own things and "create my own stuff."

Although Roger said that he still tries to collaborate with certain colleagues as much as he can, now at the end of his third year he tends to sit back and "make your own little world that works for you" because he said that there was too much drama going on with the coordinators in his institution. Roger said that, for him, freedom to be creative is important and to deliver his classes in a way he sees as the best fit for his students' learning. As he said, "I teach the way they want me to, but I also teach a little bit of what I want to." An example he gave about this was the way he uses the textbook now in that he tries to create his own exercises. The previous week he noted that his class was focusing on noun clauses and that one of his academic activities was where they read something, then report something from it by using it in a paragraph; Roger called this a "very realistic" type of activity. The following day Roger said that he had his students move about the classroom using reported speech in spoken contexts to each other. He noted that his students enjoyed the mix of writing and speaking as an activity, but this was not in the textbook as this just focused on repeated drills that he said his students did not like. As Roger remarked, "the textbooks only do repeated drills and I've observed that most students don't like that, so I like to create my own things that would help different students learn in different ways."

Roger said that, as an individual doing his own thing, it is somewhat of a "bittersweet" experience because "yes, I get to develop my own curriculum somewhat", which he said is a "nice experience", but at the same time he noted that it is very time consuming. As Roger remarked, "I don't have time and I don't get paid enough to develop the curriculum and teach." Roger said this made him somewhat angry because the coordinators get paid for this and it is their job to do it, not his. He said no wonder he has taken an individual role more so in his third year given that "a lot of half-baked ideas that got sent our way and then we just have to somehow interpret it. You want to sort of get through it somehow." Now at the end of this third year of teaching Roger said that he realizes that he often prefers "working alone on things rather than together with other people."

Reflective Break
- What is your understanding of teacher as "individual"?
- What do you think of Roger's experiences of this role in his third year?

Didactic

Another professional identity role that emerged for Roger during his third year as a teacher was that of being "didactic", or moralistic to his students. This was a similar role for Roger in his first year and was for when he was telling his students about what is right and wrong (such as plagiarism); what is or should be appropriate behavior in a multi-cultural environment, as well as appropriate behavior in an academic setting; and how to acculturate to the local cultural and academic setting. As Roger said, "my job, is to teach, not to just hand them work and say, just do it, whatever." As a result, Roger said that he would structure his classes so that his students are "forced to talk and to interact with each other" so as not to let them get away with too much just because they do not want to do this. He said he let up the previous first semester of his third year and "did not push them as much as he should" because he said he was having a "bad term with a bad class who did not care much." Now, on reflection, Roger said that he will be "stricter than I normally am in the next semester" although he does not like this.

Roger said that one of his skills as a teacher, that he now realizes, is that he can "explain things well in a way people can understand" and that will come in handy when he has to tell his students why they must work harder. Roger said that, as a teacher, he "knew I could help other people because I have that skill of explaining things. So, it's just a way to make a difference in someone's life." He said that other people had also told him that they noticed such a skill and that was another reason he said he felt comfortable becoming an ESL teacher.

Sometimes, Roger said that he feels like a personal fitness trainer who tries to help students by similarly explain why they need to learn something and how they should learn it. Roger remarked:

> you're teaching students what you're learning now, you're learning it for this reason. First you would show them how it works. So, this is the teaching part. This is what you do, this is how it works, whatever. And then after that you say, ok, now you try. And hopefully this is something that you can do on your own. But you don't expect them to be able to do it on their own yet.

Roger said he developed this metaphor in the final term of his third-year teaching because the previous term he did not even want to think about his teaching; as he said, "I didn't think too deeply about that because I didn't want to know." Roger said also that he thinks his students would consider him as a psychologist of sorts because as clients need to trust their psychologist to make progress, so too do "ESL students need to trust them before they can believe what they say." Roger went on to say that he believes that "a lot of students are hesitant to learn" and because of this he has the "moral duty to not let them slide" and that is a balancing act for him. Roger remarked, "in the past two years we've let things slide. we've passed students that shouldn't have passed. I'm not totally sure why, but I'm sure it has to do with money."

However, as an ESL teacher, Roger notes that he tries to be careful not to be influenced by this trend as he has a "duty to teach them and show them the way." This becomes difficult he notes when some of the students do not come to class and are "lumped together by some teachers as being lazy or they don't work." Some of these teachers have told Roger that they do not care and that they "just give up. Don't care, yeah. Actually, just today I heard a teacher say pretty much that exact thing." Roger says that because they complain to the school administration about their low marks, they can get them changed and this adversely affects what their teachers think about them. However, Roger said that he tells his students that they are "responsible for their low marks."

Roger said that he thinks that his ESL students are more vulnerable than regular students because they "can't defend themselves." He said this is especially true if someone says something negative or offensive to them, they do not understand fully; but for him, as an ESL teacher, this is wrong because they do not have the language skills to defend themselves. Roger said that he always tries to make sure that his students are respected in conversations and that he respects them.

Reflective Break
- What is your understanding of teacher as "didactic"?
- What do you think of Roger's experiences of this role in his third year?

CONCLUSION

This chapter presented Roger's role identity development during his third year teaching with four main roles discussed in order of frequency: *Engager*; *Pedagogical and Language Expert*; *Individual*; and *Didactic*. Although these are similar to the roles he outlined for his first year teaching, which are explored in Chapter 3, there are some differences as to how he interpreted them during his third year. For example, he noted that he would engage his students more during the final semester of his third year which was a direct result of having a "bad class" the previous summer term; and, although he is still confident in his qualifications as a language teacher and language expert, his knowledge now stems more from his actual classroom experiences rather than his book knowledge from his teacher education program. His final two roles – that of individual and didactic – also seem to come from actual experiences in the classroom and working with some of his colleagues and within an institution that does not seem to take his knowledge seriously. The contents of this chapter seem to suggest that, whilst he is in his third year of teaching, Roger is still struggling somewhat with his role identity as he continues to seek a balance between his personal ideals, his students' reactions and the requirements of his institution. The next chapter outlines and discusses Roger's principles of teaching and learning during his third year.

Chapter 10

Reflecting on Third Year Principles

INTRODUCTION

In Chapter 4, Roger's first year principles were outlined and discussed. As mentioned in Chapter 4, a teacher's principles are made up of a teacher's assumption, beliefs and conceptions of teaching and learning a second or foreign language, in this case, English as a second language. These principles are usually held tacitly but can be expressed or implied in a teacher's overall conversation about their practices. What is most important about a teacher's principles, are that they are usually a reliable guide to how a teacher's thinks about teaching and even how the teach their lessons. A teacher's principles thus are closely linked to the characteristics, traits and personality of the teacher as well as his or her thoughts about their teaching roles and their students' learning roles. This chapter outlines and discusses Roger's third-year principles.

ROGER'S THIRD YEAR PRINCIPLES

Roger's most frequent beliefs that emerged from the data were his beliefs about his students, grammar, vocabulary, group work, lesson planning, and his beliefs about his role as an ESL teacher.

Students

Just before the beginning of this third year of teaching, Roger was assigned a class to teach during a break in the usual calendar (I cannot give more details) and this class was to have an impact on all of his third year of teaching as he said his students were "bad students". This perception was to shape a lot of his principles related to his teaching in his third year so that, although we were not engaged in any reflective practice activities at the time, Roger did detail some of his reasons for his current teacher principles that relate to his experiences.

Roger remarked, "I had a class full of duds. And it was like talking to a bunch of rocks. That's how much they interacted with each other, with me. It was awful." I wondered how he had reached such a conclusion and he noted that they were all "weak" in English "with very low motivation to learn." Roger continued, "So, when I went into the classroom after a few weeks of having them, I was not looking forward to it whatsoever because I knew exactly what was coming, which was nothing from them." Roger said that when he began teaching this group, he thought they were just quiet as a group and had not "gelled together yet" but as time went by, Roger noted, "it just never happened." At the end of the class, he said he just wanted to go on vacation and forget it all but the chance to reflect again in his third year brought all the memories back. So, Roger said that he would reconsider his beliefs about his students after the bad experiences so that he would be ready for this third year of teaching and reflecting with me.

Roger noted he felt "drained" after the experience with the previous class – that this negative feeling was "lingering" still as we had our first meeting of his third year of teaching. Roger remarked, "I'm kind of worried, what if that would happen again this term to the students I have now, how would I deal with that back-to-back?" Thus, Roger wanted to reconsider his beliefs about his students with the current group he was starting with during his third year – and he already noted that he believes the class is different, with more motivated students. Although he realized that he was "a little less excited to teach" at the start of his third year, these reflections were forcing him to reposition himself as a teacher. Roger said that he is trying to "find ways to make teaching more exciting" but his class seem quiet. Roger continued, "they are pretty quiet. They're all from the same country, all around the same age" and now he said that he believes this has led to some changes in his teaching behavior.

So, for this new term Roger said he wanted to try to make his classes more enjoyable for his students and also for himself. This was beginning to happen as the term progressed. Roger reflected,

> I was so jaded after last term. Even at the start of this term, the first two weeks, you know, the students are a generally a little quieter, right? They had to gel together a little bit at first. And for me, the first two weeks this term, was like oh, my students are quiet again, without even thinking about why they were quiet. But now they're starting to perk up.

After about five weeks Roger was teaching a class and noticed a student did not participate but was very quiet. Roger said, "I saw him sitting there, just kind of looking off into space." The student was supposed to be working on a project and so Roger asked him how it was going, and the student replied that he was bored. He told Roger that the topic they were discussing was not interesting for him, so he did not want to participate. Roger said that because of his experiences with students in the previous term and how "bad" they were, he decided not to probe further and let the student be. Roger wondered at that time if there was "anything I could have done to make sure he wasn't bored? His answer was not a lot because the topic was chosen by the institution as part of the curriculum and so he had already "spent a week and a half focusing on the topic, so this project needs to be done. Whether or not he is interested in this topic or not, there's nothing I can do about it." Indeed, Roger remarked that sometimes when he does ask his students if they find the topic interesting, "half of them say, 'nah, it's not really that interesting'. But once again, there's only so much I can do about it." Roger mentioned that, in the light of his previous term's experiences, he now takes more of a back seat when it comes to motivating students, but he did say that he thinks if he sees him bored again, "I would like to find out why and what I can do to find out what he can do to make it better." Nevertheless, Roger said that his negative experiences with his students the previous term have left a mark on his teaching. Roger said, "If I have a quiet class, I just go through it. I don't take the time to actually talk about it with them. You guys want to talk? Ok, fine, let's just move on."

Reflective Break
- What are your beliefs about the role of students?
- What do you think of Roger's beliefs about the role of students in his third year of teaching?

Grammar

Following on from his beliefs about his students' low motivation to learn English in general outlined above, is Roger's belief that his teaching of grammar has been impacted as a result of the low motivation. He noted that "learning grammar is not necessarily exciting or enjoyable. It's not something that most people find appealing. But it is a necessary thing for someone who's studying academic English." Thus, Roger knows that although his students need to have a knowledge of English grammar, he is struggling to make his lessons impactful. Roger explained that he believes his students don't have that same value about learning [grammar]. For them, they're here in our ESL classes because it's just a step they have to take. One step that takes them that much closer to being a university undergraduate student. So, since I know that these students don't necessarily see the value in what they're doing, it's up to me, it's my responsibility to enable them to see that there is a value for them.

Roger said that he realized he does not like teaching verbs because of all the irregularities and exceptions and, as a result, he believes his students do not like this aspect of grammar the most. Roger remarked, "I provide a summary and then focus on the things that I think are most useful for them to know about with verbs. But I have a feeling that some students were like, 'oh no, here we go again. I've learned verbs before.'" Roger said that he noted this same feeling creeping into his "last couple of grammar classes" during his third year. Roger also said that this third year he felt somewhat rushed: "in terms of planning before class I was kind of wondering, am I ready for this enough? Did I think enough about everything I wanted to say? And then even while teaching it just felt like I was kind of rushed." Roger noted also that he rushed through some grammar items in one lesson; he continued, "I think I rushed through some parts because I could feel that some students were thinking, 'ok, we've learned this before', or 'I'm not interested'. I think it was boring because the students weren't interactive in any way."

Thus, while teaching grammar in his third year, Roger said he would "just get on with it" even if he believed the students were bored. Indeed, towards the end of his first semester of his third year, he said he noticed his students have "been so dead" and then he worried that the same bad feelings he experienced the previous term were going to come back. Roger remarked, "it's just bringing back memories of last term where it's just like, 'oh no, not this again'. And I don't want to feel like I'm going through the motions and that's it."

When asked how he teaches grammar items now in his third year, Roger said that he now uses PowerPoints, which differs from his methods during his first year of teaching. Roger said, "Well, what's typically worked well, and even in the class that I have now so far, is that I'd present my PowerPoint for fifteen minutes, go over the rules, an example of everything, make sure that they understand it, and then from there, practice." Roger said this this first term of his third year teaching he believes he has been able to "captivate them mostly with the PowerPoints."

Related to his view that his students are not so motivated to learn grammar, Roger said that he believes he is relying more on the use of PowerPoints in these grammar classes. Roger said, "I often use PowerPoint as my routine as I believe I need to structure my working hours carefully for myself so that I maximize my efficiency. So, for grammar, it's always a bit of a mixture of me lecturing teaching them with

PowerPoint, writing on the board." This he finds is necessary for the kind of students he believes he is teaching in this third year, many of who he perceives are not motivated to learn grammar. Roger said, "I've kind of noticed that if students don't put the effort into it and take responsibility for their own learning, I don't, I think I tend to put in less effort as a teacher too and I think that spirals pretty quickly." As a result of this, Roger said he thinks he is putting more grammar information on the slides. Roger remarked, "I noticed that the last time I taught grammar, which was the winter of this year, I noticed that my PowerPoints are actually getting pretty long. I'm packing a lot in." He believes he is making them even longer this third year.

> **Reflective Break**
> - What are your beliefs about teaching grammar?
> - What do you think of Roger's beliefs about teaching grammar in his third year of teaching?

Vocabulary

Roger's beliefs about teaching vocabular seemed to be at odds with the institution in which he worked. Roger noted that his students are given marks for using certain vocabular words (five minimum) in their work from what he termed "sublists for specific assignments." Roger noted that the students can use the same five words "which are the ones that they already know, I'm sure," and thus he said this would not build their vocabulary. Roger said that, from his knowledge and beliefs related to research on vocabulary, using such an approach is not good for the students. However, he also said he noticed that his students are using notebooks and writing these word lists and then they "find the definition for and translate it" but it is not contributing to their vocabular acquisition.

Roger said that his beliefs are backed by research. Roger continued, "There's lots of research that shows that this [translating words into their L1] is not an effective way to, you know, to learn words, right?" Roger relayed that the idea was for the students to memorize these lists of what one coordinator said were "common academic words that students will encounter naturally in their textbooks." However, Roger said that he believed that this was "wishful thinking" because the books they use in the institute do not have so many academic words.

Indeed, Roger said that he could see that many other teachers considered this as not effective, and some students considered it "another meaningless task." Indeed, Roger said his beliefs about vocabulary acquisition were strongly based on research because he had previously conducted some research of his own, and had read a lot of the literature in this area. He said, after that reading, he has a good understanding "of what may work better than other ways", but now the institute required him to go against these beliefs and teach it differently but "this is not a good way to do it, especially in a program where you're trying to standardize across all levels." Roger expressed his beliefs about developing a vocabular program as follows:

> if you were going to develop a vocabulary development program, or whatever, at least think about what you are doing, and exactly how you want to do it, right? Can you measure it effectively? I mean, just by checking their homework to see if they are using a word correctly from a list of 50 words, and they chose the words they know, that's not doing a post test of can they use these words now.

Reflective Break
- What are your beliefs about teaching vocabulary?
- What do you think of Roger's beliefs about teaching vocabulary in his third year of teaching?

Group Work

Roger said that he believes group work is the best for developing a language. He noted that it is "valued, it's encouraged, it's a very big part of learning a language." Roger remarked that group work is the best way to foster interaction, because "how else do you learn a language aside from interaction, right?" which, he noted, in turn draws out communication in a classroom. However, he relayed that one cannot just set up a group and have students interact because there are various factors that teachers must consider to use group work "properly." Roger believed that there were important factors to consider such as the composite of the group; he said, "Who are the people within the group? Do they all have similar personalities? Are they all from the same language background? You know, those are things you might want to avoid." He also said that the number of people in a group "makes a difference. Whether it's two, three, four, or more, the amount of interaction that each student does within the group varies."

When he approaches such group work activities, Roger says that he will "mix it up" by having pairs work first then he will put students in threes or fours and "mix people so that sometimes they're working with friends, and sometimes they're working with someone who's not their obvious friend." In addition, Roger noted that students have different learning styles while interacting in groups, and these must also be considered. This depends on their personality, according to Roger, and he notes that "if there's a shy, quiet person in a group, obviously they aren't going to be 100% comfortable compared to someone who's outgoing and social, right?" So Roger will place a shy person in a pair because, he notes, "it's just one person they have to deal with. But if it's a group of five, that shy person is not going to talk."

Roger also noted that he worries that in ESL group work may be used too much as he noted in the previous terms some of his students "think, ugh, another group project" because he believes they will want to work alone sometimes. So now even though he believes some topics would be best conducted through group work, he will nevertheless let the students do it individually. Roger said he is still a bit unclear about his true believes regarding the use or overuse of group work in ESL because it is a "trend in ESL" but he said that he still wonders if it's really effective. "I think only the teachers who really reflect on that would see that, yeah, it can be, but not always." Roger remarked, "group work is such a complex thing. A lot of people think it's easy. Just form a group of three, here's five questions, talk about it, go. And then they just sit there like, 'uh, ok.'" Roger said he is still reflecting on his use of group work noting that it has "definite value" and a lot of people assume it is good, but not all the time. Roger summed up his beliefs about group work as follows, "it's not the end all of ESL learning. So, use it, but not all the time. And I wouldn't say use it sparingly, use it frequently, but you have to mix it up."

Reflective Break
- What are your beliefs about group work?
- What do you think of Roger's beliefs about group work in his third year of teaching?

Lesson Planning

Roger also talked about the need to write lesson plans before he enters the classroom. Roger said that he usually plans for a week of lessons but that he does not write "out in too much detail just because things change." Roger continued, "usually before my classes I kind of take 30 minutes, or whatever, just to make sure things are set and to plan day by day." A lot of this he said he does in his head rather than write it down specifically for each class. If any teacher must substitute for him in case of illness, Roger notes he will have that written plan for a week to give the teacher.

Roger said that the institute requires him to have such a weekly written lesson plan but that his take on it is that it is like "a table of contents where it's like we're doing this, and this, and this." As noted above for his grammar teaching, Roger said that now in his third year he plans with the use of PowerPoints "because it's a good way for them to follow along, to take notes, and for examples, right? For teaching grammar, you need lots." In such a manner then he plans more of a lecture style of transmission for his grammar classes; Roger continued, "definitely my delivery is more like a lecture style for an upper-level grammar course." Roger said that he plans in such a manner because his students will have to listen to lectures when they enter university considering they are all EAP students getting ready to take such lectures. Roger remarked, "I want to prepare them for university, where you're listening to a lecture, taking notes, just gathering things, and then from there, you're using your notes and what you just learned, now you can apply it somehow. But many of them have mentioned that they like the PowerPoints. I post them so they can look at them later." Roger said that PowerPoints are different to using the textbook because, as he says, "PowerPoints are more condensed and are more user-friendly too." Roger said that he needs to plan for supplementing the textbooks because he finds "a lot of textbooks are not laid out very well and are just kind of all over the place, so what I do is take the most important points out of the textbook and put them all in one place for my students."

That said, Roger noted that when he is lecturing he gets annoyed if anyone yawns; he considers this to be a problem and an indication that the lesson is not going well. Thus, one way he judges if a lesson is going according to plan is by looking at his students' faces to "see what they're doing, if they're taking notes, actively listening." Roger said he plans for asking students questions to make sure they are following throughout his lessons, as well as planning for some activities for them to do, because he wants to make sure his lessons are "not just me talking to them for twenty minutes straight. It's a little bit here, then some hands-on practice. Then a little bit more, and some hands-on practice. So, they're always kind of part of the lecture too."

In terms of planning for his reading classes, he said that he follows the textbook more carefully because he notes "reading is centered more around the textbook in some ways." Roger said that because everything is in the textbook for reading lessons, he plans such lessons only from the textbook. Roger said, "when I'm teaching reading, the readings the students have to do are in the textbook and everything there is all prepared and focused on those readings. So, I would say that the textbook trumps the content."

Roger said that this term he planned to create different types of activities that do not target just one type of student or one learning style. In order to prepare for this he asked his students directly what they thought about particular activities before he planned to use them. Roger said that the previous week he had polled one of his classes, and asked whether "being in a class where students are interactive and speaking a lot is more fun than being in a class where students just sit their quietly." Roger noted that although "the majority said yes, some said no." This he interpreted as some students "don't enjoy interaction." As a result, he said he plans not to do activities every day that involve interaction among the students as he wants to give them a break from always having to interact with each other. So he said he is trying to plan his lessons with a balance in mind, because "finding a mixture of that keeps them engaged for a long period of time, not just for one day, and I think that's to me something that is exciting too, that there is variation."

Roger said that he also creates his own realistic exercises and "all of them have a different focus." He gave an example from his grammar class the previous week where he was teaching noun clauses – in one of the activities the students had to read something and "report something from it, using it in a paragraph, a very realistic type thing." The following day the students had to move around and talk to others using reported speech in spoken contexts. Roger said he noticed that some students "enjoyed the writing stuff and others liked the speaking stuff, and they all learned it still." This was the type of balance he talked about above, when trying to plan different types of activities for his lessons.

Indeed, one reason he said that he thinks he must come up with more of his own activities is that he has had no guidance from the institute where he has been teaching: "I might as well come up with my own things and do that because I don't think they will even care or be able to tell or whatever. So, it's just frustrating in certain ways." Roger notes that much of his planning has become routine since his first year of teaching, because he can "maximize my efficiency since I don't have to be at work all the time." Indeed, after a few weeks of teaching in his third year, Roger said he "backed off" active involvement outside with colleagues. For teaching, Roger noted he still planned with students in mind, but with the institute he noted that since his first year he tries not to become involved with politics. Roger continued, "over the last couple years there's been a certain amount of bullcrap to work with from various levels of, you know colleagues, coordinators, management." As a result, Roger said that he prefers to sit back more and "make your own little world that works for you and make sure you're still doing what you're supposed to be doing; but sometimes if you involve less people it just simplifies things." That said, he wanted to focus his planning on finding a balance between different activities as mentioned above, and remarked, "over the next couple weeks I really want to try and balance all the different types of activities that I have and I'm making it enjoyable not only for them, but also for me again."

> **Reflective Break**
> - What are your beliefs about lesson planning?
> - What do you think of Roger's beliefs about lesson planning in his third year of teaching?

ESL Teacher

Roger also reflected on his role(s) as an ESL teacher and noted that he feels as if he is a facilitator in terms of his teaching, especially when he teaches higher-level students. Roger suggested that such higher-level students have "studied everything there is to be studied. They studied how to write a basic English essay. They've studied most of the English grammar. They know things like note-taking strategies and stuff." Thus, all they really need is to practice what they have learned and, as such, he would facilitate that learning. Roger said that, for this third year teaching higher-level students, he has a new mantra: "just because you know something doesn't mean you can use it." So he said higher-level students need to learn how to use the things they have learned up to that point. For Roger, "facilitator means, 'ok, let's quickly review these concepts, because you obviously forgot about them, and then let's do them'. So, it's kind of like a guide, where it's like 'ok, this is what you know, this is what you have to do."

Here, Roger said, he believes that a teacher's role is to get the students to do it – a "hands-on approach" – and there is thus more pressure on the students to take responsibility rather than the teacher. Roger continued, "I mean, as a teacher, the teaching part is kind of over because it's not a heavy focus anymore. The teaching part is over, not totally over, but now you're focusing on getting them to do things rather than teaching them new things." Roger noted that it is up to the students to do it and he would not force them to do anything.

For teaching lower-level students however, Roger said that he would be more like a "personal fitness trainer" where the teacher explains why they are doing what they are doing "Just like a personal fitness trainer would help you by saying this machine helps you do this." Then the teacher would show them how it works, and "this is the teaching part." Although Roger would prefer the students to do things by themselves, he noted at these lower levels they would not be ready and so the role of facilitator shifts from the students to the teacher. Roger continued,

> Thinking of an ESL perspective, they might have errors that they might make into regular habits, but if you teach them properly, then you can avoid this solidification of how you do it or this is how you use a certain grammar structure or whatever, right? And then hopefully after you've taught them how to use it, they can use it.

Later, as a teacher of students moving to higher levels, Roger acknowledged he "might be able to move into more of a facilitator."

Reflective Break
- What are your beliefs about teacher as facilitator?
- What are your beliefs about teacher as personal trainer?
- What do you think of Roger's beliefs about both of these roles above in his third year of teaching?

SOURCES OF ROGER'S THIRD YEAR PRINCIPLES

After articulating beliefs, teachers should then examine the sources of these beliefs that have been built up over a teacher's career, as mentioned in Chapter 4. As a reminder, then, one or more of the following sources of beliefs can be considered and used either individually or in combination (adapted from Richards & Lockhart, 1994):

- *Teachers' past experience as students.* For example, if a teacher has learned a second language successfully and comfortably by memorizing vocabulary lists, then there is a good chance that the same teacher will have his or her students memorize vocabulary lists too.
- *Experience of what works best in their classes.* This may be the main source of beliefs about teaching for many second language teachers and, as such, many practicing teachers may not want to break an established, and perceived successful, routine.
- *Established practice within a school.* These practices can be difficult to change because the school has always used this method or that teachers would have to complete a particular unit in a specific time period.
- *Personality factors of teachers.* This can be an important source of beliefs as some teachers really enjoy conducting role-play or group work in their classes while others are more comfortable conducting traditional teacher-fronted lessons.
- *Educationally based or research-based principles.* This can also be a source of teachers' beliefs in that a teacher may draw on his or her understanding of research in second language reading to support use of predicting style exercises in reading classes.
- *Method based sources of beliefs.* This suggest that teachers support and implement a particular method in their classes as, for example, when a teacher decides to use total physical response (TPR) to teach beginning second language learners, he or she is following a method of suspending early production of language for the learner.

The following top six categories, for Roger in his third year as a language teacher, were identified in order of their frequency as follows: personality, research-based practice, established practice, approach or method, own experience as a teacher, and experience of what works best. These results indicate that Roger was influenced a lot by his personality when teaching in his third year as well as what the research suggests. The data suggests that Roger was reflecting internally throughout this year to determine what would best suit his teaching style rather than what was suggested in his master's degree as was the case for most of his first year. Indeed, in one exchange he had with me near the end of the third year, Roger said that he did not have any specific teacher he could emulate as a role model and wondered if that was still normal. Roger continued, "I guess I didn't really know I wanted to teach until Grade 12, but you'd think I would have had one teacher who I thought was an awesome teacher. But then I look back at other things I could have role models for and I realize there aren't many people who I know that would represent or epitomize the ultimate role model of whatever it is." Roger then said that he thinks he now tries hard not to be exactly like others but to "be different and not always follow the norm."

As such, he says, he believes in himself and his personality as a teacher to direct his lessons.

Reflective Break

- What do you think about the sources of Roger's beliefs in his third year of teaching?
- Compare the following top six categories for Roger in his first year as a language teacher were identified in order of their frequency to his third-year sources of beliefs:

    1   Approach or Method
    2   Personality Factors
    3   Educationally-based or Research-based Practice
    4   Own Experience as a Teacher
    5   Experience of what Works Best
    6   Established Practice

- What similarities and what differences do you notice?

CONCLUSION

This chapter outlined and discussed Roger's principles about teaching and learning English as a second language, as well as the sources of his principles in his third year as a teacher. Again (as in Chapter 4) the results were presented mostly in terms of his stated beliefs as well as any he implied throughout his third year of teaching. The results indicate that Roger's most frequent beliefs were those related to his students' approaches to learning, the teaching and learning of grammar, vocabulary, how he approached group work, and lesson planning, and his beliefs about his role as an ESL teacher. The chapter also examined the sources of his beliefs and the following six categories for Roger in his third year as a language teacher were identified in order of their frequency as follows: his personality, research-based backed practices, established practice, approaches and methods, his own teaching experiences including what works best (or not) for him. What emerges in this chapter, with regard to his principles, is a teacher with more classroom experience, not all of which is positive. As such, Roger seems to have retreated somewhat into himself, relying more on his personality traits to get him through his lessons rather that his knowledge of the different approaches or methods which he used more during his first year as a teacher. In addition, Roger had a difficult semester before entering his third year which, of course, could have impacted the principles guiding him as an ESL teacher. The next chapter examines Roger's third year theory during his third year of teaching.

Chapter 11

Reflecting on Third Year Theory

INTRODUCTION

In Chapter 5 I outlined and discussed Roger's theory in his first year of teaching. Once more, theory explores and examines the different choices a teacher makes about particular skills taught (or they think should be taught) or, in other words, how they want to put their theories into practice as they teach. A theory is "something we use to give understanding and attempts to answer the question 'why?' in order to increase knowledge of practice and realign thoughts regarding this" (Farrell, 2015: 67). At this stage, the teacher focuses on how they plan their lessons, more specifically, their planning (i.e., backwards, forwards, or central planning) and choice of activities, techniques, and methods. By reflecting on theory, one is able to label what happens in the classroom and understand how it influences the role of both the teacher and students during a lesson. Another means of accessing our theory is to explore and examine critical incidents (any unplanned or unanticipated event that occurs during a classroom lesson and is clearly remembered) because they can be a guide to a teacher's theory building. This chapter covers Roger's third year theory and his experience with critical incidents.

ROGER'S PLANNING IN THIRD YEAR

When planning for his classes during his third year at the same institution, Roger noticed that some of the centrally developed plans or syllabi that he was now required to follow had some challenges before he even entered the classroom (you will remember back in his first year he said that he had more freedom to make his own plans generally, as recounted in Chapter 5). An example was when he was required to teach a high-level speaking course, and one of the assignments in that course is that over the course of that term the students were supposed to reflect on their assignments by submitting a portfolio at the end of the term with all their reflections on what they learned, and what was good or bad about this assignment. Roger pointed out that this was a speaking class, and such an assignment is a written portfolio which would require his students to write at least a 1,000-word essay explaining what was contained in their portfolios. As he was also teaching the same students a writing class during this semester, he was fully aware that these same students were also required to write major research essays and, indeed, he said that he heard from other teachers of these same students that they also required written work. So, Roger worried about the time his students would need to write their assignment, as well as the quality of such work. Roger continued, "for them [his students] in that time to write, it's just a lot of work and I don't think it would be very good quality work." Roger said that while planning for this he had to also follow his beliefs about what is good practice and bad practice for his students' learning and he said although "this portfolio may be appealing, I just don't believe in that." So, Roger decided to drop the written requirement and, instead, he decided to interview each student about the contents of their portfolio. At the beginning of the semester in this class he asked all his students if they would "mind changing how the assignment was completed from written to interview", and he said all agreed but that he got them to sign a paper with the agreed changes on it.

This type of pre-planning for Roger was for the benefit of his students as he speaks of putting "my students first: what are they learning, how are they learning, what are their motivations like, right? And how can I get this specific group of students, or even this specific student to learn most effectively. Right? And to me that's something that is important." In addition, when he is planning his lessons now in his third year, he said that he always asks himself if what he is teaching them will be useful to them in the future. Roger noted that, for him, the students were always more important than the content he was teaching regardless of whether he was required to follow a centralized syllabus. Roger said that when he plans, he "would suit the content to what the students know, what the students need, what they're able to do." At the same time, however, Roger also said that he realizes that he must cover particular content within the program because there is more than one class in each level and so he realizes he must also deal with "the issue with standardization." That said, Roger adds that he will always try to rearrange any centralized syllabus to suit his students' needs and, further related to student needs, he plans his teaching to "the most common denominator." For this, he explained that he would only spend more time on an issue if he figured most of the class were struggling but not if only a few did not seem to get what he was teaching. He said he decides on the focus based on "how important is that thing that you're teaching, and how many students are actually having difficulty with it."

In terms of planning – for teaching specific skills and the use of textbooks and materials for these courses and his adaptations – these were different than for his first year where he had more freedom (see Chapter 5). Roger seemed to be most interested in teaching grammar because he suggested for him it is "more like a content course rather than a skill-based course" and, as such, he said that he plans his teaching around a university content course mode where he will plan lectures and seminars. For this he said that he uses lots of PowerPoints while giving them lectures on particular grammar points. Roger said that he also plans for some activities from the textbook that they practice in class and/or for homework.

Roger outlined how he plans a "typical grammar week" where he starts to teach the "basics" by presenting the fundamental concepts of a particular grammar structure and then provides some grammar exercises "just to refresh their memories." As an example, he said that he planned the following week's grammar focus on adjective clauses and that he intends to start the class on what an adjective clause is because he noted that although they are an advanced class, "somehow they forget what it is from one term to the next." After that, he said, he plans to give them some exercises to practice what they know and then, throughout the remainder of the week, he will focus on "more specific [grammar] points and then I'll give them some more practice." Roger noted that he creates his own exercises, which differ from those in the textbook, and give them an alternative focus. He gave the following example of how this all works:

> So, for example, this past week we were focusing on noun clauses. So, one of my activities was more an academic type activity where they read something, report something from it, using it in a paragraph, you know, very realistic type thing. And then the next day after that it was more like a stand up, move around, talk to your partners, use reported speech in a spoken context. And I could tell that some students enjoyed the writing stuff and other liked the speaking stuff, and they all learned it still. So, for me, trying to balance it all out like that, and not just only use the textbooks, because you know, only doing repeated drills, I've observed that most students don't like that, so I kind of like to create my own things that would help different students learn in different ways.

For his advanced level grammar students Roger prefers to have them presenting what they consider to be the grammar structure rather than him just telling them at the beginning. Roger said that the previous week he focused on adjective clauses, and on the first day of that "grammar week" he decided not to directly tell them what an adjective clause was. Roger continued, "so the first day, rather than me introducing it, I had a group of students present on it just to get the students' minds thinking about the topic of adjective clauses. From there, I focused on the issues related to the adjective clauses that I thought would be useful, but also to the textbook."

When asked about his use of textbooks while planning, Roger noted that textbooks guide his lesson plans "a little bit" and he uses them because he is not only expected to use them but also because he noted "textbooks are not cheap." Roger said that because he is given textbooks for each course he teaches, and he is required to use them, he shapes his planning of their use to his own specifications. Roger remarked, "when I get a textbook, for grammar anyway, I don't say let's start on page one and go to page 300. It's kind of like what's in the textbook, how can I order it in a logical way that makes sense, right? So, I might start with Chapter 5, and then go on to what I think is important." Roger said this is necessary because some of the textbooks he is given are not always up to date, but the institute must use them all before any changes can be made.

Roger relayed how one course he was teaching the "textbook" was put together by the administration, using a textbook that was out of print (but with the permission of the author). They inserted a printed copy of the syllabus in the back of the book, "the outline, and all of the rubrics and that stuff," but did not sell enough of the copies of the book in that term, so they could not use a different textbook in the next term. Roger continued, "we couldn't use a different textbook this term because he needs to sell a certain amount of these textbooks before any changes could be made, so for that reason, because it was in the syllabus, the assignment couldn't be changed, apparently." This frustrated Roger and his planning because he said he was "tied" to this "dry" book which he considered not very useful. Thus, Roger said that after teaching them using the textbook, "I also create my own exercises, all of them kind of have different focus" that were useful for his students.

Reflective Break
- How do you plan your teaching of the various skill areas?
- What do you think of Roger's approach to planning for teaching grammar? Do you have a different way of teaching grammar?
- Are you required to use textbooks? If yes, how do you use them? Do you start at the beginning and go page by page in sequence?
- What do you think of Roger's opinion and use of textbooks?

ROGER'S CRITICAL INCIDENTS THIRD YEAR

I now outline and discuss a major critical incident Roger said he experienced during his first semester of his third year of teaching. I relay the whole incident as written by Roger and sent to me as a response to the question: "Did you experience any incidents you consider critical during your first semester of your third year?" In fact, Roger writes about one particular incident and outlined a week-by-week development over the 14 weeks of that semester he was teaching. I now present the complete incident in Roger's own words as follows.

Critical Incident: Students Not Engaged

Last semester I experienced a dramatic and quite impactful critical incident while teaching an upper-level ESL writing course. I've taught upper-level writing courses a lot over the past couple of years and have typically enjoyed them, even though there is a large amount of marking associated with teaching this type of course. The students in this class write a large research essay (around 1200 words) and several smaller essays (around 400–600 words), so the work is quite intensive and requires a lot of dedication and focus on the students' part. Normally I have groups of students that exhibit various levels of interest in writing and demonstrate a variety of work ethics: there are students who enjoy writing and have a high level of writing skill, students who don't enjoy writing, and students who don't particularly work very hard, which results in variety of grades ranging from As to Fs. Last semester was different.

Week 1

Normally there are a number of students who don't show up in week 1, simply because they don't see the value in it. In this class, it was the same, but there were even less students attending than usual. The students that I did have were very quiet and did not seem very excited to be there already. I thought that they were just having a hard time putting themselves in the right frame of mind for studying and, since it was summer, it's not always easy to be in the classroom. I expected that soon enough most of these students would become more interested as the week went on. I jumped right into things and had them writing academic paragraphs right off the bat to show them that this class is not easy and requires a lot of their attention. Usually, I take this approach when starting an upper-level class to set a more serious tone in terms of how much work the students need to do. I still tried to connect with them on a personal level and get to know them better. But, they didn't talk much.

Week 2

Finally, more students showed up and, by the end of the week, most of the students were present. They were all from [the same country] except for one student. That didn't faze me much as it happens more often, but I knew right then that it would be more difficult to have a social and interactive environment in the classroom, based on my experiences teaching classes with predominantly [name of country] students. Nothing against these students, but they are typically quieter and more reserved in class. Most of my students attended every class, which I saw as a positive sign but, as the week went on, I realized that most of them were physically attending my class, but not mentally as they were quite disengaged and disengaging. At the end of this week, I collected their first assignment, which was a basic five paragraph essay, that focused on essay structure and organization. I just wanted to see what they could do in terms of writing.

Week 3

I marked their first essays and was appalled. These students could not, or did not, write an organized essay to save their own life. Or so I felt. I wasn't able to understand over half of their essays due to the abundance of grammatical, organizational, and logical errors in their essays. These essays could have been written by students just learning to write essays for the first time. Most of the students got a failing mark on this essay. The strange thing was that when I handed them back, the majority of the students who failed seemed genuinely surprised at their low marks, as if they thought that simply by completing the assignment they should have passed. Throughout the first few weeks of teaching them, using the textbook with them, and observing them work individually and in pairs, I noticed a lot of disturbing trends. They would complete each task as quickly as possible, they didn't speak English unless asked to so specifically, they did not engage actively while I was teaching them (no note-taking, no questioning, nothing). Every time I asked them a question, I would get a blank stare from each student, but no response unless I specifically chose someone to answer. At this point, I noticed very quickly that this group was going to be nearly impossible to teach and that I was in for a long semester.

Week 4

I collected more work from them, this time their topic and thesis statement for their major research essay. It was obvious that hardly any of them had given a second of thought about their essay and just quickly written something down and handed it in. I had to review how to choose a topic, how to write a thesis statement, and why it is necessary to actually think about what you want to write. These are all things that these students learned before and shouldn't have had much difficulty with. Now I was wasting time going over things they should have been at least adequately capable of doing. I tried to connect with them more on a personal level, but I couldn't. They either didn't want to or were actually so lacking in personality that they really had nothing interesting to offer to the class. Each day I dreaded going to class already because I knew it would just be me talking to blank faces and to students who were quite obviously just going through the motions. Even now, just thinking about this, re-evokes a certain anger and frustration in me!

Weeks 5–7

These few weeks just were kind of a blur and not particularly memorable in any way aside from that I just continued to receive lackluster and less than mediocre work from my students. They just showed up, every day, not really doing anything in class. They didn't speak to each other or to me unless prodded and when they would speak to each other, it usually was in their native language. I felt so bad for the one student [who did not speak their language] because he was so obviously ostracized by the other students and at this point neither he nor they tried to collaborate or interact as it was nearly impossible to genuinely interact. It was as though every student in this class put up some kind of facade and didn't want to connect with each other. It was like teaching a group full of individuals with a few pairs of friends here and there. After the midterm exam, I handed back the exams and told the class that over half of them had failed and the majority of them were failing the course at this point. I went over different ways that they could improve their marks, attitudes, and motivation and had a great discussion with them about it. They all agreed that they need to work harder and find ways to motivate themselves. I really didn't want to create a negative environment in the classroom, so I tried to take a positive approach to situation at this point in time. Now that I reflect on this, I realize that the classroom was already a negative environment, not by my doing, but based on the students' attitudes and work habits. I can't control the social environment in the class completely as there is a strong dependence on the students themselves to bond with each other and try and make their daily learning environment a positive place to work and learn in. The responsibility is not all on the teacher to do all the work in creating a good environment. It's not my fault that this group of students had the personalities and attitudes that they did.

Week 8

After two days of students working hard and staying focused, they reverted back to their previous ways. I had to continually tell them to speak English, stay on task, do their work more carefully, and take things seriously and realize that they did not in fact have the skills to pass this course and be a successful university student. It was at this time that I realized that the majority of the students in this class were not able to see the big picture. They didn't know why they were studying English. Or perhaps why they were studying at all! I mentioned to them that their ESL classes are a steppingstone to university and that they needed to learn how to use English before they can use English to learn something else, like math or business. Without having the requisite English skills, they would fail their university courses or at least need to expend a lot more energy while taking them. Most of the students did not react to this. It simply did not faze them that their English was poor and their academic skills, such as writing, were not adequate. This really frustrated me because I knew right there and then that I couldn't do much more to persuade them or motivate them to take this writing course seriously. It was at this point that I slowly started to not care so much about taking the time to carefully plan and prepare my lessons for this class. But I had to go through five more weeks of teaching them so I would just do what I can do provide them with basic academic writing skills. I would still do my part and teach them what they need to know, but I wouldn't push them much more or try to make it connect with their disconnected minds.

Weeks 9 and 10

I collected more essays and noticed very little improvement or none at all for most students. There were two (2!!) students who I noticed genuinely were trying to improve and actually taking the time to improve. Others were trying to improve, or at least wanted to, but didn't put in the effort or time. The majority of the class did not put the time into writing carefully, which resulted in consistently poor work. I pointed this out on several occasions, but none really seemed to bother with doing it. For them it was just about task completion, not about quality work. This really bugged me. Another thing that bugged me during this time was that we had a guest speaker come talk about academic misconduct at university and most of the students did even pay attention to him talk. They didn't answer his questions. They didn't laugh at his jokes. They just sat there, like they did every day, silently and with a bored, blank look on their faces as if we were wasting their time by asking them to come to class and learn. I started to become angry with this class around this time, but I tried my best not to let that influence my lessons. Perhaps it would have been better if I had burst out in anger one day and reamed them out. Maybe that would have been one thing that I did that would have stuck with them!

Weeks 11 and 12

I collected the first drafts of their major research essay. Garbage. Several of them had blatantly plagiarized, even though they knew what plagiarism was and what it looked like at this point as we had discussed it many times that term. The amount of simple grammar mistakes that they had in their essays was appalling. The most frustrating part was that when I met with them to discuss their essays, the majority of them were able to identify and correct mistakes when I asked them to. Once again, they didn't take the time to prepare a good quality essay. Another thing I noticed was that the majority of the students were making the same mistakes over and over, even though I had given them individual feedback on previous assignments and taken time in class to go over common errors they had made and how to fix them or avoid them. It was obvious that the whole 12 weeks before this had simply been a waste of time and really, genuinely, only 3–5 of them had actually improved, but only as a result of them putting effort into their work. The rest of the class had just sat idly by all term. What a waste of time for them! It also felt like I had wasted a lot of time with them because they hadn't learned. But learning is a two-way street that requires effort from both parties and I felt like I had done my job, but they hadn't done theirs. Was there more I could have done to get them to do their work better?

Week 13

This week was spent meeting one-on-one during class and conferencing about their first drafts. I had given them written feedback the previous week and asked them to read over it and come prepared with questions so I could further direct them to improve their first drafts. About half of the class was genuinely interested in getting feedback and came prepared with questions and a desire to improve. Other students had no questions and wanted no feedback, even though they desperately needed it. Others just wanted me to fix all their mistakes and tell them exactly how to improve their essay. I did not do so, as that wouldn't benefit them in the long term at all. In fact, that just made me want to not help them at all as I would basically be doing all their editing and revision for them. At this point, and probably the previous few weeks before this, I found myself just focusing on the few students who demonstrated an interest to improve their writing skill, not just their marks. Most students asked me to give them higher marks because they needed to pass. I told them I don't just give them marks; they earn them based on what they hand in. Once again, this did not really seem to faze them. The one good thing that happened this week was that the couple of students who wanted to improve came to see me a few more times to make sure what they were doing was good. I also had one student come see me begging me to pass her because she just need to get a degree. She didn't need to learn anything. She just wanted a piece of paper saying she graduated from a Canadian university. So, if I could pass her, she would be very grateful. I just laughed.

Week 14

This week was very frustrating and exciting all at the same time. This was the last week. I couldn't wait to be done with this group. I told them half of them were still failing and that their final drafts and their final exam would determine if they passed. The frustrating part was that the majority of them had final drafts that were not too bad overall. They were capable of it all along, but never bothered to hand in good essays until push came to shove, or in this case, a matter of passing or failing. Their final exams too were just enough to get a few of them to pass. They were capable of doing mediocre to decent work, but just never really felt the need to do it until it was completely necessary. This part really bugged me because it was obvious that so many of them didn't really work hard until they needed to. All they cared about was just scraping by and just passing with doing the minimum amount required. And they dragged me through the whole process and made me nearly go insane doing it. I was so happy to see them go. Only two students actually went through a legitimate learning curve over the semester and improved like my students normally do when I teach an upper-level writing course like this one. The exciting part of this week was after exams were done, I didn't have to see their pathetic, lazy, and disengaging faces anymore. I know it sounds mean, but this is truly how it felt to me at the time.

Roger's Reflection

So, after reflecting on this long and torturous critical incident I have come to realize that there wasn't much that I could have done to change things. I put my full effort in for the first few weeks, but when I realized that my efforts weren't being appreciated or reciprocated, I slowly eased off and just stuck with the basics because I knew that was all I could get out of this group. They were simply not capable of doing good work or of even doing advanced level writing. Maybe it was because they hadn't paid attention in previous levels, and this was just the result of them having barely gotten by for several terms. Also, their motivation was so low, and I tried what I knew to try and increase it, but if they don't want to change or don't try to change, there is so little I can do. I just wish I had been able to impact them more than I did. I want to make every student feel like they can succeed and that my classes are useful to them in some way. However, this class I felt like I just couldn't reach them, no matter what I did. It was painful to come to class and watch them just go through the motions and hand in crappy work. I knew that they were wasting their time. I knew that they wouldn't be prepared for university and that they would feel the effects later of not working hard. I just wish there was something I could have done to make them feel the same way, but I know that I can't. Or can I?!?!? This is the issue that really got to me after this term!

> **Reflective Break**
> - Have you ever experienced a class similar to the one Roger was teaching the first semester of his third year?
> - What would you do if you had a class of students who were not engaged in your teaching or their own learning?
> - Do you think it is the teacher's fault that such students remain uninterested or unmotivated?
> - Do you think a teacher can build in specific plans that can change the structure of such a class?
> - What is your understanding of how Roger felt throughout the semester as revealed in his semester write up?
> - What do you think of Roger's reflection on the whole incident/term with this class?
> - Have you ever wanted the term to end because you had a group of students you considered not to be motivated?

CONCLUSION

This chapter outlined and discussed Roger's theory that included his approach to planning and his experience of a major critical incident that he also experienced during his third year of teaching. Roger noted that during his third year of teaching at the same institution he was required to follow a syllabus and use textbooks more than during his first year. That said, the chapter revealed how Roger always tried to put his students learning needs first when making detailed lesson plans, especially regarding the way he plans grammar lessons, and how he tends to manipulate required textbooks rather than follow the pages and chapters in the sequence they are published. In addition, the chapter detailed a critical incident about one course he was teaching where the students were not engaged throughout the whole 14-week semester and how this was impacting Roger's planning and execution of his lessons adversely. This incident again made Roger reflect on the fact that there are no easy or simple solutions to the complexity of teaching students from a different cultural background. The chapter also introduces Roger's actual classroom practices during his third year of teaching.

Chapter 12

Reflecting on Third Year Practice

INTRODUCTION

In Chapter 6 I outlined and discussed Roger's actual practice during his first-year teaching. In this chapter I outline and discuss his practice during his third year. To remind, the fourth stage, *practice*, is what constitutes the tip of the iceberg and examines observable actions while teaching. This stage is strongly connected to the first three stages as development of awareness of the convergence or divergence between belief and practice is the start of "a process of reducing the discrepancy between what we do and what we think we do" (Knezevic, 2001: 10). The convergence of beliefs and practice can be impacted by situational constraints, experience, changes in beliefs preceding changes in practice, incompatible propositions, conflicting beliefs and tensions between core and peripheral beliefs (Fang, 1996). Classroom observations can be used to compare what a teacher says they do and what they actually do using category instruments, or audio and video recordings. This stage of practice can bring to light the reasons for convergence or divergence by helping teachers draw connections between their philosophy, principles, theory, and practice to develop the ability to reflect during a lesson (reflection-in-action), after a lesson (reflection-on-action) and reflect prior to teaching (reflection-for-action). As in Chapter 6, I provide details of his observed classes as well as detailed transcripts of three of his lessons that I observed, and which Roger reflected on. Thus, the chapter again suggests that to capture what really happens in a classroom it is best to have concrete data that can be gathered by observation, recording (audio and video), transcription and analysis.

ROGER'S ACTUAL TEACHING THIRD YEAR

Roger said that when he makes decisions about what to do in his lessons, he tries to make sure that these are for the benefit of his students' learning. Roger continued,

> anytime you're teaching, obviously you should be putting the students first. What are they learning, how are they learning, what are their motivations like, right? And how can I get this specific group of students, or even this specific student to learn most effectively. Right? And to me that's something that is important.

Roger said that he would tailor the content to what the students know, what they need and what they're able to do; but that also he must consider particular content that they must cover in the program. For this, Roger said that when he mentions "students" he means them all as a class and so he will try to teach to "the most common denominator" rather than the few. As Roger notes, if most of his class are not "grasping something", he will not move on with some new concept until he thinks the class have understood the previous concept. Thus, he said he "would spend a little more time on it than say was planned by other people."

In his third year, Roger said that he likes teaching grammar more than the other skills (similar to what he mentioned in his first year) because he considers it to have more content than the other skills-based courses. He also noted that the way he teaches grammar is more like the way teaching is conducted in a university setting. Roger said, "the way that you do things can be more like a typical university content course where you have your lecture-seminar type thing. So, for grammar, for me, it's always a bit of a mixture of me lecturing teaching them, you know, with PowerPoint, and writing on the board and they after do some textbook activities."

Roger said that for him a "typical grammar week" teaching a high proficiency level class sees him start with the basics of a grammar concept and structure, and from there he would give them some grammar exercises "just to refresh their memories." Roger said that the following week he intends to teach adjective clauses to his high proficiency level class and so he will get them to present on them on the Monday class because he thinks they will have forgotten them from past classes. After that he said he will give them exercises to practice on and then he said, "throughout the week I'll be focusing on more specific points and then I'll give them some more practice." Roger said that because the textbook he uses is prescribed by the institution, he will supplement it with his own exercises that focus on other aspects of grammar the book did not cover. As Roger remarked, "I like to create my own things that would help different students learn in different ways." Thus, Roger said that he has a lesson plan in his mind but not in writing, before he goes in to teach and, as noted above, Roger said that he uses lecture-style mode of teaching with lots of PowerPoints in his grammar lessons as many of his students he said, "mentioned that they like the PowerPoints."

For Roger, as noted before, grammar was his favorite skill to teach because he was happy to impart knowledge of the content as the other skills are more practice oriented rather than content heavy. Roger noted that his students must be able to learn the rules of grammar for all the skill areas and they must learn grammar terminology as he said, "this gives them a means to talk about the language. However, he said that he only focuses on what he thinks his students need in terms of grammar rather than wasting "time trying to fill my students' minds with rules that aren't important as they should focus on learning what they need."

In terms of the actual teaching, Roger said that now, in his third year, he has "created habits/routines in how I teach grammar based on what works." Roger summed up his overall approach to grammar lessons as follows:

> I think grammar is a content course in a sense and to be able to talk about the structures we learn, we need to give them names. However, I don't expect my students to memorize or remember the terms long term. As long as they are able to use the structures they learn properly. Students need to learn by doing tasks and using the grammar structures as this is how they will become more proficient. In terms of learning grammar, I strongly believe that practice makes perfect, so students need a lot of chances to use the structures in context so they can apply it and use it in the future. Just learning rules is not enough, but they need to know how to use them in real life.

Roger's Grammar Lessons

Roger was interested in reflecting on his teaching of his upper-level proficiency grammar classes for one week during his third year and asked me to observe some of these lessons. For these lessons, Roger said that his main objective for the week was to have his students review the main and specific uses of perfect verbs and to practice using them, as well as a written in-class assignment. He would be using a textbook to help deliver these lessons. Roger invited me to observe his second, third and fourth grammar lessons of that week because he said his first lesson would be focused on reviewing homework from the previous week and preparing his students for the week ahead, whilst his fifth and final grammar lesson of that week would focus on an in-class assignment. Thus, he said, he would learn more from observations and video taping of the middle three lessons. Each lesson was transcribed, and

I present the transcriptions below with Roger's immediate comments below them and later a detailed reflection and analysis of them.

Transcript 1

The following is a transcript of Roger's second class of the "grammar week" that he said was to focus on verb review using PowerPoint as a mode of lesson delivery.

1   R: How's your day going so far? Pretty good? Not so good?

2   Student: So far so good.

3   R: So far so good? That's like the standard response, right? You guys have to learn more than so far so good because what does so far so good always mean?

4   Student: Good?

5   R: Yeah, at this point you're good, but you're expecting your day to be worse?

6   Students: [laughter]

7   R: Right? When I hear so far so good, it's like, are you waiting for something bad or what? It's like, are you expecting worse things to happen later on? Alright, um, today we are going to be starting something different, verbs. So, um, after midterm, obviously we had our midterm tests and you guys were all very happy with it, right?

8   Students: [mixed responses]

9   R: No? Well, maybe. Ok, I want to encourage you guys to focus on the areas that you still have problems with, ok? So if you're not really familiar with for example adjective clauses, try to find ways to focus on that. If you need extra help I am here for you. All you need to do is ask. It's important to recognize what you can do and what you can't do, right? In this class, it's what you can do. Not do you know it, can you use it. Yeah, so, so far we've talked about things related to nouns, right? Noun clauses, noun clause, quantifiers, adjective clauses, they're all connected to nouns. But, from now we're going to change our focus here. We're going to change our focus to a different type of phrase. Any idea? [pause]

10   R: Verb phrase. If you don't have one, you don't have a sentence, right? So today we're just doing some basic review. So, very quickly, we've got three things to think about when talking about verbs. We've got the tense, the voice, and the aspect. Hmmm. Do you guys know what any of these words mean? It's not really important that you know exactly what they mean, but they are important when you're talking about verbs. It's important to kind of understand how they work. So, when we talk about tense, what are we actually talking about here?

11   Student: Time

12   R: Time. Ok, so what would mean we have what? In English, which tenses do we have?

13   Students: Past, Present, Future

14   R: Yeah, past, present, future, and? [pause]

15   R: Yeah, we have no more.

16   Students: [laughter]

17   R: So we just have the three. This is all review for you hopefully. Next we talk about aspect. What does that mean for you? Any guesses? So we have four aspects, although some people would argue only three. The textbook mentions four and I kind of agree. I think that's more accurate. What do you think aspect might be? We've got past, present, and future. Aspect. When you hear the word aspect, what does it mean to you? [pause]

18   R: Maybe you don't know this word. How you look at things. A point of view. A way of looking at time. We've got the simple aspect, the continuous aspect, the perfect aspect, and what's the last one?

19   Student: Past

20   Students: [laughter]

21   R: This is where the debate kind of lies. Perfect continuous. So this is how we look at time, right? Is it at one point in time, is it over a period of time, is it before one point in time. And voice, what are we talking about. When we're talking about verbs and you hear the word voice, what are we talking about? Loud and soft? No.

22   Student: Active and passive

23   R: Yeah, active and passive. So who's doing the action of the verb. Is it, you know, the person who is the subject of the verb or not. So, we'll look at these in more detail over the next couple weeks. Um, so before we do that I have a few questions that I want to ask you guys. How many verb tenses are there in English? [pause]

24   Student: Three

25   R: Ok, yes, three technically. But how many verbs do we have in English?

26   Student: Twelve.

27   R: Yeah, most people would say there's twelve. Three tenses with four aspects, that's twelve in total, right? Which verb is used the most in English? Simple, or...

28   Student: Simple present.

29   R: Actually, it's interesting. They've done research on it and it's not very common. It may be easy to use, but it's not very common, especially in a classroom setting.

30   Student: The past.

31   R: Yeah, the simple past. Any idea why?

32   Student: We talk about things in the past.

33   R: Yeah, we always tell stories and that's why it's the most common. Which one do you think is used the least?

34   Student: Future.

35   R: Future?

36   Student: Perfect.

37   R: Perfect? Yeah, one form of the perfect is used the least.

38   Student: Past perfect.

39   R: Yeah, that form of the perfect isn't used a lot, especially in spoken English we hardly use the past perfect. So that is one that we don't use very often. At least not in speaking. Now this is based more on your experiences. So which verb tenses are the easiest to learn based on your experience?

40   Student: Simple.

41   R: Yeah, the simple, so the past, present, and future. Ok. Anyone else? No? Alright, which one is the most difficult to learn based on your experiences?

42   Student: Past perfect.

43   R: The past perfect? Yeah, that one is not easy. How many of you would agree that the perfect tenses in general are the more difficult ones?

44   Students: [mixed answers]

45   R: Yeah? Good, because that's the one we're going to spend the most of our time on in this class is focusing on the perfect verb because, yeah, they are difficult because there's a certain understanding of time that you need to know. Last question here. And this is what I'm interested in, just to see what you think about it. According to your opinion, or your experience, what is the best way to learn English verb tenses? [pause]

46   R: I'm not asking for the professional answer, but based on what you've experienced. [pause]

47   R: Really? No ideas at all?

48   Student: Use it.

49   R: Use it? Yeah, that's a good one. Learn it somehow and then just use it? Yeah, I would agree that's a good method. Yeah, you said something too.

50   Student: Practice.

51   R: Yeah, practicing. That's a very good trend I'm seeing here. But, before you practice, you have to learn it too. So how do you learn verb tenses most successfully? [pause]

52   R: When someone tells you the rules or when you figure out the rules yourself? [pause]

53   Student: When someone tells.

54   R: Ok, you think when someone tells you the rules. Does anyone disagree with that? [pause]

55   R: No, you guys are still not very active? Reading Week sucked all the English out of your brain?

56   Students: [laughter]

57   R: Alright, let's move on here. So today what we're going to focus on is we're going to do a very quick overview of the simple verbs, as well as the progressive or continuous verbs, ok? We're only going to spend about fifteen minutes talking about those verbs, and that's it. Ok? And then also today we are going to have an introduction to the perfect verbs by the students who are presenting today. Um, so, these two aspects, the simple and the progressive, are ones that at this point you should be very familiar with. Whether you joined us in Level 1, or Level 3, or whatever, these are verbs you should have learned a lot before. So if you do have issues with them, it's important that you try and identify it and if you have any problems, come talk to me and I can help you out. Ok? But there's definitely some self study that's required here as we're not spending much time on it in class, ok? So today we'll just quickly have an overview of those ones and if there's still something about them that's confusing, see if you can figure it out. So, the simple form. Generally we only have a verb with it, there's nothing else. There's just one verb, ok? And that's why people think they're easy. So for example, if I had a sentence like "I play squash twice a week", right, you look at it and say, oh, that's a very simple sentence. The verb's easy. However, this is where I notice problems occur. As soon as you start to use the negative form or, if it becomes a question, we have to add words. Ok? Um, so, something like this: "I don't like giving low marks", or "I eat a couple hamburger every day". Here's where I notice problems. So, once again, when I ask you to try to identify problems, look for can you use this properly. So, when you have the simple form in a question, add, you know, do, or something like that. So focus on that you can use this type of structure, especially in writing. Last term I taught Level 5 writing and I was shocked at how many types of errors there were with this type of structure. So yeah, people are like, oh, the simple verb tenses are easy. They're simple to learn. But can you use them properly? Try and keep track of that. The future. When we use the simple future, we add "will" or "be going to". So, I'll give you a thousand dollars if you get over 98% in this course.

58   Students: [laughter]

59   R: Yeah, seriously. So, if you can do it, come talk to me. We'll figure something out. Or your girlfriend told me that she's going to break up with you tomorrow night. She told me, but... Anyway, in this case notice how we use

"will" and "be going to" together with the base form. Right? And hopefully this is all simple stuff for you. Now, when do we use the simple? [pause]

60 R: Any idea? So, simple present is used when?

61 Student: Habits.

62 R: Yeah, talk about habits. Regular activities. So I always eat an egg for breakfast. In this case you're saying it's a habit. And that's probably the most common use right there. Um, when you're describing things. Like a process or instructions. This is when you would use the simple present as well, right? For example if you say something like first you pick you up the phone, then you dial the number, and then you ask for a pizza, right? And that's how you order pizza. And this is a process, so therefore I would use the simple present. Now, more specific for you guys when you're writing essays, this is also when you would use the simple present quite a bit is if you're reporting information or summarizing an article or something, often times we would use the simple present. For example, research mentions that students who don't study often get lower marks. Right? So notice how here all the verbs are in present simple. Why? Because, well, they're true right now, it's something that's always true, we kind of go back to the regular activities part. When something is consistent we would use that verb tense. And, when we're talking about things like movies, books, stories, yeah, we also use the simple past, but many people use the simple present too. So if you're talking about a movie, see if you can guess which movie this is from. So a guy goes to Paris and kills six people, and then he does this, and bla, bla, bla, notice how we use the simple present. Why do you think we would use the simple present and not the simple past?

63 Student: It's not real.

64 R: Ok, yeah, it's not a real story, I guess. Maybe. But you want it to sound real, right? And the present does that. By the way, which movie is this from? Any idea? [pause]

65 R: No? Has anyone ever seen the movie *Taken* with Liam Neeson?

66 Students: [mixed response]

67 R: I'm sure you have. It's a very popular movie. Anyway, so that's the simple present. Not very much to talk about since you've studied it a lot before. But there is one problem area that I want to focus on, ok? And by Level 5, everyone's like, oh, yeah, of course subject-verb agreement with the simple present is easy. I never have problems with that. But then I see sentences like this: Roger give a lot of homework.

68 Students: Gives.

69 R: Yeah. Everyone's like oh yeah, of course, you have to add an "s". But when you actually use it, are you actually adding the "s"? I don't know. So just

make sure that you watch out for these kinds of mistakes. They are very easy to avoid, right? You know about it, you've studied it a lot, so just pay attention, especially in writing, that you're not making simple little errors like this. Uh, so, the simple past. When do we use that? [pause]

70   Student: [unintelligible]

71   R: Sorry?

72   Student: Describe the past.

73   R: Ok, to describe when something is happening, but when we're also using dates or specific times in the past. So in 1995, the world was cursed when Justin Bieber was born.

74   Students: [Laughter]

75   R: So in this case, notice how I'm referring to a specific point in time. So as soon as I'm referring to a specific point in time, you have to use the simple present, er, simple past. So we'll focus on this later this week, when to use the past perfect, or present perfect, and when to use the simple past. Can you think of any other situations where we would use the simple past? [pause]

76   R: I know, your brains have to work now. It's tough. [pause]

77   R: Oh, we've got one more example. In 2013 you came to Canada. What about completed events that are not connected to anything? So, once again, one instance in the past. So if there's no connection to anything we would use this. So, when I went to Cuba, I tried a coconut there. There's no connection to the present, no other time in the past, we just use the simple. Also, when you talk about past habits. Ok, so hopefully you can see a trend here. Simple present we talk about habits, past habits we use the past. So for example, when Bob was young, he only spoke Chinese. Right? Because we're talking about what he did in the past. It's over now. It's completed, right? So hopefully you can see a trend here. When something was completed in the past and there's no connection to the present anymore we would use simple past. Are there any questions so far? Alright, last thing that we're focusing on with the simple is the future. When do we use simple future?

78   Student: [something unintelligible]

79   R: Sorry?

80   Student: Prediction?

81   R: Yeah, that's one example of when we can use it. Anyone else?

82   Student: [something unintelligible]

83   R: Yeah, just to talk generally about future events. Right? So this is probably the easiest verb tense. Often we use "will" or "be going to", it's the most common. Right? Um, and often there is no meaning between "will" and "be going to". Sometimes there is a small difference, but in many cases there is

not. Now "will" is the more general use of this. "Be going to", we typically talk about if the thing or event in the future is planned. That's the biggest difference there. So if we're just predicting something, we're just talking about something in the future that's not planned, use "will". Or "be going to". That's fine too. Often times I find students get really hung up on whether they should use "will" or "be going to", but really there's not a huge difference. If you use these in every day English, people will understand you. Um, but I do want to show you a little bit of a difference. I will visit Zimbabwe someday or I'm going to visit Zimbabwe someday. Is there any difference to you? [pause]

84 Student: [gives her idea about the difference]

85 R: Yeah, the first one is just more general, right? I will visit it someday, I don't know, maybe, maybe not. But when we use "be going to" it's more like we plan to do it, and that's definitely the biggest difference that you should know. Alright, hopefully this is not too easy for you today. Ok, the last thing that we're going to look at today is the continuous aspect. Um, so obviously we know that we use a form of the verb "be" and a verb ending in -ing, right? It's also called the progressive. Textbooks call it one or the other. Basically, in general what this is used for is to show that something is in progress at a certain point in time. Right? So the present continuous, we're talking about something that's happening now. Can anyone give me an example? [pause]

86 R: An example of the present continuous being used.

87 Student: Murilo is drinking water.

88 R: Yeah. Wow, he is yet too. Awesome. Yeah. Or Rudy is listening very carefully. So in this case what is going on right now? He's listening carefully. Molly is thinking about Montreal at this moment. You went there during Reading Week, no?

89 Student: No.

90 R: Oh, I must have been thinking of someone else. But anyway, what, yeah. Notice that there is something attached to this sentence. At this moment. And next week, or no, later this week, we'll talk about using time words to help you use different verbs. We've also got the past and future continuous, right? And basically we use these to show that in the past or in the future something is happening at that specific time. Ok? So just think about progressive verbs need specific time. Ok, just to show that it's happening over that specific period of time. Any questions? [pause]

91 R: Ok. Oh, we've got one example here. Jing was playing video games at this time last week. Is it true?

92 Student: No.

93   R: No? Really? Another one. Paula will be swimming in the ocean on December 25th. True?

94   Student: No.

95   Students: [laughter]

96   R: It's too cold? Anyway, but notice here we have specific dates right? For homework tonight I would like you guys to do this. Write 10 sentences using different verbs in each one. Um, what you're going to do is exchange with a partner tomorrow and you're going to look for errors. We don't have any time to do this in class right now since we have a presentation today. Um, and then if you would like some optional extra practice from the textbook, if you want to double check how well you're able to use the simple or continuous forms, you can find them here. So today was just a very quick overview of the verb tenses that we're not studying, and then now we're going to have our introduction to perfect verbs, and then tomorrow we're going to look more closely at how to use perfect verbs because that's not always easy to do. Alright, that's it.

The above class was followed the next day by another grammar lesson that Roger said would focus on perfect verbs mainly using PowerPoints for lesson delivery as well as practice exercises from the book and some of his own handouts. Before the lesson Roger told me he thought that his lesson the previous day had gone "pretty well as the students seemed to pay attention" and that he was happy with his PowerPoint presentation. However, he wondered if his students "were learning new information or just reviewing information." I now present the transcript of Roger's third grammar lesson that week.

Transcript 2

1   R: Alright, everyone ready to start? Good to go? Perfect. Uh, so the homework from yesterday, don't worry about it now. We'll do something with it later this week, ok, but make sure that you still finish it. [more students walk in]

2   R: Hi guys, come on in. And we'll wait for Paula. Hi, have a seat. Uh, ok, so today we're going to continue with verbs. We're going to focus on perfect verbs, ok? Not verbs that are perfect, but the verb tense, right? And, more specifically, we're focusing on use. So that's something that at Level 5, you all know how to make verbs, how to create them, what the structure looks like, but how many of you think you're really good at using verbs? [pause]

3   R: No, how about some verbs?

4   Students: [mixed response]

5   R: How about perfect verbs?

6   Students: No.

7   R: No, ok, you're in the right place today, that's good. Um, so, perfect verbs, the big question is what distinguishes a perfect verb from the simple or the progressive? What's really the big difference? Why is a perfect verb a perfect verb? [pause]

8   Student: Have done.

9   R: Yeah, so "have done" is an example of a perfect verb. But what is unique about perfect verbs? [pause]

10   R: In their relation to time. What is... so in relation to time, how do perfect verbs work?

11   Students: [mixed responses]

12   R: Ok, so that's one example. If something else is finished before another thing. But, even more generally, what can we say about perfect verbs? We can say that there is a connection between... two points in time, whereas a simple verb or a progressive verb there's not. So when we have the present perfect, we have a connection between the past and the present, right? With the past perfect there's a connection between two past events. Right? The past perfect, I kind of like to call it the past tense, because really it's far, far in the past. And future perfect. Two connections, um, a connection between two future events, right? One is further in the future than the other one. So that's what's special about perfect verbs, right, is there's a connection between two points in time. Now think about your language, your first language. Do you have a verb tense similar to this?

13   Student: [shakes head]

14   R: No? So, Chinese no. What about Portuguese, Spanish?

15   Students: Yes.

16   R: Yeah, so some languages have it, some languages don't. If your first language doesn't have this then it's more difficult to learn because you have a whole concept of time before you really know how the verbs work. So a few questions for you before we get into it. Can perfect verbs be used by themselves? [pause]

17   R: What do you think? Or maybe the first question, do you think? What do you think about this? [pause]

18   R: Don't be shy. [pause]

19   R: There's two choices, yes, no, three I guess, maybe. [pause]

20   R: Who says yes, raise your hand?

21   Students: [no reaction]

22   R: So you guys, ok, no?

23   Students: [some raise hand, others say yes]

24   R: Yes! And we'll look at some examples later. Are perfect verbs always used with another verb? [pause]

25   R: Yes or no? [pause]

26   R: Come on, you guys aren't paying attention?

27   Students: [some say yes to the question]

28   R: No! Come on read the question. Can perfect verbs be used by themselves? Yes. Are they always used with another verb? Obviously no. If the first answer is yes, the second one has to be no. So, the question though that we need to think about is do perfect verbs always be used, need to used with another point of reference? And by point of reference I mean a time reference. [pause]

29   R: Yes, completely. Once again, a perfect verb connects two points in time, and we need to show how. Ok? So, some examples, alright. I have five examples here. They all have different points of reference, but there's always two. So the first example. Effy had already eaten dinner when Kuang invited her for dinner. Ok. Now in this case what are the two points in time?

30   Student: [something unintelligible]

31   R: Yeah, she had eaten and then Kuang asked her, hey, do you want to come for dinner? So we have two points of time in the past. So we've got two time references. How about this one? I've just recently arrived, so I'm quite tired. [pause]

32   R: So what two time references do we have.

33   Student: Recently

34   R: Recently, yeah. So it's not too far in the past. What about the other time reference?

35   Student: Now.

36   R: Yeah, now. But how do you know that?

37   Students: [mixed answers]

38   R: Yeah, the verb tense. So it's not explicitly stated, it's not obvious, but you know there's a connection to now. So past and present. Luis has been to Thailand before.

39   Student: I wish.

40   R: Yeah, you wish. That would be nice. So the two time references here?

41   Student: Go to Thailand

42   R: When he went Thailand. And what about the other one? [pause]

43   R: Hmm, there's only one verb, so how can we have two time references?

44   Student: Before.

45   R: Yeah, before when?

46   Student: Now?

47   R: Yeah, before now. But it's not explicit, but it has to be there. So if I said Luis has been to Thailand, yeah, that's ok too, but in that case we still understand that it's before now, right? By the time you finish Level 5, you will have learned to hate winter in Canada. So, we have two future time references, right? Which one is first? Finish Level 5 or hate winter?

48   Students: [mixed answers]

49   R: Winter, yeah. First you'll hate winter, then you'll finish Level 5. Right? So before, or by the time you finish Level 5, this will have happened, right? So there's two points in time here. Last one. I had never eaten McDonald's before yesterday. So, in this case, what are the two time references? [pause]

50   Student: Yesterday.

51   R: Yeah, so yesterday is one that's the closest. And the one further in the past is eating McDonald's right? So hopefully you can see that a time reference can be stated, it can be obvious either by using another verb or a word like yesterday, or it can be implied. But, either way, you have to know that there are two points in time. And that's what's special about the perfect verb. So before you're able to use these verbs, you have to understand that there are those two connections between one point in time and another. So, any questions so far? [pause]

52   R: Perfect. Now, in terms of use this is where I find students often have the most questions. When do I use the perfect, when do I use the simple? Or when do I use the regular perfect or when do I use the perfect progressive? These are all questions that I'm sure you have too. Um, so today we'll focus on comparing use between the perfect verbs and simple verbs, and hopefully this is something that will happen in your writing especially, but also in your speaking. So, comparing the present to the simple past, ok? So simple past is used to talk about specified time. We talked a little bit about this yesterday. If you have a specific time in the past you can only use the simple past, right? So we have a sentence like Murilo went to Malawi in 1994. Ok, now in this case I have a very specific date, right? So I can't say Murilo has gone to Malawi in 1994. This just doesn't logically work. Why? Because there is only one point in time, right? Were you even alive in 1994?

53   Student: No.

54   R: No, maybe even not. Now, whereas the present perfect, we can use that with an unspecified time in the past, ok? And in this case we got a sentence like Murilo has been to Malawi before. Before when?

55   Student: Before now.

56   R: Before now. So that's the connection between the past and the present. But one common error that I see is that students use a specific time with

perfect verbs, and that just doesn't work logically. Uh, so simple past is used to talk about completed events. [students whispering to each other]

57   R: Oh, Malawi is in Africa. Yeah, it's a really obscure country. Anyway, finish events. Right, they are complete. What does that mean? There's no connection to now. For example, my friend smoked from 1992 to 2012. Does my friend still smoke? No. Right? It's finished, it's complete. But if my friend still smokes, I have to use what? The present perfect. Right? So a sentence like my friend has smoked since he was 14. So in this case it tells you that now he's still smoking, right? Or at least he could be. But in any case, you know, it's unfinished or it appears to be unfinished. So that's the biggest difference between the present perfect and the simple past. If there's only one point in time, we have to use the present simple. If not, we can use the present perfect. Um, a similar thing here. The simple past is used to talk about things that won't happen again. So it's the same idea as events that are completed, but in this case it's the idea that the events were repeated a few times. So for example, I went to Spain three times while I was in university. Now in this case, will it happen again? [pause]

58   R: Could I go to Spain again?

59   Student: Yeah.

60   R: I could, but am I in university right now? Well, as a student? No, so in this case there's no connection between the past and the present, right? But if I tell you that I still want to go to Spain, or that it could happen again, what do you think the sentence would look like? [pause]

61   R: What about something like this? I've been to Spain three times so far. And what does that mean?

62   Student: Plan to do again.

63   R: Yeah, I plan to do it again. If I had enough money, that's the first place that I'd go to. Spain is amazing. So, in either case, I hope you can see the difference here. In this situation, this situation can't happen again unless I go back to university, but I don't really feel like doing that right now. So, in this case, I'll just use the present perfect to show that I still want to do it. Now, one small little area that's a little confusing sometimes is with recently completed events. We can use often the simple past and the present perfect, but the meaning is slightly, it's kind of a little different. So here we have the sentence Shelley just bought a new pair of shoes. Alright? Now is there any connection to now? Not really. She just bought a pair of shoes recently in the past, that's it. But I can also use the present perfect to show that she just completed something. So Shelley has just bought a new pair of shoes, so she's really happy. Now what's the difference between these two sentences? [pause]

64   R: Why would I use the simple past in one and the present perfect in the other? [pause]

65   R: Well, in this one there's a connection to now. She's really happy now. So in that case I can use the present perfect. And this is something that might be a little confusing. Oh, it's in the past, but it's just in the past, so there's still a connection to now, or at least you can make the connection. So any questions about using the simple present versus the simple past? [pause]

66   R: Alright, good. Now this is the verb tense that I find most people have difficulty with is the past perfect. Why is the past perfect difficult? [pause]

67   R: For you maybe. Or just in general. What makes it so difficult? [pause]

68   Student: Time.

69   R: Ok, time, yeah, so you're not, you have to think about which action is first. I think another reason might be that it's not used very often, especially in speaking. A lot of people don't use it unless there's an obvious need for it. So, the simple past, as we mentioned, describes one event in the past. So, Jim went to Las Vegas last week. Ok, that's it, just one event, one verb. But, when I wanted to describe an earlier event before that action, that's what the past perfect is for. Alright? So, Jim had taken out a lot of money from the bank before he went to Las Vegas. Right, so in the case I would use the past perfect just to show, hey, that happened before this. That's quite, you know, that's probably the simplest reason for why we would use this. However, this is where a lot of people have some issues is that the past perfect is often optional. This means we don't really need to use it when the meaning is clear. And this is something that's especially common in speaking when if we don't need to use the past perfect, we don't. So a sentence like this. After Helen ate breakfast, she went to school. Right? Now we've got two verbs, they're both in the past. Which one happened first?

70   Students: [mixed responses]

71   R: Ok, so I could say after Helen had eaten breakfast she went to school. And that's fine. Because the meaning is so clear in which action happened first, we don't use it. Same with this sentence. We could go back to that. Jim took out a lot of money from the bank before he went to Las Vegas. No one is going to wonder, oh, which one happened first. I don't know. Right? It's clear because of the time words that we use. But what about this sentence. Steven went to school when he noticed he was late. Which action happened first? [pause]

72   R: We don't, we, we can probably guess. Steven went to school when he had noticed he was late. Maybe he noticed first and then went to school. But we can also say Steven had gone to school when he noticed he was late. So he first went to school and then noticed he was late. Right? So in some contexts

it's not completely clear, so in those cases we would use the perfect to make it more obvious. But, in many cases, we don't need to use it. And that makes it tough because if we don't use it, or you don't hear it, you don't learn it as quickly. [pause]

73   R: Let's move on to the future perfect and compare it to the simple future. So, the simple future once again talks about one event. Right? Simple just means one. So, we will graduate on December 12, 2014. Hopefully. Right? So here we're looking towards the future, just one event. It's also used to express a state of being. So how we feel, how we appear. I will be 67 years old by 2044. Oh, that's a long time from now. Good. So in this case, just one event. But if we want to show that there's a future action happening before another, we have to use this verb tense. There's no other way, ok? We have to use the future perfect. You will have spent 40% of your life sleeping by the time you are 25. Is, oh, it's probably true. If you add it up in total. So in this case, which action happened first? [pause]

74   Student: Sleep.

75   R: Yeah, first you spend 40% of your life sleeping then before you are 25. So we're showing that one thing happens before another in the future. That's the only verb tense that we can use to show that. So, that's obviously the main function. Alright, so that's kind of comparing the future perfect with the simple. Now let's compare using perfect with the perfect progressive. What's the difference? I'll ask you first. Any idea?

76   Student: [something unintelligible]

77   R: Ok, to show an unfinished action. [pause]

78   R: Any other thoughts, ideas? [pause]

79   R: Ok, so present perfect progressive is used to emphasize. Ok? That's the main function. We use this to show that something just happened recently. So we've got we've been eating too much pizza lately, said no one ever, of course. No one says that. But imagine if someone said this sentence. We've been eating too much pizza lately. What does it mean? [pause]

80   R: That over the last period of time, we've been doing too much of that. So I'm emphasizing that fact. It's not that it's repeat, it's just, you know, going on too much. We can also emphasize how long something happened. So a sentence like we've been studying grammar for seven weeks. Now, in this case probably it is ongoing, but it could also be finished right now. It's not necessarily that it's continuing, but we're emphasizing that it's been going on for a period of time. And that's the biggest difference between the perfect and perfect progressive. So the present perfect then, just the regular present perfect, we use this to show that something has been completed. So that's more of, it's a final thing. So, for example, Stella has travelled a lot

in the past. In this case she could still travel more, but I'm not focusing on that. I'm just saying before now she has travelled, and that's all I'm talking about. Or if we want to mention the quantity of something. How many times we've done something in the past. Paula has sung in ten singing competitions. Right? You have a beautiful voice right? But, in this case I'm just adding things up. Until now, this many times. Maybe she'll sing again, but I not focusing on that. Ok, so the perfect progressive just emphasizes either the continuation of something or the length, or that something just happened recently. Now, they can have the same meaning though. So, in most cases though, they would have the same meaning. What about these two sentence. She's been living here for 67 years. She's lived here for 67 years. Is there any difference here? [pause]

81   R: No. She still lives here now. Um, the second sentence could mean that she's moving now, but it doesn't necessarily have to mean that. Same with the first one. She's been living here for 67 years and now she's moving. Right? So either way, they have the same meaning. Another example. Let's see if they have the same meaning. My pet fish has been jumping out of the water a lot lately. Or my s..., oops, I just changed this sentence. It should be my pet fish has jumped out of the water a lot lately. Any difference?

82   Students: [laughter]

83   R: Yeah, I had my secretary has worked a lot lately, but I changed it to something more interesting, but I forgot to change one of the words. That's awesome. Any difference in meaning here? [pause]

84   R: No. And that's probably the most common thing is that you'll find that there's not a big difference. But if you do want to emphasize something like duration or how long something has been, use the present perfect. Any questions? [pause]

85   R: Ok. And one last thing. We're comparing the future perfect versus future perfect progressive. So same idea. The future perfect progressive emphasizes the length of time. Ok? Just to show that something has happened, or will be happening over a period of time. So I will have been working at Brock for 45 years by the time I retire. I only have 40 more years to go. And I'm not even that old. Ok. That's fun. So what am I showing in this case? I'm just showing 45 years, wow. Right? Future perfect just refers to a completed action. I will have worked at Brock for 45 years by the time I retire. In this case it's just more of the idea that in 45 years, it'll be done. But they can have the same meaning. Or they do have the same meaning. This one is just more emphasizing how long. So, any questions about using the perfect verbs? [pause]

86   R: Hopefully I was able to answer some questions for you that you may have had. So, the perfect progressive verbs, they are not as special as you might think they are. They are just used to emphasize. That's probably why they are one of the biggest questions people have. Alright, so, don't be scared, it's a lot of work. I don't expect you do to it all. Yesterday I talked about monitoring your own ability to use certain things in grammar. These are all the activities from the book that I think would be useful for you. However, the ones that I want you to focus on that we'll take up in class are these ones. Ok? So we'll take these up probably Friday, maybe tomorrow. We'll see exactly. Um, so if you want a lot of practice because you think you need a lot of practice, I've given you more things to work on. Ok? But, at least work on these ones. [pause]

87   R: And feel free to work together in groups, or by yourself, whatever you like. If you have any questions, just raise your hand and I'll be happy to help you. [pause]

88   Student: When do I use the future perfect?

89   R: So the future perfect, we use that to show that there are two future events happening, one before the other one.

90   Student: One happening before another one.

91   R: Yeah.

92   Student: But we can use the future only for this?

93   R: Uh, just the regular future? If we're just talking about one event in the future. So for example if we say next summer I plan... no. Next summer, I'm going to go to Mexico. Ok, so obviously in that case there is only one event, so I use the simple future. I'm going to go. Or I will go.

94   Student: So future perfect for two events?

95   R: Yeah, so I can say before we go to Mexico, I will have bought new sunglasses.

96   Student: Oh.

97   R: So in that case, you know, I'm going to Mexico. But before that, at this time, I'm, you know, I want to buy new sunglasses. So think of it as like the future future tense. Right? So one of them is further in the future than the other one. So for the future perfect there is always two verbs.

98   Student: Two verbs?

99   R: Yeah.

100   Student: So one is future and the simple future. Or just simple right?

101   R: It would be simple present, yeah.

102   Student: Ok, thank you.

103   Student: Should I use had or have?

104   R: Should you use had or have?

105   Student: Is this past perfect or present perfect or past.

106   R: So what do you think?

107   Student: [gives explanation, unintelligible]

108   R: Uh, ok, so in this case the issue, or the city has... Yeah, so it depends on... so here you would use a simple past. The city issued a beach warning because a shark had attacked. So before, well, it had attacked before we arrived. So, in this case, this happened before this. This is in the simple past, so this should be the simple present... or, the past perfect.

109   Student: Oh, so this is right, right?

110   R: Yeah.

111   Student: [asks more questions, unintelligible]

112   R: Yeah, yeah, so this verb and this verb are not really connected. It's this verb and this verb. Yeah. [pause]

113   R: Alright, you guys all look really hungry right now.

114   Students: Yeah.

115   R: Yeah? You are? Make sure you finish these nine exercise tonight because we will take them up in class, alright? So, please make sure that you finish only these ones. It should take you only 15 minutes, half hour, which really isn't that much time. So, have a good day, enjoy your lunch, and see you tomorrow.

Roger said that after the lesson he was not so satisfied as he thinks the students believed that they knew all he was teaching. Indeed, Roger said that the lesson "seemed pretty boring" to him. So he said that he hoped they would do the exercises he assigned them at the end of the class because he thinks they need the practice. Then he said that he hopes that "they liven up a bit soon." In terms of using his PowerPoints as a mode of lesson delivery, Roger said that after two days of this he may need to mix it up a bit and make his class more interactive given how passive his students were in his previous class. I now present the transcript of his fourth grammar class.

Transcript 3

1   R: Yeah, so tomorrow's Friday and after that you get to sleep for two days straight, and then we get to do it all over again! So hopefully you finished the homework from yesterday. We're going to take it up now. It's quite a bit of exercises, but it should go quickly because a lot of them are just, you know, fill in the blank type answers. So we'll start off with exercise 3.4, which was on page 41. Page 41, exercise 3.4. So what we'll do is start on this side here and just go around the room and you guys can each take a turn answering a question. Um, if you don't have the answer to the question, just

say pass. That's ok. Um, if you have any questions about the answer, just raise your hand and say stop, or whatever. Make sure that you get an answer to your question. So Molly, we'll start with you. If you could just say which of those sentences is used in that.

2   Student: A

3   R: So, 1A we use A? Does everyone...?

4   Student: B

5   R: Yeah, it's B. Why couldn't she make it to the party. Is that in the past or in the present?

6   Student: Past.

7   R: Yeah, so in this case we need a past response. B. Her occupation for the last 30 years.

8   Student: I think it's B.

9   R: B? She sang in the coffee house.

10   Student: A?

11   R: Actually they're both correct, but they have different meanings, right? One means now she's finished, the other one means she's still doing that career, right? Uh, C.

12   Student: A.

13   R: Yes, A. Definitely. And D?

14   Student: [answer]

15   R: How did she earn a living... yes, B. We have to use the simple past. Uh, Rudy, so, next one. Why does Mark look so happy? A or B?

16   Student: B

17   R: B? Does everyone agree with that?

18   Students: Yeah

19   R: Yeah, that's correct. John.

20   Student: A. Uh, B.

21   R: Which one? B? Both?

22   Student: B

23   R: Yup, B works. C?

24   Student: A?

25   R: Yes, he saw... yes it's talking about the past. How about D?

26   Student: B?

27   R: Yeah. Ok. If he's dead. But he's not. He's alive. So it's actually B, ok? Mike doesn't care if he goes to another concert in his life because he has seen Whitney Houston. Alright, let's move on to, what's the next one, 3.8. Uh, so where are we at. Stephanie? So if you could just read the first sentences here.

28   Student: [gives answer]

29   R: Yup have you ever gone. And the answer?

30   Student: [gives answer]

31   R: Have gone?

32   Student: [gives answer]

33   R: Went. I went there three years ago. Why not had gone, or has gone?

34   Student: [gives answer]

35   R: Yeah, three years ago. It's a specific time, ok? Ok, Shelley next. Two.

36   Student: [gives answer]

37   R: Yes, that's correct. She has been to Disneyland five time before and Jill took and they came. That's correct

38   Student: [gives answer]

39   R: Yes. Has never seen that's correct. Jing?

40   Student: [gives answer]

41   R: Yeah, I have just had an accident. That's correct. Have just had. And Bob, number five.

42   Student: [gives answer]

43   R: Yes, that's almost correct. The only one that wasn't correct was the third one. Three of the doctors...

44   Student: [gives answer]

45   R: Were sick. Last week, right? So I had to fill in. That's good. Sorry I didn't write you, I have been busy. Alright, Ade, if you can do the next one.

46   Student: [gives answer]

47   R: No, the next one on the next page.

48   Student: [gives answer]

49   R: So you said had gone? Does anyone have anything different?

50   Student: [gives answer]

51   R: Yeah, went. Next sentence. Steven?

52   Student: [gives answer]

53   R: Uh, not that. Not never saw. I?

54   Student: [gives answer]

55   R: Yeah, have never seen. Next sentence? Luis?

56   Student: [gives answer]

57   R: Almost. Were. Yeah, the simple past of be is were. Next sentence?

58   Student: [gives answer]

59   R: Yeah, that's correct. Were, slipped, and fell. Paula, next one?

60   Student: [gives answer]

61   R: Yeah, she broke her leg, they took her to the hospital immediately. Yeah. Kuang, next one?

62   Student: [gives answer]

63   R: Ok, I didn't make?

64   Student: [gives answer]

65   R: Haven't made? Yeah, that's a better choice there. Any questions about these? Ok, next one. 3.14. So, page 49. So same thing. We'll just take a sentence and go around the room.

66   Student: [gives answer]

67   R: Hmmm, the first one wasn't correct. What do you guys think?

68   Student: [gives answer]

69   R: Yeah, decided, yes. My parents decided because they had never been there before. Had never been. Yeah, we're talking about the past. Decided is the nearest past action, but before that they decided, or had decided. Sorry. They had never gone. Uh, next sentence.

70   Student: [gives answer]

71   R: Not had woke up.

72   Student: [gives answer]

73   R: Yeah, just woke up. We all woke up. Next sentence?

74   Student: [gives answer]

75   R: Yeah, packed and made. Next?

76   Student: [gives answer]

77   R: Yeah, we piled. That's good.

78   Student: [gives answer]

79   R: Yeah, sweltering day. It was. Next.

80   Student: [gives answer]

81   R: Yeah, so had broken. Had not had the time. And left. Ok, next sentence. Effy. No, not Effy. Sorry, where are we? Candy?

82   Student: [gives answer]

83   R: Yeah, so arrived. We could say lost, or also had lost. In this case the past perfect is optional because it's clear which action came first. Jim?

84   Student: [gives answer]

85   R: Yup. Issued and had attacked. That's correct. Next.

86   Student: [gives answer]

87   R: Yeah, when I think. And the last one.

88   Student: [gives answer]

89   R: Yeah. Had never gone back. That's correct. Uh, so any questions about the past perfect here. Ok, let's move on to 3.16. Future or future perfect. So number one.

90   Student: [gives answer]

91   R: Mmmmm, not will have had. Will have. So why do we use will have and not will have had? Any idea?

92   Student: [gives answer]

93   R: Yeah, there's just one point in time. There's no connection between two points. Uh, two.

94   Student: [gives answer]

95   R: Hmmm, will have perform?

96   Student: [gives answer]

97   R: Will perform. Yeah, that's correct. Three?

98   Student: [gives answer]

99   R: Yeah. Will mean. Next.

100   Student: [gives answer]

101   R: Yeah, will have found. So in this case we have to use the perfect because there's a connection between two future times. Number five?

102   Student: [gives answer]

103   R: Yup. Will have discovered. Six?

104   Student: [gives answer]

105   R: That this will not be the case. Yeah. Oh, we got another one here. So just say the verb. That will speed up time a bit.

106   Student: [gives answer]

107   R: Will have worked? Yes. That's correct. Any eight?

108   Student: [gives answer]

109   R: Not much will have changed. Is that correct? Or will change?

110   Student: [gives answer]

111   R: Yeah, so by the next century, not much will change. Alright, let's take up one more here. And rather than reading the whole thing, just read the verb so we can speed up a bit. So Kuang, if you could read 3.18.

112   Student: [gives answer]

113   R: She will go? Yeah that's correct. Two?

114   Student: [gives answer]

115   R: Yeah, will wear for both. Don't worry about reading the whole sentence. You can read just the sentence.

116   Student: [gives answer]

117   R: Yeah, will go. Or not?

118   Student: [gives answer]

119   R: Yeah, will have gone. Because if by tomorrow at 6:00 she will have gone and will have picked up and will have bought. Ok? So in this case we have to use the future perfect for all of those. Four?

120   Student: [gives answer]

121   R: Ok, the last two are correct. The first two are not. Yeah, those are just the regular future. The simple future. Why? Because it's just this afternoon. We're looking towards the future. So this afternoon he will rent and will get. And number five.

122   Student: [gives answer]

123   R: Will be? Yes, that's correct. Alright, so any questions at all? Alright, good. So today we're going to focus on one more thing with focus words and that is time words that we use with them. Now, when you hear the word time words what do you think of?

124   Student: [gives answer]

125   R: Sorry?

126   Student: [gives answer]

127   R: Yeah, so today, tomorrow.

128   Student: [gives answer]

129   R: Yeah, so any words that describe time. So why do you think these types of words are really important when you're using perfect verbs?

130   Student: [gives answer]

131   R: Yeah, these time words, why do you think we have to use them with perfect verbs? Why are they so important?

132   Student: [gives answer]

133   R: Yeah, so we can mention specific time. But it's because we need to show that there is two points of connection between time, right? So in many cases, without these time words, the meaning of the verb is not exactly clear. Ok? So there's a lot of different time words that you can use. And today, what you're going to do is I'm going to give you a handout with all the most common time words that we use with perfect verbs. And I want you to try to use them with the different verb tenses, ok? So in some cases, certain time words only work with the past perfect or present perfect or future perfect. So I want you guys to try and figure it out, see if you can find any patterns, and of course in your textbook there are some charts, but I want you to try it without the textbook first so you can see if you know these time words and how they're used and if you can figure out which verb tense they work with. Ok, so I'll hand out a copy to you guys. And you can work together in pairs, so this way it can save you some time, but it's kind of a mix and match type thing. See if you can figure out which time words match up with which verb tense. [pause]

134   R: Alright, so yeah, work together in pairs, with a friend. If you don't have friends, make one. Ok. Um, and I want this to be interactive as well, ok? So this way you can help each other figure out the answers. I'm not collecting this. It's for your own purpose. And once again, try not to use your book, ok? [pause]

135   Student: Can I use the same time word more than one time?

136   R: Um, you can, but try to use as many different ones as you can. [pause]

137   R: One other thing, try not to use the same time word more than one time with one verb tense. So for example... actually I'll explain this a little more clearly. You'll see there is space for present perfect, present perfect progressive, past perfect and past perfect progressive, and then future perfect. So I want you guys to write sentences using those verbs, but adding in one of these time words. So try to use as many different time words as you can and then at the end here there are spaces to use the time words that you didn't use. So you need to try and use as many of these as you can to see if you can use them. And if you're not sure after you're finished, refer back to the textbook and see if it's correct and if you have any questions, just raise your hand. [pause]

138   R: Oh, and one more thing. Speak English, ok? [pause]

139   R: And since this practice, it's not a quiz or a test, if you want me to check to see if your answer is correct, just raise your hand and I'll come help you out. [pause]

140   R: By the way, if you're not sure what the verb would look like in the perfect tenses, right, so with the perfect verb tenses we use a form of have with the past participle. So in your books on pages 411 to 414, there's a list of all the irregular verbs and what the form would look like. So if you ever have questions about what the verb form would look like, just turn to those pages and check it out there. [pause]

141   Student: [asks question, unintelligible]

142   R: For the progressive?

143   Student: [gives answer]

144   R: Well, why don't you try it. Why don't we change this to the progressive.

145   Student: [gives answer]

146   R: Ok, so what do you think?

147   Student: [gives answer]

148   R: A period of time, yeah. Exactly. So if you would add the word studying in here, I've been studying in Canada for one year, then you have the present perfect progressive. Yeah, so it can be used with.

149   Student: [asks another question]

150   R: Yeah, but try and use as many different words as you can rather than just the same one.

151   Student: [asks another question]

152   R: Yeah. [pause]

153   R/Students: [conversation about the new iPhone 6 Plus] [pause]

154   R: Any questions about anything guys?

155   Student: [asks question]

156   R: Sorry?

157   Student: [asks question about placement of time word]

158   R: Yeah, you can add it at the end or at the beginning too.

159   Student: Thank you.

160   R: Yeah, no problem. [pause]

161   Student: [asks question]

162   R: Yeah, barely and yet are used similarly. Barely is an adverb, so it would come before the verb.

163   Student: Thank you.

164   R: You're welcome [pause]

165   R: Any questions over here?

166   Student: [mixed answers]

167   R: Yeah?

168   Student: [asks question about meaning of time word]

169   R: So thus far means up to now. And by then means by a specific point in time.

170   Student: [asks follow-up question]

171   R: Not after. So like, here's our point in time. By then something will have happened. Yeah, thus far means up to now. By then, by a specific time in the future or in the past. [pause]

172   R: Any questions over here?

173   Student: [asks question about meaning of time word]

174   R: Ah, up to now means by now. So far...

175   Student: [gives answer]

176   R: Yeah. By then refers to a specific point in time in the future or in the past. Here's our point in time and some action will happen by then. [pause]

177   R: Any question, Jim?

178   Student: [asks question]

179   R: Ok, um, what do you think?

180   Student: [gives answer]

181   R: Uh, I have eaten my dinner by that time. Oh sorry, not the present perfect. That refers to the past, past perfect.

182   Student: [asks question]

183   R: The past perfect? Yeah.

184   Student: [asks question]

185   R: They're a little bit different. By that time refers to the past. By the time refers to the future. Yeah. [pause]

186   Student: [asks question about one of his answers]

187   R: Yeah, Rudy. Yeah, we have been in Phoenix lately. Yeah, that makes sense. Yeah. [pause]

188   Student: [asks question]

189   R: Yeah, you can make that negative, too. For example, I haven't been feeling well lately. Yeah.

190   Student: Up to now?

191   R: I haven't been feeling well up to now? Yeah, you could, but that sounds kind of awkward. I'm trying to think about why… You would use that to refer to if something started until now. It would be like, so imagine if you took a trip to Cuba and then four days into your trip I haven't been feeling good so far. While I've been on vacation. Or, if you came to Canada and then three months in, oh I haven't been eating well so far since I came to Canada. So it's kind of like up to that point in time.

192   Student: Ok, thank you.

193   R: Yeah. [pause]

194   R: Any question about anything?

195   Student: No.

196   R: Do you guys have any questions?

197   Students: No.

198   R: No? Alright. [pause]

199   R: Do you have any questions?

200   Student: No, not yet.

201   R: Not yet? Alright.

202   Student: [asks question]

203   R: Um, not all of these. So probably a lot of these will work with the present perfect progressive.

204   Student: [asks another question]

205   R: Yeah, that makes sense. [pause]

206   R/Students: [discussion about spinning pencil on fingers] [pause]

207   R: You guys have any other questions?

208   Students: No.

209   R: Alright. [pause]

210   R: Do you have any questions about anything?

211   Student: [asks question]

212   R: Ok, why doesn't that make sense.

213   Student: [gives answer]

214   R: It's correct. It kind of depends on the context. So if you would say I haven't been cooking much lately, that's correct. Or I haven't cooked much lately because I've been so busy.

215   Student: [asks follow up question]

216   R: I haven't cooked lately? That makes sense too. Like why do you eat at McDonald's every day? Oh, because I've been so busy. Right? Or I haven't

been studying much because I've been playing too many video games. Right? So it often depends on context.

217   Student: [asks another question]

218   R: No, that one doesn't work.

219   Student: Why?

220   R: Because at that point you're looking towards the future.

221   Student: Oh yeah.

222   R: Right? So if you say haven't been cooking, that's now.

223   Student: Yeah, yeah.

224   R: Any more questions?

225   Student: [asks to check answer]

226   R: I've been waiting for the midterm mark since last week? Yeah, that's perfect. The teacher had come... hmmm, that one doesn't work.

227   Student: [asks why]

228   R: Well, what are you trying to say here?

229   Student: [gives response]

230   R: Oh, ok. So in that case the time doesn't work with when. So you can say when the teacher, um, after we had become quiet. So you can fix this. The teacher had come when we become quiet.

231   Student: [asks question]

232   R: Um, sometimes. But it's not always the case. So I can use when. I can say I had studied a lot when I came to school. That works. So really, the verb where the action came first, that one always needs the past perfect.

233   Student: Thanks.

234   R: No problem. [pause]

235   Student: [asks question about answer]

236   R: What do you mean by that?

237   Student: [gives answer trying to explain]

238   R: No, because the time doesn't work. You have to use present perfect. Also, the verb be doesn't really work in the present perfect. It's not very commonly used in that form [pause]

239   Student: [asks question about time word]

240   R: No, after doesn't work with this one.

241   Student: which ones?

242   R: With the present perfect. So after, that one we can only use with the past perfect verbs.

243   Student: Oh.

244   R: Everything going ok? Not too confused?

245   Student: [gives answer]

246   R: Any more questions?

247   Student: [asks question]

248   R: Yes. Yeah. [pause]

249   R: Alright, so as you probably notice, there's some homework for tonight. There's four exercises that you should do that are connected to time words. Ok? Also, on your handout I've given you the page numbers where your textbook talks about time words. So if you're not sure about something, just refer to those pages. And then, there's also two exercises that I would like you to do. You don't have to if you don't want to. These are two exercises that use all the verbs we've talked about. So if you want to test yourself to see how well you can use all English verbs in one place, there's two exercises there. So that's it for today. We'll take up this exercise at the beginning of class tomorrow and then we'll have a little in-class assignment that we'll work on. Ok? Any questions?

250   Student: No!

251   R: Ok, enjoy your day.

ROGER REFLECTS

Roger said after the last class (Transcript 3) that he was very happy with the way the lesson went and that he noticed that all his students were active. He accredited this to change of delivery mode he decided before the class to make it more interactive. He said that he was also happy that they asked lots of questions and good questions at that. Roger said, "Now that I look back on the last three days [as in Transcripts 1, 2 and 3], I see the value in changing up the lesson in terms of how it's carried out and what types of activities we do. I think the students value a change as well." Roger said that if he had a chance to redo each of the lessons again, he would have been more interactive throughout each and not have so many what he called "formal activities." In other words, Roger said his lessons were too academic for the students and so he wanted more "social type lessons" that were less formal.

Roger also said that he noticed that he had too many PowerPoint slides and that he would need to edit them more if he was teaching the same level again to break up his delivery to get his students to "stop and think" more. So, Roger said that after looking at the transcripts and after reflecting on his own teaching he realizes that he has been teaching too many things the same without thinking much about it. He said, "I've been doing too much of the same thing, you know. Recently it hasn't been working so well, so as a result I should be trying to change it up." Roger said that he was [after those three observations] trying to mix things up in his teaching and changed his plans as a result. Roger gave the following example:

This past week we were doing modals, even then I changed what I had planned. We were going to do a jigsaw type activity where each student was responsible for a certain meaning of a modal or whatever. They were responsible for looking it up, knowing what it means, giving some examples, and then they share it with each other. But I noticed on Monday or Tuesday that this class already has a really good grasp on using modals, or at least they know them really well. So, I had to change it so that they would be doing something where they just use them and not so much focused on trying to learn them. So, that's what I ended up doing was having an activity that focuses completely on use.

Roger said that he gave them a scenario that they had to use these grammar modals in groups with other students, and he said that he thinks it went very well. He also said that for the first time during his third year he did not use any PowerPoints because he had become too dependent on them for his whole lesson, and he realized that they did not ensure any interaction among his students. Roger said that he had not realized that he had allowed himself to "slide into a routine" and although he was vaguely aware of this and did not consciously want to be in a routine, he nevertheless conceded "sometimes it's easier. It's cushy. You're in a pattern and you don't have to think much."

Reflective Break

- At the beginning of the reflection period in his third year before the classroom observations, Roger said that he had "created habits/routines in how I teach grammar based on what works". Do you think this would be typical behavior for teachers in their third year because of their teaching experiences?
- What did you notice first when you read each of Roger's three transcripts above?
- How would you interpret each transcript in terms of his students' learning?
- Why do you think Roger mainly used PowerPoint slides to deliver his grammar lessons?
- Do you think his mode of delivery was effective? Use evidence for or against from the transcripts.
- Why do you think Roger himself perceived his second observed lesson (Transcript 2) "pretty boring"?
- What do you think of Roger's reflections on his transcripts directly after teaching each lesson and his overall reflections at the end?
- Each of Roger's three lessons had a different grammatical focus. How would you teach each of these and why?

- As in Chapter 6, if you do teach each of these three grammatical items, record you class and write transcripts of any aspect of these lessons you are interested in and then analyze them. Compare them to Roger's transcripts above for similarities and differences.

CONCLUSION

This chapter outlined and discussed Roger's actual classroom practice during his third year with detailed examples of three recordings and transcripts of three grammar lessons he planned during a "grammar week" he had designed. The chapter also includes Roger's reflections on these lessons directly after teaching each, as well his overall reaction after reading the transcripts. As a result of his reflections, Roger began to notice that he tended to follow routine in all his lessons and his preferred mode of delivery was with PowerPoint slides with lots of grammar information on each slide. Roger said that although he thought this was a good way of delivering what he called the "content" of grammar, such a way of teaching "seemed boring" even to him. As a result he said he would change his mode of delivery to develop more interactive lessons with fewer slides, if any. The chapter that follows outlines Roger's reflections in his third year beyond practice.

Chapter 13

Reflecting on Third Year Beyond Practice

INTRODUCTION

Chapter 7 presented Roger's reflections beyond practice, which explored his emotions both inside and outside the classroom. This chapter presents Roger's emotions on all aspects of his practice during his third year of teaching. Indeed, even for many seasoned teachers, the act of teaching can be stressful because of severe hectic pace, or the "hot action" (York-Barr et al., 2006: 2), which they are constantly involved in throughout each day of each term. At the center of this "hot action" is a person-as-teacher rather than a mechanical robot; and it is impossible to separate the person-as-teacher from the act of teaching because emotions constitute a fundamental dimension of teaching and of being a teacher (Kelchtermans & Deketelaere, 2016). As Teng (2017: 118) points out, "emotions are part of the very fabric that constitutes the teacher's self." Thus, it is not surprising, given such a hectic pace where teachers must juggle various multiple tasks while making thousands of different on-the-spot decisions each day, that the risk of burnout because of emotional and physical exhaustion is very real (Byrne, 1999). As in Chapter 7, I analyzed Roger's reflections during his third year for affective language using White's (2000) approach which includes examining the data for *adverbials*: "happily", "angrily", "fearfully", "proudly"; *attributes*: "I'm <u>sad</u>". "He's <u>frightened</u> of spiders"; *nominals*: "His <u>fear</u> was obvious to all"; and *verbs*: "This pleases me". "I hate chocolate". Thus, by applying the above categories of affect to the linguistic expressions which appeared in Roger's reflections, a deeper scrutiny of his use of affective language was possible during his third year of teaching.

ROGER'S EXPRESSED EMOTIONS THIRD YEAR

A scan of all the data related to Roger's reflections during his third year revealed his experience of teaching involved negative emotions for the most part that included his main feelings such as "bored", "drained", "not excited", "exhausted", "frustrated", and "jaded". I note that *bored/not excited* could be put together as can *drained/exhausted/jaded* which leaves three main groups including *frustrated*.

Bored/Not Excited

From the very first meeting to set up the reflective process for his third year, Roger articulated a whole relay of mostly negative emotions, in which he expressed a lack of excitement because he had just finished a short summer semester. In fact, when we set up this new reflection period for his third year proper, it was the emotional distress of that previous summer term that triggered Roger to want to engage in a set of further reflections to get him out of what he called a "slump".

Roger said that he felt "bored" with teaching as a result of the whole experience of being with "terrible students" and that he worried somewhat that he was not excited to begin the new semester that was to start his third year of teaching proper. Roger said that he realized that students change with the changing semesters and years and that "you have an ever-evolving audience, I mean, one class to the next your students are different, even from one semester to the next obviously you have different students, so you got to target them in different ways." However, even with this realization Roger said that he did not feel any excitement towards teaching because he had had such a "a class full of duds" during that summer term. Roger said that for him it got so bad that he felt like he was "talking to a bunch of rocks" because there was no interaction whatsoever in his lessons. In addition, he said that when he "went into the classroom after a few weeks of having them, I was not looking forward to it whatsoever because I knew exactly what was coming, which was nothing from them, but yeah I found myself thinking is this class almost over yet."

We met by chance one day and I asked him how it was going. Roger said that, because it was his worst semester so far, he would like to reflect on that bad experience as well as enter new reflections for the coming semester of his third-year teaching. Roger mentioned at the time that when he was beginning to get ready to start the fall semester of his third year, he worried about what might occur if he were to encounter such a class again, or have similar experiences – and what he would do about them. Roger remarked that his negative experiences from the previous summer term "are still lingering, and although I don't have a fear that'll happen again, but I'm kind of worried, what if that would happen again this term to the students I have now, how would I deal with that back-to-back, you know." Hence, Roger said that he was happy to meet me to engage in more detailed reflections (of course I should note here that I was also happy to facilitate his reflections as I could also learn more about the lived experiences of a teacher in his third year of teaching and compare these to what the *same* teacher had experienced during his first year of teaching). As Roger reflected, "I said to myself, like listen, I can't do this again where I just go in with an attitude of like, well, whatever, who cares, right? Because that's not fair to the student and for me either, uh neither, I mean, I have a level of professionalism I have to maintain as well."

Thus, during the first few meetings during the fall semester of his third-year teaching, Roger focused on explaining some of his negative experiences of the previous semester and how he intended to avoid having such a negative attitude. He decided that he would have to structure his classes "in a way that forces them to have to talk, to have to interact with each other. And I would just be a lot more strict than I normally am, which I don't normally like wearing the strict hat, but, if it comes down to that..."

Roger added that he was not excited because of the administration. He knows that he must continue working with them, and some of their unreasonable, added, hidden working hours. Roger recounted that the previous semester he "worked most weeks 35–40 hours, instead of the 30 I get paid for, right? If not more than that. So that, you know, that was always in the back of my mind where I'm like, ugh, I'm working for free right now." This made Roger feel "even less excitement" for the coming fall semester if he had to maintain such a work week and he could not look forward to any work–life balance. Roger, said that he had realized this over the past few years and that he now had to "structure my working hours carefully for myself so that I maximize my efficiency, and I don't have to play catch-up at other times if I go home early as I did previous semesters, right?" He realized that he usually took his marking of essays home with him before, but he will try to avoid this in the future.

Roger said that his loss of excitement for the fall semester was also most likely related to the working environment the past few years that he said was becoming more high pressure and he said that this pressure was "trickling down to me." All of this, Roger noted, has forced him to plan more carefully because the institution now wants to standardize more tests within levels and so all the teachers must do the same types of assignments, and the same number of assignments and he said that this limits what he can do. Roger said that "whereas before, a couple years ago, where there wasn't such a heavy focus on being standardized, we were able to be a little more creative in how we would test our students, or what types of assignments we would have." As a result, Roger was not feeling any excitement with all the new planning he was faced with for the new fall semester. He continued, "I have days like that where I know it's something that's not necessarily exciting to do or to learn, because, you know, if you're teaching grammar sometimes it's just not exciting." Roger said that before this he liked teaching grammar. But now, in his third year, he said, "if there's no interaction happening in the classroom between students, between teachers and students, it's tough to feel excited too." Roger attributed his lack of interest in teaching to his students' lack of interest in the subject and this has grown a lot since his first year. Roger said, "recently I find it's kind of increased a bit where I'm not as interested sometimes because the students aren't. Or they don't appear to be."

In fact, Roger attributed his lack of excitement most to his issues with where he was working and how the atmosphere there was becoming difficult with "the management." Roger continued, "over the last couple years there's been, I don't know, a certain amount of bullcrap to work with from various levels of, you know colleagues, coordinators, management." As a result, Roger said that he has decide "sit back" and not get involved and "make your own little world that works for you and make sure you're still doing what you're supposed to be doing, but sometimes if you involve less people, it just simplifies things." Roger said that he only voices his opinion about issues he really feels strongly about, but that mostly he just does his own thing.

Roger gave an example of an issue he did feel strongly about that occurred the previous semester concerning his teaching of speaking to high level proficiency speakers of English. Roger noted that one of the assignments in that course was that, over the course of that term, the students were supposed to reflect on their assignments by submitting a portfolio at the end with all their reflections on what they had learned. The problem, as far as Roger was concerned, was that the portfolio was a written assignment which he pointed out "probably amounted to 800 to 1000 words, which is a lot for an ESL student in a speaking class." Roger said he realized this was not a good idea because he was also teaching the same high level writing class at the same time and they were required to write a major research essay as well as their other classes with written assignments. Roger said he did not believe in using written portfolios for this assignment, so he decided to interview them instead. Roger continued,

> Imagine that a speaking class, you ask them to vocalize what they learned, right? So followed pretty much the same parameters, they had to choose presentations, assignments, quizzes, whatever, and I'd ask them questions like what you learned, how did this help you improve your speaking, what were some of the negatives, and so on, and to me that just made sense.

Later Roger said he mentioned this to a supervisor and although the supervisor said he thought it was a great idea, nevertheless because all the other classes required a written portfolio, then he should too. Roger said he just continued doing what he had decided regardless of any complaints that might be voiced (there were none).

That experience along with others during the previous term and even years led Roger to feel little excitement with the coming fall term and this lasted well into the third year to the point that he was worried his whole approach to teaching was impacted. Roger said that even well into the fall semester, he was still not feeling excited. Roger remarked, "I'm still in that mindset that when I get to class, this will happen, based on what happened last term. It had a pretty big impact on me, for sure." Roger said that in order to motivate himself, he would continuously remind himself that this was a different term with different classes: "when I go to class, I have to keep on telling myself, you know, this is a different group of students, they are better, and I have to treat them better than I did last term." The previous term Roger said that he got so bored with his students that he actually "gave up on trying to make my classes interesting."

Roger gave an example of this when he noted he changed his teaching pattern at the time so that he was not putting as much effort into such lessons. Roger remarked, "If I'm standing there teaching things that I think are important and they're not really reacting to it in any way, that's kind of boring and I just want to say let's just get on with it. If you guys don't want to participate, I'll just give you some work to do." In such a manner, he would pull back from direct instruction as he did not want to go through the motions of teaching. As a result, Roger said he noticed he had created "routines in grammar based on the past and what works." These routines included presenting his "PowerPoint for fifteen minutes, go over the rules, an example of everything, make sure that they understand it, and then from there, practice."

Drained/Exhausted/Jaded

Most of Roger's expressed feelings above – of not being excited, and even bored – stemmed largely from being "drained", "exhausted" and/or "jaded" from the previous term. This meant that he felt that he had to get away, even if only for a few days, before the fall semester. Roger remarked,

> ... I just wanted to do physical work, mindless work. I wanted to go on vacation because my mind was fried. It was draining, marking these essays that didn't make sense, that were full of grammar mistakes that shouldn't have been made, it was just, you know, and repeated over and over, they were making the same mistakes and stuff, so you know it was draining.

Then, when beginning the fall semester, Roger realized that he was still exhausted mentally because of his experiences and that he did not have enough time to recover really. Roger said that he was "so jaded after last term that even at the start of this term, I was still exhausted and the first two weeks, the students are generally a little quieter, and I was like oh, no, my students are quiet again, without even thinking about why they were quiet." Then Roger began to reflect on his students this term because the previous term they were so inactive, and how after two weeks he noticed that he is "spending a lot more energy in finding ways to get my students to become more active, but it's kind of draining in some senses."

Thus, Roger began his third year teaching still drained from his previous term experiences with what he called inactive students and as a result said he was determined to try not to become negative about his students' quietness this fall term and so he wanted to "try and get back to where I was in terms of my level of enthusiasm" (most likely to when we first met during his first year of teaching). As the third year progressed Roger found himself changing a lot of his teaching methods and activities because he realized that he was "still jaded at the beginning of the term and then once I had a class full of quiet students again, I was like uuuhhh… not this again and I just set the bar low." So he wanted to make sure that he was on top of his negative feelings and emotions throughout the fall term of his third year of teaching. As Roger remarked, "as the term went on, I realized there were a lot of things I should be doing, things I can't do, can do, and need to do, so my approach, my attitude, how I treat them, those changed."

Frustrated

Another negative emotion that Roger frequently expressed during his third year was that of frustration, mostly related to his students' lack of motivation and his exasperation with the institution where he worked. Regarding his students, Roger said that although, as a teacher, he knows that they need to learn English to transfer into the university, they do not always see this – mostly because they are what he describes as "adult/ young teenagers who mostly act like teenagers who are not quite sure what they are doing or why they are doing things." Roger said that they know that they have to learn English, but "they don't necessarily know why. Or for what purpose."

Roger said that he gets frustrated with them and this in turn makes him not enjoy what he is doing. Roger continued, "So for me, if I don't enjoy what I'm doing, then I won't impact people the same way, so for me, I enjoy what I do because I can see results." Roger noted that in the previous semester he was so frustrated with the whole process and his students because he did not see any results from his teaching. Roger noted that, as a teacher, he has a responsibility that his students are "equipped" to go up to the next proficiency level in his institution. However, he also notes that sometimes this is difficult and "a little frustrating because they are not always eager to make sure that they get there too." Roger said it is frustrating because there is only so much he can do but that they must take some responsibility for their own learning. Roger continued, "if they don't take their own responsibility for learning, that's the frustrating part."

Roger also said he was frustrated with the institution that was affiliated with a university in which he worked because they treated it like a business and not an educational environment. Roger asked how they can "balance a good quality education with a successful business model?" because he realized, after his second year and into his third year, that the institution was "focusing too much on the business aspect and the actual learning and teaching is not being attended to so well." Roger connected this frustration to his expressed frustrations with his students above because he said the result of such a focus on business is "get crappy students with crappy curriculum because they are not focusing enough time on improving what we have." Roger said that he was not the only one to notice this decline as some told him that they were getting "a little bit of a bad name" as a result.

For example, in all his time there he said he never had an official professional development day or conversation as instructors with other instructors, and especially nothing with the management of the institution. This is ironic because at the same time the management were asking the instructors to help them "and talk about how we can make our students happier." Roger realized that he had a solution, but he did not raise it with management: "you know, for a lot of teachers, it's an easy fix. Just turn on the passion again, turn on the light. Show the students you're there and you care. But you can't really say that, can you?"

Part of his reason for not saying anything was his expressed frustrations with trying to work with his immediate supervisors as he said they did not really care to listen to his ideas. For example, for one of his classes he created what he considers a really creative mid-term examination for a listening/speaking class and wanted to share it with them, but they did not care: "It's frustrating sometimes because I created a creative and when I asked them to look, they just give this crappy little answer, like 'oh, just make sure you focus on listening and incorporate speaking.'" So, he decided to send it to them anyway, but he never heard back from them about it. His frustrations with these supervisors extended to other projects as well such as implementing new curriculum ideas that they come up with as they did not explain what the teachers should do or, as Roger stated, "but actually implementing it in the classroom, it seems like it's half-baked. There's been a lot of half-baked ideas that got sent our way and then we just have to somehow interpret it and then implement it, but when you're standardizing it, it becomes tricky."

Roger said he got so frustrated with them because he realized that they really did not know what his students were and were not capable of doing and, indeed, Roger was incredulous when he noticed they "seemed shocked that my students might have difficulty with that [new curriculum initiative]. As a result, Roger said that this was "just another reason why I don't really feel like collaborating or working with people. If the people who are running and supposed to be organizing it don't really know what's going on, then why even bother?" Hence, Roger realized that he should just come up with his own things because he said "it's just frustrating in certain ways." So, Roger decided that during his third year the only way he would ask his supervisors for any assistance was if he was not sure about some assignment but, regardless, he also knows that he will "still have to adapt it a bit because of the group of students that I'm teaching right now."

Reflective Break

- Why do you think Roger felt *bored/not excited*, *drained/exhausted/jaded* and *frustrated* during his third year of teaching?
- For each of these three groups, did you have any similar negative feelings as your teaching career progressed? If yes, give examples.
- After reading about Roger's expressed negative emotions, try to note any other negative emotions while teaching *after* you first year and compare them to Roger's emotions as expressed in this chapter.
- Can you point to how your negative emotions affect:
  - ▶ your use of English when teaching English?
  - ▶ your interaction with students?
  - ▶ your response to unanticipated classroom incidents?
  - ▶ the extent to which you make use of particular methods or activities?
  - ▶ the kind of feedback you provide?
  - ▶ the level of satisfaction about your career choice as an ESL/EFL teacher?
- Do you think any of the above six items were impacted by Roger's negative emotions in his third year of teaching? If so, which ones and how were they impacted?

CONCLUSION

This chapter outlined and discussed Roger's expressed emotions during his third-year teaching.

The findings reveal the three main groups of negative emotions he experienced, such as *bored/not excited*, *drained/exhausted/jaded*, and *frustrated*. These are all negative feelings that Roger lived with during his third year for the most part, and if unexpressed may have prevented him from accomplishing his goals throughout his career as an ESL teacher. Roger himself realized that he was expressing such negative emotions only after reading the entire transcripts of each meeting we had during that third year. Roger was not excited and even bored with his teaching and the thoughts of teaching through another semester because he was jaded, exhausted and drained from a previous term's negative experiences. He was also frustrated with his students as a result of the negative term where he perceived them as totally inactive. He was also frustrated with the lack of support and interaction from his institution and its management and supervisors. However, rather than giving up, Roger decided to enter into more intense reflections throughout his third year which resulted in his realization that he must begin to change things so that he could thrive throughout his career and not just survive it. The chapter that follows gives an overall appraisal of Roger's third year as an ESL teacher.

Chapter 14

Analyzing the Third Year

INTRODUCTION

The previous five chapters outlined and discussed Roger's third year reflections on his philosophy (Chapter 9), his principles (Chapter 10), his theory (Chapter 11), his practice (Chapter 12), and his reflections beyond practice (Chapter 13). This chapter summarizes some of the important findings from all these reflections so that we can portray an overall image of Roger that illustrates his lived experiences during his third year of teaching. The chapter also outlines Roger's own reflections on what he has learned during his third year of teaching.

THIRD YEAR REFLECTING FROM PHILOSOPHY TO BEYOND PRACTICE

In this section I provide a summary of Roger's major reflections on his philosophy, principles, theory, practice and beyond practice during his third year of teaching in the same institution.

Philosophy

In reflecting on his philosophy during his third year, Roger identified the predominant professional roles he took on, in order of their frequency, as *engager, pedagogical and language expert, individual* and *didactic*. During this third year of teaching, Roger noted that he took on the role of engager, identifying the need to create more exciting lessons that would be valuable for his students. Roger added that such engagement provided an incentive for his students to put more effort into their learning, because he wanted them to take more responsibility for their own learning rather than relying on him all the time. In fact, this most frequently identified role of engager was directed at his students from the very beginning of the semester of his third year because he had had such negative experiences with students in a short summer course prior to this semester and, as he noted, he did not "have much time to recover." Thus, he continuously pointed to (and at) his students' lack of effort and how this had negatively impacted his teaching throughout his third year until he finally got a hold on it towards the end of the year through his reflections. Such negative experiences left Roger practically lifeless in terms of planning his lessons and activities, not to mention his self-confessed lack of energy executing his lessons, which made him realize that he would need to engage more with the whole teaching process.

The next most frequent professional role that Roger identified throughout his third year – either explicitly or implicitly – is that of pedagogical expert. Similar to the definition of this role as outlined in Chapter 3, as he noted during his first year of teaching, is his sense of confidence in his knowledge as a language expert and his confidence in how he can measure his students' needs, but also the further development of his pedagogical expertise from his experiences over the past few years. Roger said that his pedagogical and language expertise is now not only the result of his initial training (although he acknowledged that he relied much less on this as the years progressed), but also his continued reading of research which he said generally informs his practices. In addition, Roger noted that he has gained a lot of new knowledge from his teaching experiences on "what actually works" for him in the classroom over these past three years rather than what he learned in his MA program, which now seems limiting for him. However, Roger also noted his frustration with the administration of the institution in which he teaches as he noted they did not care much about his expertise. Indeed, although Roger said that he was willing to share it with the other teachers, they did not seem to have any avenue (such as professional development days or the like) or any intent to provide such avenues for other teachers to share their knowledge as well.

The next most frequent professional role that Roger identified throughout his third year – either explicitly or implicitly – is that of an individual; the definition of which is similar to that which was identified in his first year. Every teacher is different and has different styles, methods, preferences, and choices in regard to how they go about teaching; values freedom in follow one's own way, discovering what works best for that person. One reason Roger said that he had embraced this individual professional identity role during his third year was because of the lack of clear instructions from the administration and supervisors in the institution in which he worked. He again became so frustrated that he stopped trying to figure out what they "wanted" him to do, and just did what he "wanted" to do. This was particularly true when it came to assessments, as the institution's required methods of assessment were not suitable for his courses, according to Roger, so he ended up making his own assessments to show what "his students" were learning. So, as the third year progressed, Roger acknowledged that he no longer followed many of the directions that "came down from the administration" and followed his own path. However, Roger said he was not always comfortable with this decision because he usually likes working in collaboration – not in isolation, which is as he said he feels he was in his third year. As a result, Roger noted that he may have created "a shell" around himself which added to his sense of individualism.

Another professional identity role that emerged for Roger during his third year as a teacher was that of being "didactic", or moralistic to his students. This was a similar role for Roger in his first year and was for when he was telling his students about what is right and wrong (such as plagiarism), what is or should be appropriate behavior in a multi-cultural environment, as well as appropriate behavior in an academic setting, and how to acculturate to the local cultural and academic setting. In contrast to this role in his first year, however, Roger saw himself telling his students more about what not to do in his lessons in terms of learning and then what they should be doing. Roger acknowledged that a lot of these "didactics" probably emanated from his negative experiences in the summer before his third year officially began. Roger said that he feels like a personal fitness trainer who tries to push students by explaining why they need to learn something and how they should learn this. He said he let up during the summer semester of his third year and "did not push them as much as he should" because he said he was having a "bad term with a bad class who did not care much." Now, on reflection, Roger said that he will be "stricter than I normally am in the next semester" although he does not like this.

Reflective Break

- Looking again at the four identity roles (*engager, pedagogical and language expert, individual* and *didactic*) that Roger (either explicitly or implicitly or both) took on during his third year, which of these identity roles would you take on and why?
- Comment on their frequency. Would you rank them similarly? Why, or why not?
- Which identity roles would you not take on and why?
- Do you think any of these roles are opposite (e.g., "engager" and "didactic") to each other in the light of Roger's experiences?
- Can you think of any identity roles that third year teachers might take on that could clash without their realizing such a possibility?
- List any identity roles you think Roger missed during his third year of teaching.

Principles

Roger's reflections on his principles during his third year indicate that his most frequently stated beliefs were related to his students' approaches to learning, the teaching and learning of grammar, vocabulary, how he approached group work, and lesson planning, and his ideas about his role as an ESL teacher. His negative beliefs about his students' work ethic emanated mostly from his experience in the previous summer semester: "I had a class full of duds. And it was like talking to a bunch of rocks. That's how much they interacted with each other, with me. It was awful." Thus, he said, he tried to focus his instruction in more engaging ways to avoid such negative experiences. His beliefs relating to his students throughout his third year seemed to be based on the worry that he would be put in the same situation with a similar group of students and "how would I deal with that back-to-back." I am not sure that Roger was ever able to shed his negative beliefs about his students' work ethic and perhaps he was correct that he probably needed a more extended break beyond the two weeks he had between his summer term and his official start to the third year.

Regarding the sources of these beliefs, Roger identified in order of their frequency as follows: his personality, research-based practices, established practice, approaches and methods, his own teaching experiences as well as what works best (or does not work) for him. Roger seemed to be reflecting internally throughout this third year to determine what would best suit his teaching style rather than what his students really needed and did not look back at what he learned in his initial training program. This retreat into himself shaped his stated beliefs related to teaching the skills mentioned above and how he planned (or did not plan in many instances) his lessons during his third year. Towards the end of this third year Roger noted that he no longer had any role model for teaching in mind, and further stated that "there aren't many people who I know that would represent or epitomize the ultimate role model of whatever it is." As such he says he believes in himself and his personality as a teacher to direct his lessons. What emerges related to Roger's principles is a teacher with more experiences in the classroom, not all of which are positive. As such, Roger seems to have retreated somewhat into himself, and began to rely more on his personality traits to get him through his lessons rather than his knowledge of the different approaches or methods on which he had relied during his first year as a teacher. Roger's difficult summer semester prior to officially beginning his third year may have impacted his principles of what guides him as an ESL teacher during his third year.

Theory

Roger reflected on his theory during his third year and again mostly about how he planned his lessons but also how he dealt with some interesting critical incidents. Roger noted that during his third year of teaching at the same institution he was required to follow a syllabus and use textbooks more than during his first years. This was especially true in the instance where the institution's planned assignments for his high-level speaking course were totally inadequate for his students' needs and these would have been a huge burden for his students in terms of their work load. Roger mentioned that the required written portfolio of his students' experiences in his speaking class were counterintuitive to a speaking class because they also had other written assignments with him in his writing classes. Thus, Roger had to re-plan everything and even added to his own workload by interviewing each student about the contents of their portfolio instead. Roger noted that his type of pre-planning was for the benefit of his students as he said he always puts them first. In terms of planning for teaching specific skills, Roger said he always prefers to plan for and teach grammar because it is more of a content type course rather than the other skills he is teaching.

In addition, during his reflection on his theory during his third year of teaching, Roger detailed a critical incident about one course he was teaching where the students were not engaged throughout the whole 14-week semester and how this was impacting Roger's planning and execution of his lessons adversely. Roger ended up writing about this incident each week (see Chapter 11 for the details) and, after reflecting on what he called "this long and torturous critical incident", he said he did all he could to engage his students more. But, after a lot of effort the first weeks, he gave up. As Roger unfortunately noted, "they were simply not capable of doing good work or of even doing advanced level writing." This incident again made Roger reflect on the fact that there are no easy or simple solutions to the complexity of teaching students from a different cultural background, regardless of how many years teaching experience one has.

Practice

Roger's actual classroom practice during his third year focused on one week ("grammar week") and detailed examples of three recordings and transcripts of three grammar lessons he taught. Roger again noted that he likes to teach grammar most because (and as noted above) he sees it as a content course which is most like university type courses that his students will have to experience soon when they graduate from his institution. Thus, he said, he teaches this grammar course in a lecture-seminar manner where he gives a lecture on a grammar point through the medium of PowerPoint slides with the details of the item on each slide. When observed teaching all three grammar classes as well as analyzing the transcripts, Roger takes on this role by providing information in lecture format while also asking related questions in intervals following a typical IRE (Initiation, Response, Evaluation) classroom communication format thus showing that he controls the floor much like a professor in a lecture. Roger also provides some textbook activities for his students to complete in each of the classes.

Roger then reflected on all three lessons that were audio/video recorded and later transcribed and said that, overall, he noticed that these lessons "seemed boring" to him because it looked as if everything was following a routine. He also noted that his PowerPoint slides were loaded up with too much content but that he was happy just to lecture this content to his students in such a routine manner that he wondered if they too were bored. Although he said that he thinks the lessons were successful in terms of what he wanted to teach and what he thinks his students learned based on their participation as noted on the transcripts, he also worried that he was slipping into too much of a routine way of teaching. Roger said he did not realize this until he dialogued with me as the facilitator after these lessons. In fact, Roger said that he looks as if he is into the teaching of grammar while on video but now he wonders if he was faking it a bit by just blindly following his PowerPoint slides while teaching.

Beyond Practice

When reflecting beyond practice, I again chose to focus on Roger's expressed emotions during his third year of teaching, as with his first year of teaching, through the use of the Appraisal Framework which explores the language for expressing attitudes such as affect, to refer to language used for expressing emotions. Thus, by applying analysis of affect to the linguistic expressions which appeared in Roger's reflections during his third year, a deeper scrutiny of his use of affective language was possible. For the most part, Roger seemed to express mostly negative emotions with the three most frequently found in all the data being his use of *bored/not excited*, *drained/exhausted/jaded*, and *frustrated*.

From the very first meeting to set up the reflective process for his third year, Roger expressed a whole relay of mostly negative emotions that highlighted a lack of any excitement for his third year. In his own words, he was in a "slump". He also noted that he was drained because of his previous summer of negative teaching experiences and felt jaded just thinking about another semester. This feeling of being exhausted mentally did not change a lot during his third year as he worried that he would meet similar students and what to do about this. He felt he did not have the energy to muster up any strength to liven up his lessons. In fact, during his third year he analyzed that his students were not mature enough (they were mostly teenagers or young adults) because they were away from home for the first time and in a new country. Roger was also frustrated with the institution because they treated it like a business and not an educational environment. Roger suggested that they accept any paying student regardless of the educational quality of that student's background. As a result, he said, he suffered in the classroom as many were not able to follow his lessons because of their poor proficiency levels and poor study habits. Thus, the negative emotions that Roger expressed during most of his third year were preventing him from producing his best teaching, but he did not realize he was expressing such negative emotions until he read the transcripts of all of the third-year meetings we had had. Such a late reflection though allowed Roger to begin to make changes to his thinking and his practice during the second semester of his third year.

> • If you have more than one year teaching experience, what were your emotions during your second and third years? Compare these to Roger's expressed emotions during his third year.

ROGER REFLECTS ON THE THIRD YEAR

Roger reflected on his overall experiences during his third year, and I present his answers in his own words.

> Well, first of all, last summer term was just bad all around. Yes, it soured me. And I don't think I had enough time off between terms either to really feel like I'm ready for the next term to start. Yeah, it hit me hard and it took a while to recover from it, right? But yeah, over the course of this term I started to realize that there are hardworking students in my classes and students do listen to me when I talk. What brought me around to seeing this?
>
> Well, just, for example, last week I was marking something. It was paraphrasing. And it was like, wow, this paraphrasing is actually really good. And so is the next one. And the one after that too. Last term this never would have happened. Students actually listen to me when I talk when I'm teaching paraphrasing structures and they're using it successfully. I think as the term went on, yeah, I was changing continually because I was still jaded at the beginning of the term and then once I had a class full of quiet students again, I was like uuuhhh... not this again and I just set the bar low. And then as the term went on, I realized there were a lot of things I should be doing, things I can't do, can do, and need to do, so my approach, my attitude, how I treat them, those changed.
>
> I think I often rely more on what I think works than what others may think works; I have a feeling I may need to involve others more in my decision making or planning and share ideas more often. I still am really frustrated by the lack of involvement from my students. It's like they are scared to say the wrong thing or something, even though I'm constantly encouraging them ask questions and be involved. I realize now that I often prefer working alone on things, rather than together with other people (I often preferred that in the early years). You asked whether or not I was creating a shell around myself... maybe I am!
>
> I have also had a change of mind about teacher metaphors. After reflecting on it, I realized that the *personal trainer metaphor* fits better

with middle level students. I came up with a different metaphor for teachers teaching low level ESL students. I mentioned it during the meeting but wasn't able to flesh it out or think about it on the spot enough. I would say a teacher teaching a low-level ESL classroom is a tour guide. They are knowledgeable about everything they teach (since it's very simple English) and essentially the students know very little (only maybe preconceived notions about things they picked up here and there). The teacher takes the group through the "world of English" and tells them everything they know about it. However, there is no expectations for students to be able to reproduce or do exactly what the tour guide (teacher) does. Instead, they are expected to listen, observe, notice, and gather in the information (learn). Then, at a later time if they want, they can review what they learned (by looking at their "pictures", since they are tourists!) and try and piece things together again. The emphasis here is on the fact that teachers don't expect these students to use the things they learn like they would in higher levels, but rather just try and piece the language together and make sense of it all.

I find it strange in a sense that I didn't really have a specific teacher role model. Is that normal?!? I guess I didn't really know I wanted to teach until Grade 12, but you'd think I would have had one teacher who I thought was an awesome teacher. But then I look back at other things I could have role models for, and I realize there aren't many people who I know that would represent or epitomize the ultimate role model of whatever it is. I think I try to hard not to be exactly like others, but to be different and not always follow the norm. I think that's why I had a hard time coming up with a teacher role model.

This was a really tough year for me, and I had a hard time motivating myself to really get into what I was doing in the beginning of the fall semester especially. I was really exhausted after that summer term, and I had no real break before I went straight into the fall semester of my third year and so I felt jaded before I even went into the classroom. I was going through the motions I think and dreaded that I would meet a class group similar to the one I had in the summer. At the beginning of the term in the back of my head I worried what I would do and how I would react if I had had such a bad experience again. I do not think I could have taken it if I had to face such a group again. Indeed, when I met you that day early on I was happy that we decided to enter into a reflective process again as it helped me a lot to sort out my head in that year. I realize now that I had to overcome such negative thoughts and after this new reflection period, I'm happy to see that I still have passion to teach after last term, and of course after three years of being an ESL teacher. I know that I was pretty beat up after last term, and I'm slowly recovering from that, but I'm starting to notice some joy and excitement in me to teach every day

Reflective Break
- What do you think of Roger's reflections on his third year of teaching?
- Why do you think that Roger is beginning to experience more joy towards the end of his third year of teaching?
- Do you think that the issues he faced in his third year are common among teachers? If yes, why? If not, why not?
- What would you do if you were faced with what you consider to be an uncooperative class of learners? How would you respond?
- What were the main issues for you during your third year as a teacher and why?

CONCLUSION

This chapter has summarized Roger's reflections throughout his third year of teaching as well as his overall analysis of his third year as a teacher. Roger's reflections on his philosophy, principles, theory, practice and beyond practice as defined by Farrell (2015) revealed a somewhat negative experience overall that began before he officially started the third year. In fact, during the short summer semester just before this (which also technically counts in his third-year teaching) the negative experiences were so impactful that they laid the groundwork for much of his third year negative feelings – of exhaustion and frustration – and these only began to lift through the power of reflection with this author. Have I won you over? The following chapter outlines and discusses how language teachers can continue their professional development after they graduate from their teacher education programs and into their early career years, just as Roger experienced as expressed in the previous thirteen chapters.

Chapter 15

Professional Development Through Reflective Practice

INTRODUCTION

The preceding chapters have outlined and discussed Roger's first year and his third year of teaching, through the lens of the framework for reflecting on practice (Farrell, 2015). There are five stages: philosophy, principles, theory, practice and beyond practice. This framework helps us to enter Roger's professional life and to view a snapshot of his lived experiences from his very first day on the job through to his third year as a teacher. Roger said that he engaged in such intense reflections in order to learn more about himself as a novice teacher during his first year on the job. Then, after a difficult summer semester before his third year officially began, Roger approached this author with the idea of continuing his reflections during his third year because he said he was a bit worried about what he thought was happening negatively to his motivation to teach. In this chapter I first attempt to re-visit some of Roger's lived experiences during his journey from his first to his third year of teaching. Then I outline what we can learn from Roger's experiences and how other teachers in their early career years can engage in similar reflective practices so they can navigate any challenges before them in order to avoid the type of third year slump that Roger experienced.

ROGER'S JOURNEY

The First-Year Excitement

From the very first day on the job, Roger said he felt the excitement of walking into the classroom to teach his own students and as he walked in that first day, he noticed that "right away these students look at you as if you're that teacher." From the beginning he told them that they could just call him Roger as many were of similar age. He remarked, "I don't feel like I really need that title of teacher." Roger felt confident in his ability to teach from the very beginning because he had just finished his MA in teaching English to other speakers. He said he had all the education necessary to be a successful teacher and that he was eager to put into practice what he had learned. Indeed, after his first week teaching, Roger said that he really felt like a teacher now because he had actually given lessons. He continued,

> I have students do work that I've assigned, I've assigned homework. I definitely feel like a teacher now. I have my own classroom now that I'm in charge of. I can control what happens in this classroom. I can say, "we're going to do this today, we're going to do that today" and the students will have to do it. [laughs]

As a result, he said that at the end of that first week he felt very excited about his life as a teacher, remarking that he had a lot of confidence in all aspects of handling a class regardless of what might come up. Roger noted that this was the first time after his MA degree that he had stepped into a classroom to teach as a career, and that was exciting for him because he was "loaded with this new knowledge from the master's program about classroom management, classroom control, teaching methods, and so on."

Roger also noted that he was excited at that time to reflect on what he was doing with this author acting as his facilitator because he said he wanted to step back to "take a look at what I am doing." Roger mentioned that he was interested in getting a different point of view of what he was doing and why. As Roger remarked, "Is it things that I just made up or things that I learned from my classes or things I just learned from life experiences or from watching other people?"

Roger also realized that he was still a novice teacher during this first year, with a lot to learn from others. However, he also was trying to be himself – an individual – while finding his own way of what works and what does not. That said, Roger tempered his desire to go it alone from his point of view only and said he was full focused on providing student-centered lessons. Roger also noted that he believed that students should not use their L1 in lessons as it can distract from their learning. Regarding teaching the skill areas, Roger noted that his beliefs clashed sometimes with how the institution wanted him to teach, but he was confident from the knowledge that he had obtained in his MA program that he was on the correct path here. Roger was particularly focused and interested in teaching grammar as he believed that his students needed a good knowledge of this as a basis for all their learning of English as a second language in academic settings such as a university where most of his students will enter upon graduation.

Although Roger noted above that he was confident in the knowledge that he obtained from his MA courses, he also realized that they did not prepare him for everything he encountered during his first year, such as how to deal with the issue of his students discussing inappropriate topics during lessons. In addition, Roger said he was shocked when his students did not, or were not able to, follow his instructions when using APA referencing and that this was a real wake-up call for him from his teacher education program. Roger seemed happy with his actual teaching of grammar and, from the evidence obtained in the transcripts of his lesson, he noted that his students were learning and that he accomplished what he had intended. Overall, Roger seemed pleased with the results of his first-year reflections and remarked that at the end of the first year he "would say that I am a student-first, learner-centered, easy-going, novice teacher." Roger expressed his "excitement" about his new career, not only in language but also in his animated use of that language, and that he was "confident" he had chosen a great career as an ESL teacher.

The Third-Year Slump

A chance meeting in a narrow corridor brought us back together at the beginning of Roger's third year for the fall semester. I must say that he did not look at all as bubbly as he had previously (the "spark-plug; go-getter" as I noted at that time) and, in fact, seemed a bit down. I asked him how it was going, and this question led ultimately to our third-year reflections as a continuation from his first year reflections. I learned that the excitement he felt (and I felt) during his first year of teaching had long vanished – especially at this moment when he had just finished teaching "a horrible short summer semester" two weeks previously and that he was still jaded from that. In fact, this was the reason he wanted to engage in reflective practice again because he said he was worried about his negative attitude and low motivation before he even began his third-year fall semester. He said that he felt that he was now in a slump because he worried that he would have the same bad experience this coming semester as he had just experienced, and he did not know what he would do about it. So, he was delighted that he'd bumped into me and that we had agreed to "continue" his reflections in the same manner as we had during his first year of teaching. I should point out that Roger's desire to (re)engage in reflective practice during his third year shows what a professional he was turning out to be, noting that he had negative feelings that he wanted to address rather than to let slide as he had the previous summer term. Indeed, I was to discover that these negative experiences he said he had with "a class full of duds" who would not participate made it like "talking to a bunch of rocks" for Roger and, as such, one wonders what would have occurred had he not reflected on his practice during the third-year slump? Statistics suggest he may have left the profession which would have been a horrible shame as I was to find out again what a wonderful, caring ESL teacher he truly was. The problem was that he allowed himself to go into that slump for the beginning of his third year because he had lost his sense of curiosity, his excitement with teaching, his student-centered approach to teaching and his overall joy of being with his students in his own classroom for the first time.

Thus, in the first few weeks of his third semester, Roger, noting that his reflections about his negative experiences the previous semester with this facilitator, and the already early signs in the first weeks of his third year that he may have to face similar students with possibly negative effects, decided to try to take a different attitude and role. Some of the changes from his first year were his comments almost exclusively about his students' approaches (or non-approaches) to learning and how he was planning his lessons in a type of vacuum where he felt suspended between his reality and his professionalism but where exhaustion was also preventing him from full investment. This was particularly visible in his teaching practices where he was observed using PowerPoints almost exclusively and each slide was loaded with lots of information. It is possible that, from the very beginning of the third year, Roger was trying to make his teaching and materials so generic that they could shield him from any negative feedback from the students and that he was going through the motions of teaching compared to the excitement he felt during that first year when he was eager to try anything to motivate learning.

Reflective Break
- How do you compare Roger's first year excitement to his third-year slump?
- How can teachers be prepared for the challenges they may meet in their early career years and be better able to avoid any slumps?
- How did you survive your early career years (assuming you did)?

THE IMPORTANCE OF REFLECTIVE PRACTICE

It is interesting to note that very little research appears to have been published regarding the lived experiences of ESL teachers in their third year of teaching and definitely no published studies to this author's knowledge that compare the first- and third-year teaching experiences of ESL teachers. I believe the work outlined in this book could be considered a longitudinal study of Roger's lived experiences during these important years. If we look at Huberman's (1993) teacher career cycle for reference points during these early career years we can see that his first two phases could be covered in this longitudinal account, that of the initial exploration phase, or Roger's first year of teaching, and Huberman's (1993) second phase where teachers seek some kind of stabilization, or Roger's third year of teaching. The first phase is really where a teacher attempts to make a smooth transition from the teacher training program to the first year(s) of teaching, and this can be full of ups and downs with success often depending on the quality of the initial teacher training as well as the teacher's own motivation for entering the profession. In Roger's case, his first-year approaches as a teacher mainly emanated from his supreme confidence in his knowledge about language learning and teaching that he attributes to his undergraduate and graduate education in linguistics and language teaching. As the first year progressed, he seemed to be able to adjust what he realized the program and training did not prepare him for by implementing his own ideas as necessary. This again was a result of his confidence in his abilities that never waned throughout his first year.

Then it all slumped in his third year because of some negative experiences with what he called a "bad group" of students during the summer preceding the fall semester of his third year. His early confidence in his abilities was shaken to the extent that he began to question himself and his decision to become a teacher. In other words, he did not reach the stabilization that Huberman (1993: 245) suggested, where he could make a "durable commitment to teaching, begin to consolidate a basic repertoire of pedagogical skills and materials at the classroom level, and begin to feel a greater ease, sense of relaxation and increased psychological comfort." In fact, Roger's lived summer experiences seemed to completely destabilize him as an ESL teacher and erode much of his confidence obtained in the previous two years of teaching. Roger seemed to be plagued with self-doubt at that time directly after the summer and into the early weeks of his third year of teaching. In fact, I believe if it were not for our chance encounter that fateful day when I met him and asked him about his teaching career, Roger may not be a teacher. I am happy to report he is still teaching (at a different institution now) and really enjoys it but I think it is only because he entered into a period of deep reflection about his experiences at that time in his third year that he survived and thrived. Roger stabilized during the fall term of his third year of teaching as a result. Thus, reflective practice leads to stabilization. I will now outline Roger's reflections on reflective practice to give his perceptions on how he became more stabilized through the reflective process. As he said, "reflection definitely helps."

Reflective Break

- Do you think engaging in reflective practice can lead to stabilization for a teacher in their third year of teaching? Why or why not?

Roger Reflects on Reflection

I now present Roger's reflections on reflective practice that he engaged in during his third year of teaching and what he said he gained from the process.

I now realize that the process of reflection helped me 100%. It definitely was a real factor. If I hadn't sat down and reflected on the past and things now, I don't think it would have been the same. I would have kept on going down that same path of let's just get this done and over with. Yeah, just doing everything faster, so yeah, by reflecting it gave me a chance to sit back and reflect on my practice. Who I am as a teacher, how I teach. Second of all, am I targeting these specific students the way I should because they aren't the same group of students as last term. Once I realized they were more motivated students and more interested, then I could do more things with them. I think I had to change my attitude and the way I thought about things. It was the glasses I was looking through. I think halfway through this term I started to appreciate the students and what I do again. So, if I was going to advise other teachers after my experiences, I would give them a few ideas. For example, I would say try and develop some routines, but be careful not to fall into a routine where you're always doing the same thing. I would also say to always try new things because if you have a certain set of routine things and then mix in new things, you're not always doing the same thing over and over and fall into a rut, and then you're in autopilot. I would remind them that they are teaching different students all the time and just because you have a bad group of students one term, it doesn't mean the next term is going to be the same.

In terms of reflective practice, I would say at the end of the term, by yourself, or chatting with other teachers, look back at what you did and what worked well and didn't. During my reflections in the third year, I did something interesting that helped me a lot with my own reflections and that was related to all the meeting transcripts. I actually wrote out all the transcripts, and this process allowed me to see what we were talking about, as well as reflect on it in real time. Yeah, that was pretty cool actually. I think it helped me even more by doing that. Just talking about it here, you talk about it and then you leave. You may or may not think about it after, but the fact that you transcribe it, I had to think about it again and then reflect on my reflections. It just gets to that deeper level where you wonder why did I say this about this. Now how could a novice teacher do that? They could record a conversation and transcribe it, but that's not really what people like to do. They could talk to other teachers. Maybe find a critical friend.

Maybe over the course of a couple years, find someone who you can tell, hey, I'm struggling with this or need help with this, or something like that. Kind of like a buddy system, where you can help each other out.

The last time we did this [Roger's first year of teaching], we recorded the conversations and then before those I wrote a journal. But I think this time around, it's been more effective for me anyways. First of all, sitting down to write a journal is not always something you want to do. And when I wrote a journal, it was always a page or a page and a half, like 1500 words. When I type out our conversations, it's like 5000 words. And a lot of them are my words. For sure 2500 words. You get more, and you also get the double reflection aspect. For me it worked well. Really well.

I also found the classroom observations very helpful. Probably if I would have sat back and thought about it myself, and noticed my own question practices, I might have noticed, hey, I'm not waiting long enough and answering my own questions. But the fact that you came in and noticed that it caused me to kind of change how I do things and made it better. Observation was a kind of mirror for me and after recording them, we transcribed them too. Yeah, that was interesting too. But I think when someone else comes and tells you, oh you're doing this and this, it's more powerful than if you would just notice it yourself because there is no pressure to change it, right? If someone else notices it and they ask you later on if you fixed the issue, then there's more pressure. In fact, I do not feel nervous or scared being observed by someone in the room and I don't think I even really noticed you [author] sitting there. But, for me, I don't care if people watch me. I don't think there's anything that I do that's crazy. Other people might be a bit nervous, but that's a personality thing maybe too.

Reflection changed me. Yeah, I was definitely primed for it. I had lots of things to reflect on and I recognized it. Other teachers might say, no I don't want to do that, even though they should maybe. But yeah, I think it's something that every teacher should go through at some point, whether it's three years, five years, or every point. I just want to say again thank you [author] very much for taking me through the reflection process. After that and a nice long break, I feel the most refreshed (mentally and physically) that I ever have going into a new term/year. I'm really excited to have a renewed point of view towards what I do. I have a very positive vibe about this coming term/year. After this past term/year, I really understand now why you are so excited to spread the good news of reflective practice. It works, and it's necessary to look back and reflect on every aspect of being a teacher. I'm more than happy to promote reflection myself and to possibly even find ways to incorporate it into everyday teacher practice and teacher training. You've won me over :)

Reflective Break

- In terms of the reflective process, Roger wrote out his own transcriptions of each meeting we had. How do you think this facilitated his reflections and his journal writing?
- Why do you think Roger is not intimidated by being observed while teaching?
- Why do you think many teachers may be intimidated by being observed in the classroom while they are teaching?
- Are you intimidated by being observed while teaching? Why or why not?
- Why do you think Roger said engaging in reflective practice has changed him?
- In what way(s) do you think engaging in reflective practice throughout his third year has changed him?
- Why do you think Roger appreciates the power of reflective practice now after this third year?
- Do you think that engaging in reflective practice using the Farrell (2015) framework (reflecting on your *philosophy, principles, theory, practice* and *beyond practice*) can help you better navigate your teaching life in the years to come? Why or why not?

PROFESSIONAL DEVELOPMENT
THROUGH REFLECTIVE PRACTICE

In this section I outline and discuss how ESL teachers (and teachers of all subjects) can engage in reflective practice as part of their professional development so that they can thrive throughout their teaching careers.

There are many different models and approaches about how teachers can reflect, too numerous to cover in this article (but see Farrell, 2019 for a comprehensive review of many of them). The first model of reflective practice I developed emphasized a practical approach, with the idea that practicing TESOL teachers would be better able to "locate themselves within their profession and start to take more responsibility for shaping their practice" (Farrell, 2004: 6) rather than relying on publisher produced materials and books that were rampant in the TESOL profession at that time. I saw a need for teachers to be able to break away from relying on these badly produced textbooks with teacher guides to *tell* them what they should be doing rather than taking responsibility for their own direction while *teaching their students.*

My initial framework attempted to encourage teachers to look at their own practice with other teachers and decide their own future direction in terms of providing opportunities for their students to learn. This framework (Farrell, 2004) of reflective teaching is composed of five components: (a) a range of opportunities and activities, (b) ground rules, (c) provision for four different times or categories of reflection, (d) external input, and (e) trust. This framework (Farrell, 2004) is explained as follows:

1   *Opportunities.* A range of activities should be provided for teachers to reflect on their work. In this model the activities that were emphasized were group discussions, journal writing and classroom observations. These activities can be carried out alone, in pairs, or as a group. A group of teachers may decide to do one of the activities or a combination of any or all of them.

2   *Ground rules.* In order to avoid groups or individual teachers just drifting off into something other than reflection, this framework suggests a need for a negotiated set of built-in rules or guidelines that each group or pair should follow in order to keep the drifting to a minimum. The model can be adjusted to individual group needs. Indeed, suggestions three through five are actually ground rules that can be built into the activities. For example, who will chair the meetings and other such related question? For observations, certain understandings need to be negotiated ahead of time. For example, what are the responsibilities of the observer? Is intervention possible or desirable in the class? Will the class be videotaped, audiotaped, or neither? If you use a video, how will this be analyzed and why? What is to be observed and how? For journal writing, groups/pairs should negotiate the number of frequency of entries and the type of entries. The following list of general questions may help get a writer started: Describe what you do with no judgment? Why do you do it? Should you continue to do it or change it? What do others do? To suggest a set of built-in rules for critical friends while observing is not easy because there must be an element of trust and openness present in order to avoid putting emphasis on the critical while overlooking the friend. The friend can provide another set of eyes that both support and challenge us to get at deeper reflections of our teaching. To encourage this openness, the initial conversations between critical friends (or all conversations) should be taped and analyzed. This analysis can include the use

of questions in their relationship, in terms of type, power structures established, focus of observation, and usefulness. In this way critical friends can negotiate what they want to achieve. Of course, all of the above activities and built-in guidelines cannot be accomplished quickly; like all valuable things, they take time. This introduces the next component of the model: time.

3   *Time.* For practicing teachers to be able to reflect on their work, time is a very important consideration. Groups can consider four different views/types of time: *Individual, Activity, Development, Period of Reflection*
   - <u>Individual</u>: A certain level of commitment by individual participants in terms of time availability should be negotiated by the group at the start of the process.
   - <u>Activity</u>: Associated with the time each participant has to give the project is the time that should be spent on each activity.
   - <u>Development</u>: Another aspect of time that is important for teacher self-development groups is the time it takes to develop. Analytical reflection takes time and only progresses at a rate which individual teachers are ready to reflect critically.
   - <u>Period of Reflection</u>. The time frame for the project as a whole is important to consider. How long should a group, a pair, or an individual reflect? Having a fixed period in which to reflect allows the participants to know what period during the semester they can devote wholly to reflection.

4   *External input.* The previous three suggestions utilize the idea of probing and articulating personal theories, which is at the center of teacher professional self-development. This involves process of constructing and reconstructing real teaching experiences, and reflecting on personal beliefs about teaching. However, at this level, reflection only emphasizes personal experiences – but what do these mean in the greater professional community? Thus, external input of some kind is necessary to see what other teachers and groups have done. This external input can come from professional journals, other teachers' observations, and book publications of case studies.

5   *Trust.* The above four components of the model all pose some threat and associated anxiety for practicing teachers. Inevitably, there will be a certain level of anxiety present. Therefore, trust will be a big issue when teachers reflect together, so a non-threatening environment should be fostered in the group by the individuals themselves.

The most important aspect of this early framework (Farrell, 2004) is to encourage reflection and to give teachers the opportunity to reflect, and I believe this framework is still relevant today: I have used this framework successfully and very recently with experienced TESOL teachers in a teacher reflection group in Canada (e.g., see Farrell, 2014), and it is still worthwhile for teachers wishing to reflect on their practice and especially with a group of teachers.

In more recent times I began to work on a different framework that focused more on individual teachers reflecting holistically on their practice rather than a group of teachers reflecting together as with the early model above. I call this the framework for reflecting on practice (Farrell, 2015, TESOL). As outlined in Chapter 1, the framework has five different stages/levels of reflection: *Philosophy; Principles; Theory; Practice; and Beyond Practice*. This was the framework we used for Roger's reflections in his first and third years of teaching. The framework is descriptive rather than prescriptive in that it does not suggest mapping out so-called best practice. As Edwards and Thomas (2010: 404) cautioned, "reflective practice cannot be a prescriptive rubric of skills to be taught [to teachers]; in fact, to see it in this way reverts to the very technicist assumptions reflective practice was meant to exile." Over recent years, I have also conducted such evidence-based holistic reflective practice research using the above framework (but without specific reference to the emotional aspects of reflecting on practice that are present in this Element), with the idea that the teachers will benefit as a means of making their own informed decisions about teaching (e.g., Farrell & Kennedy, 2019; Farrell & Avejic, 2020; Farrell & Macapinlac, 2021; Farrell & Moses, 2023).

The framework can be navigated in three different ways: theory-into-(beyond) practice, (beyond) practice-into-theory or a single stage application. Teachers can take a deductive approach to reflecting on practice by moving from theory-into-practice or from stage/level 1, philosophy through the different stages to stage/level 5, beyond practice. Some may say that pre-service teachers who do not have much classroom experiences, would be best suited to take such an approach because they can first work on their overall philosophical approach to teaching English to speakers of other languages and work their way through the different stages of principles (stage/level 2), theory (stage/level 3) when they reach the practicum stage, they will be well placed then to reflect on their practice (stage/level 4) and eventually move beyond practice (stage/level 5). This theory-driven approach to practice where philosophy and theory have an initial influence on practice is probably a natural sequence of development for novice teachers because they do not have much teaching experience. When their early practices are observed, it is most likely that theory can be detected in their practice; however, over time, and with reflection, it is possible that their everyday practice will begin to inform and even change their philosophy and theory and they may come up with new principles of practice.

Experienced teachers too can also choose to begin their reflections at stage/level 1, philosophy especially if they consider their philosophy as a significant basis of their practice with principles second, theory third and so on through the framework. For experienced teachers, some of whose practice can be theory-driven if they have been reading and experimenting with applications of particular theories throughout their teaching careers, most likely describe their work in terms of their overall philosophical approach to teaching English to speakers of other languages and this description probably embeds a lot of their values, beliefs, principles and well as theories behind their practice. When such teachers are observed teaching their lessons, we are likely to see that their approaches, methods and activities often reflect the influence of these theories.

Many teachers are very busy and as such may consider the above approaches too time consuming for them to engage in. I agree to a certain extent that it can be time consuming, but it would be time well spent. I would also suggest that teachers begin at whatever stage they feel comfortable with above (e.g., your philosophy or your principles) when you have the time and work your way around the framework as you see fit. In this way teachers can use the framework as a lens through which they can view their professional (and personal) worlds – what has shaped their professional lives – as they become more aware of their philosophy, principles, theories, practices and how these impact issues inside and beyond practice. I believe that such a holistic approach to reflection produces more integrated second language teachers, who have the self-awareness and understanding to be able to interpret, shape and reshape their practice throughout their careers. The information that is produced from reflecting during each stage can be compiled into a teaching portfolio and used for collaborative teacher evaluation purposes. In such a manner the teacher is not separated from the act of teaching when reflecting or being evaluated.

As noted above, teachers are very busy in their schools so I will only suggest the three main tools of reflection that we used for Roger to explore his first and third year of teaching: dialogue, writing, and classroom observations that readers may also find useful if they want to navigate the frameworks above. Of course, talking is important for humans, and as Roger and myself met regularly through dialogue, such discussions enabled us to reflect together in a supportive manner. We were able to discuss what happened and analyze and make interpretation as well as discuss what Roger was planning for events in the future. When teachers come together in a similar manner to discuss their experiences during their journey through the framework, they can become more aware of who they are and who they want to become as language teaching professionals. Mann & Walsh (2017) also note the importance of dialogue as crucial for reflection as is allows for clarification, questioning and enhanced understanding.

Teachers do a lot of writing within their workday, be it on lesson planning, reports on students' progress or the like, but they seldom take time to write for themselves professionally about their practice. As I mentioned in Chapter 1, writing has its own built-in reflective mechanism; the process entails that writers must stop to think and organize their thoughts and then decide on what to write (either using a pen or a computer). After writing they can "see" (literally) their thoughts and reflect on these for self-understanding. This I call reflective writing and I use it all the time to help me with my own reflections.

For teachers, such reflective writing can include written accounts of their thoughts, classroom observations, assumptions, beliefs, attitudes, and experiences about their practice both inside and outside the classroom (Farrell, 2013a,b). Teachers can include records of critical incidents, perceived problems/issues, and insights that occurred during lessons (reflection-in-action) in order to gain new understandings of their own teacher learning and instructional practices. I actually take a notebook with me to jot down events as they happen while I teach in case I forget after the lesson – I am usually fully invested in the act of teaching during a lesson, so I cannot remember exactly what has happened after the event and I worry that I may have a selective memory. Thus, when teachers take the time to write about their practice they can express their opinions, hypothesize about their practice, and of course reflect later on what actually happened during their practice and compare results.

Teachers can also use writing as a tool for reflection with or without dialogue depending on time available. Roger also used writing along with our dialogue sessions and found it a very useful tool for him to reflect on his work. There are different modes of writing for reflection, some of which include teacher journals and online writing in blogs, chats, and forums all of which are useful. Teachers may also consider different types of levels of writing they can engage in. Hatton & Smith (1995: 85) identified four levels of writing.

- *Descriptive writing* (not reflective) reports events that occurred or is a report of something you have read in the literature. There is no attempt to provide reasons or justifications for the events. Its main purpose is to provide a support or a starting point for the framework.
- *Descriptive reflection* attempts to provide reasons and justifications for events or actions but in a descriptive way. Although there is some recognition of alternative viewpoints, it is mainly based upon personal judgment, e.g., *I chose this problem-solving activity because I believe the learners should be active rather than passive.*
- *Dialogic reflection* demonstrates a "stepping back" from the events/actions leading to a different level of mulling about discourse with one's self through the exploration of possible reasons, e.g., *I became aware that a number of students did not respond to written text materials. Thinking about this, there may*

have been several reasons. A number of students may still have lacked some con-fidence in handling the level of language in the text.

- *Critical reflection* demonstrates a level of awareness that actions and events in the classroom (and beyond) are explained by multiple perspectives. It involves giving reasons for decisions or events, which takes into account the broader historical, social, and/or political contexts, e.g., *What must be recognized, however, is that the issues of student management experienced with this class can only be understood within the wider structural locations of power relationships established between teachers and students in schools as social institutions based upon the principle of control.*

Teachers can also engage in classroom observations, similar to what Roger experienced, of what they do while they teach. Roger was able to note if his principles (beliefs) are present or not in his actual classroom practices. We used a variety of approaches to his observations such as a general approach to collecting data by using such instruments as written ethnography and lesson video recording. At times we also took a more detailed approach by using some form of category instrument to collect data, such as SCORE (Seating Chart Observation Record) analysis (Farrell, 2018a). Regardless of the focus of the observation or the instruments used to collect data, teachers can use classroom observations as a means of examining and analyzing teaching events as part of their overall reflections on their work.

Reflective Break
- Which of the reflection approaches and tools would you prefer to use as you reflect on your practice and why?
- Oberg and Blades (1990: 179) maintain that reflection "lies not in the theory it allows us to develop about practice or reflection but the evolution of ourselves as a teacher. Its focus is life; we continually return to our place of origin, but it is not the place we left." Do you think that teachers can and should engage in reflective practice throughout their teaching careers?

CONCLUSION

This final chapter outlined and discussed Roger's lived experiences, from his first-year excitement as a teacher to his third-year slump, and how engaging in reflective practice led to stabilization for him. The chapter then outlined Roger's thinking on his experiences using reflective practice and how it really helped him overcome the challenges he faced during his third year of teaching. Finally, the chapter outlined and discussed two of my reflective practice frameworks and the three major reflective tools we used for Roger's reflections during both years: dialogue, writing and classroom reflections. The purpose of encouraging ESL teachers to reflect on their practice is *not to look for best practice*; rather it is to get a holistic view of oneself as a TESOL professional. As Fanselow (1988: 116) has noted, "each of us [teachers] needs to construct, reconstruct, and revise our own teaching." I believe that the five-stage holistic framework we used as a lens for Roger to reflect provided him with details about his philosophy, principles, theory, practice and beyond practice critical reflection that helped him not only survive his third year but also thrive as he is still teaching (albeit in a different institution) and really excited about his future years as an ESL teacher.

Though generalization is always difficult from such a case study, which has obvious limitations because of the small sample size (one teacher), I believe that readers may find much of Roger's reflections has relevance for their own context, practices and reflections. As van Lier (2005: 195) points out, rigorous analysis of a case study of just one teacher can provide in-depth insights into intricate pedagogical and contextual issues that, "cannot be done adequately in any other common research practice." I agree with Fanselow (1988: 115) when he notes: "Here I am with my lens to look at you and your actions. But as I look at you with my lens, I consider you a mirror; I hope to see myself in you and through your teaching... Seeing you allows me to see myself differently and to explore variables we both use." I hope that by engaging in such holistic reflections, all TESOL teachers regardless of their experiences but especially early career teachers such as Roger, can (re)construct and (re)adjust their personal beliefs and practices to better provide optimal learning conditions for students within their classrooms.

ENVOI

It is such a delight for me that I know Roger is still thriving as an ESL teacher and his students are benefiting from his reflections on his practice.
Happy reflecting everyone!

References

Artigliere, M., & Baecher, L. (2017). Sink or swim: aligning training with classroom reality in ESL co-teaching. In T. S. C. Farrell (Ed.) *TESOL Voices: Insider accounts of classroom life—preservice teacher education*, (pp. 43–50). Alexander, Virginia, US: TESOL Press.

Bezzina, C. (2006). Views from the trenches: Beginning teachers' perceptions about their professional development. *Journal of In-service Education, 32*, 411–430. https://doi.org/10.1080/13674580601024515

Brookfield, S. D. (1995). *Becoming a Critically Reflective Teacher*. San Fransisco, CA: Jossey-Bass.

Bullough, R. V., & Baughman, K. (1993). Continuity and change in teacher development: a first-year teacher after five years. *Journal of Teacher Education, 44*, 86–95. https://doi.org/10.1177/0022487193044002003

Burns, A. (1992). Teacher Beliefs and Their Influence on Classroom Practice. *Prospect, 7*, 3, 56–66.

Byrne, B. M. (1999). The nomological network of teacher burnout: A literature review and empirically validated model. In R. Vandenberghe, & A. M. Huberman (Eds.), *Understanding and Preventing Teacher Burnout*, (pp. 15–37). Cambridge: Cambridge University Press.

Calderhead, J. (1992). Induction: A research perspective on the professional growth of the newly qualified teacher. In J. Calderhead & K. Lambert (Eds.), *The Induction of Newly Appointed Teachers, General Teaching for England and Wales*, (pp. 5–21). Slough: NFER.

Callahan, J. (1988). The role of emotion in ethical decision making. *Hastings Center Report, 18*, 3, 9–14.

Creswell, J. W. (1994). *Research Design: Qualitative & Quantitative Approaches*. Sage Publications,

Cirocki A., Madyarov I., & Baecher L. (Eds.) (2019). *Contemporary Perspectives on Student Teacher Learning and the TESOL Practicum*. Holland: Springer.

Dewey, J. (1933). *How We Think: A Restatement of the Relation of Reflective Thinking to the Educative Process*. Boston, MA: Houghton-Mifflin.

Edwards, G., & Thomas, G. (2010). Can reflective practice be taught? *Educational Studies, 36*, 403–414. https://doi.org/10.1080/03055690903424790

Elbaz, F. (1991). Research on teacher's knowledge: The evolution of a discourse. *Journal of Curriculum Studies 23*, 1, 1–19. https://doi.org/10.1080/0022027910230101

Fang, Z. (1996). A review of research on teacher beliefs and practices. *Educational Research, 38*, 1, 47–65. https://doi.org/10.1080/0013188960380104

Fanselow, J. F. (1988). "Let's See": Contrasting conversations about teaching. *TESOL Quarterly, 22*, 1, 113–130. https://doi.org/10.2307/3587064

Farrell, T. S. C. (2003). Learning to teach English language during the first year: personal influences and challenges. *Teaching and Teacher Education, 19*, 95–111. https://doi.org/10.1016/s0742-051x(02)00088-4

Farrell, T. S. C. (2004). *Reflective Practice in Action*. Thousand Oaks, CA: Corwin Press.

Farrell, T. S. C. (2007). *Reflective Practice for Language Teachers: From Research to Practice*. London: Continuum Press.

Farrell, T. S. C. (2008). *Novice Language Teachers: Insights and Perspectives for the First Year*. London, England: Equinox.

Farrell, T. S. C. (2012). Novice-service language teacher development: Bridging the gap between preservice and in-service education and development. *TESOL Quarterly, 46*, 3, 435–449. https://doi.org/10.1002/tesq.36

Farrell, T. S. C. (2013a). *Reflective Practice in ESL Teacher Development Groups: From Practices to Principles*. Basingstoke, England: Palgrave Macmillan.

Farrell, T. S. C. (2013b). *Reflective Writing for Language Teachers*. Sheffield, England: Equinox Publishing Ltd.

Farrell, T. S. C. (2014). *Reflective Practice in ESL Teacher Development Groups: From Practices to Principles*. Basingstoke, UK: Palgrave Macmillan.

Farrell, T. S. C. (2015). *Promoting Teacher Reflection in Second Language Education: A Framework for TESOL Professionals*. New York: Routledge.

Farrell, T. S. C. (2016). *From Trainee to Teacher: Reflective Practice for Novice Teachers*. Sheffield, England: Equinox Publishing Ltd.

Farrell, T. S. C. (Ed.) (2017). *TESOL Voices: Insider Accounts of Classroom Life—Preservice Teacher Education*. Alexander, Virginia, US: TESOL Press.

Farrell, T. S. C. (2018a). *Reflective Language Teaching: Practical Applications for TESOL teachers*. London, UK: Bloomsbury Publishing.

Farrell, T. S. C. (2018b). *Research on Reflective Practice in TESOL*. New York: Routledge.

Farrell, T S.C. (2019). *Reflection-as-action in ELT*. Alexander, Virginia, US: TESOL Press.

Farrell, T. S. C. (2021). *TESOL Teacher Education: A Reflective Approach*. Edinburgh, UK: Edinburgh University Press.

Farrell, T. S. C. (2022). *Reflective Practice for Language Teachers*. Cambridge, UK: Cambridge University Press.

Farrell, T. S. C., & Kennedy, B. (2019). Reflective practice framework for TESOL teachers: One teacher's reflective journey. *Reflective Practice, 20*, 1–12. https://doi.org/10.1080/14623943.2018.1539657

Farrell, T. S. C., & Avejic, V. (2020). "Students are my life": Reflections of one novice EFL teacher in Central America. *TESL Canada Journal, 37*, 3, 47–63. https://doi.org/10.18806/tesl.v37i3.1345

Farrell, T. S. C., & Macapinlac, M. (2021). Professional development through reflective practice: A framework for TESOL teachers. *Canadian Journal of Applied Linguistics, 24*, 1, 1–25. https://doi.org/10.37213/cjal.2021.28999

Farrell, T. S. C., & Moses, N. (2023). "Class Is Like A Family": Reflections of an Experienced Canadian TESOL Teacher. *Korea TESOL Journal.*

Feiman-Nemser, S. (2001). Helping novices learn to teach: Lessons from an exemplary support teacher. *Journal of Teacher Education, 52*, 1, 17–30. https://doi.org/10.1177/0022487101052001003

Freeman, D. (1994). Knowing into doing: Teacher education and the problem of transfer. In D. Li, D. Mahony and J. C. Richards (Eds.), *Exploring Second Language Teacher Development* (pp. 1–20). Hong Kong: City University Press.

Freeman, D. (1996). *Doing Teacher Research: From Inquiry to Understanding.* New York: Heinemann.

Freeman, D., & Johnson, K. E. (1998). Reconceptualizing the knowledge-base of language teacher education. *TESOL Quarterly, 32*, 3, 397–417. https://doi.org/10.2307/3588114

Fuller, F. F., & Brown, O. H. (1975). Becoming a teacher. In K. Ryan (Ed.), *Teacher Education: The Seventy-Fourth Yearbook of the National Society for the Study of Education* (pp. 25–51). Chicago: National Society for the Study of Education.

Glesne, C., & Peshkin, A. (1992). *Becoming Qualitative Researchers: An Introduction.* White Plains, NY: Longman.

Halford, J. (1998). Easing the way for new teachers. *Educational Leadership, 55*, 5, 33–6.

Hatton, N., & Smith, D. (1995). Reflection in teacher education: Towards definition and implementation. *Teaching and Teacher Education, 11*, 1, 33–49. https://doi.org/10.1016/0742-051x(94)00012-u

Holmes, M. (2010). The emotionalization of reflexivity, *Sociology, 44*, 1, 139–154. https://doi.org/10.1177/0038038509351616

Huberman, M. (1993). *The Lives of Teachers.* London Cassell.

Ingersoll, R. (2015). Revolving Door Of Teachers Costs Schools Billions Every Year. *NRP, ED.*

Johnson, K. E. (1992). Learning to teach: Instructional actions and decisions of preservice ESL teachers. *TESOL Quarterly, 26*, 507–535. https://doi.org/10.2307/3587176

Johnson, K. E. (2006). The sociocultural turn and its challenges for second language teacher education. *TESOL Quarterly, 40*, 235–257. https://doi.org/10.2307/40264518

Kagan, D. (1992). Implications of research on teacher belief. *Educational Psychologist, 27*, 1, 65–90.

Kaufmann, R., & Ring, M. (2011). Pathways to leadership and professional development: Inspiring novice special educators. *Teaching Exceptional Children, 43*, 5, 52–60. https://doi.org/10.1177/004005991104300505

Kelchtermans G., & Deketelaere, A. (2016). The emotional dimension in becoming a teacher. In J. Loughran & M. Hamilton (Eds.), *International Handbook of Teacher Education*, (pp. 429–461). Singapore: Springer.

Kindsvatter, R., Willen, W., & Isher, M. (1988). *Dynamics of Effective Teaching.* New York: Longman.

Knezevic, B. (2001). Action research. *IATEFL Teacher Development SIG Newsletter, 1,* 10–12.

Lincoln, Y. S., & Guba, E. G. (1985). *Naturalistic Inquiry.* Beverly Hills, CA: Sage.

Lindqvist, P., Nordänger, U. K., & Carlsson, R. (2014). Teacher attrition the first five years–A multifaceted image. *Teaching and Teacher Education, 40,* 94–103. https://doi.org/10.1016/j.tate.2014.02.005

Loughran, J., Brown, J., & Doecke, B. (2001). Continuities and discontinuities: The transition from pre-service to first year teaching. *Teachers and Teaching: Theory and Practice, 7,* 1, 7–23. https://doi.org/10.1080/135406000020029846

Malderez, A., & Bodoczky, C. (1999). *Mentor Courses: A Resource Book for Trainer-Trainers.* Cambridge: Cambridge University Press.

Mandel, S. (2006). What new teachers really need. *Educational Leadership, 63,* 6, 66–69.

Mann, S., & Walsh, S. (2017). *Reflective Practice in English Language Teaching: Research-based Principles and Practices.* New York: Routledge.

Martin, J. R. (2000). Beyond exchange: Appraisal systems in English. In S. Hunston and G. Thompson (Eds.) *Evaluation in Text, Authorial Stance and the Construction of Discourse* (pp. 142–175). Oxford: Oxford University Press.

Martin, J. R., & White, P. (2005). *The Language of Evaluation: Appraisal in English.* New York: Palgrave Macmillan.

Meister, D. G., & Ahrens, P. (2011). Resisting Plateauing: Four Veteran Teachers' Stories. *Teaching and Teacher Education, 27,* 770–778. https://doi.org/10.1016/j.tate.2011.01.002

Melnick, S. A. & Meister, D. G. (2008). A comparison of beginning and experienced teachers' concerns. *Educational Research Quarterly, 31,* 3, 39–56.

Merriam, S. B. (2009). *Qualitative research: A Guide to Design and Implementation* (3rd edn). San Francisco: Jossey-Bass.

Oberg, A., & Blades, C. (1990). The spoken and the unspoken: the story of an educator. *Phenomonology+Pedagogy, 8,* 161–180. https://doi.org/10.29173/pandp15136

Perryman, J., & Calvert, G. (2019). What motivates people to teach, and why do they leave? Accountability, performativity and teacher retention. *British Journal of Educational Studies, 68,* 1, 3–23. https://doi.org/10.1080/00071005.2019.1589417

Redding, C., & Henry, G. T. (2018). Leaving School Early: An Examination of Novice Teachers' Within- and End-of-Year Turnover. *American Educational Research Journal, 56,* 1, 204–236. https://doi.org/10.3102/0002831218790542

Renard, L. (2003). Setting up teachers for failure or success. *Educational Leadership, 60,* 8, 62–64.

Richards, J. C. (1998). *Beyond Training.* New York: Cambridge University Press.

Richards, J. C., & Lockhart, C. (1994). *Reflective Teaching.* New York: Cambridge University Press.

Richards, J. C., & Farrell, T. S. C. (2005). *Professional Development for Language Teachers.* New York, NY: Cambridge University Press.

Richards. J. C., & Farrell, T. S. C. (2011). *Teaching Practice: A Reflective Approach.* New York: Cambridge University Press.

Robbins, S., Judge, T., & Campbell, T. (2017). *Organizational Behaviour* (2nd Edition). New York: Pearson Education.

Shi, L., & Cumming, A. (1995). Teachers' conceptions of second language writing instruction: Five case studies. *Journal of Second Language Writing, 4*, 2, 87–111. http://dx.doi.org/10.1016/1060-3743(95)90002-0

Smith, M. T., & Ingersoll, M. R. (2004). What are the effects of induction and mentoring on beginning teacher turnover? *American Educational Research Journal, 41*, 681–741. https://doi.org/10.3102/00028312041003681

Stake, R. (1995). *The Art of Case Study Research*. Thousand Oaks, CA: Sage.

Taggart, G., & Wilson, A. P. (1998). *Promoting Reflective Thinking in Teachers*. Thousand Oaks, CA: Corwin Press.

Teng, M. F. (2017). Emotional development and construction of teacher identity: Narrative interactions about the pre-service teachers' practicum experiences. *Australian Journal of Teacher Education 42*, 11, 117–34. https://doi.org/10.14221/ajte.2017v42n11.8

van Lier, L. (2005). Case study. In, E. Hinkel (Ed.) *Handbook of Research in Second Language Learning*, (pp. 195–208). Mahwah, NJ: Lawrence Erlbaum Associates.

Varah, L. J., Theune, W. S., & Parker, L. (1986). Beginning teachers: sink or swim? *Journal of Teacher Education, 37*, 1, 30–34. http://dx.doi.org/10.1177/002248718603700107

Vonk, J. (1989). Beginning teachers' professional development and its implication for teacher education and training. *The Irish Journal of Education, 23*, 1, 5–21.

White, P. (2000). Dialogue and inter-subjectivity: Reinterpreting the semantics of modality and hedging. In M. Coulthard, J. Cotterill & F. Rock (Eds.) *Working with Dialogue*, (pp. 67–80). Tübingen: Max Niemeyer Verlag.

Wright, T. (2010). Second language teacher education: Review of recent research on practice. *Language Teaching 43*, 3, 259–296. https://doi.org/10.1017/s0261444810000030

York-Barr, J., Sommers, W., Ghere, G., & Montie, J. (2006). *Reflective Practice to Improve Schools: An Action Guide for Educators* (2nd ed.). Thousand Oaks, CA: Corwin Press.

Index

9 781781 795521